Operations Forensics

Operations Forensics

Business Performance Analysis Using Operations Measures and Tools

Richard Lai

The MIT Press
Cambridge, Massachusetts
London, England

MIT Press books may be purchased at special quantity discounts for business or sales promotional use. For information, please email special_sales@mitpress.mit.edu or write to Special Sales Department, The MIT Press, 55 Hayward Street, Cambridge, MA 02142.

This book was set in Times New Roman by Toppan Best-set Premedia Limited, Hong Kong. Printed and bound in the United States of America.

Library of Congress Cataloging-in-Publication Data

Lai, Richard, 1962–
Operations forensics : business performance analysis using operations measures and tools / Richard Lai.
    p. cm.
Includes bibliographical references and index.
ISBN 978-0-262-01866-1 (hardcover : alk. paper)
1. Production management. 2. Industrial management. 3. Performance. I. Title.
TS155.L244 2013
658.4′034—dc23
2012027960

10 9 8 7 6 5 4 3 2 1

Brief Table of Contents

Contents

Preface

This book started as supplementary material for the course Operations Performance Analysis (OPIM 650) at the Wharton School of the University of Pennsylvania. The quarter-long course is taught as an elective to MBA students. While OPIM 650 has been taught at Wharton for many years, it was only in the fall of 2009 that it began to focus on *operations forensics*, by which I mean the practice of diving into a firm's operations—beyond commonly used and publicly available financials—to better discern and influence its valuation.

There are already worthy and related books from the angles of accounting, finance, marketing, strategy, and law; this book focuses on operations, so I exclude topics such as disclosure, financial leverage, product pricing, strategic positioning, and term sheets.

This is not an introduction to operations management. Nor is it a call to some newly discovered program of action. It is a pedagogical collection—under a new perspective—of many powerful tools and frameworks, some of which are already in textbooks but spread over various disciplines, while others are only found in the research literature and have not percolated into a book for practitioners and students. As this is a collection, the style here is direct, without many motivating examples. This also keeps the book short.

Finally, as in class, I welcome feedback to make this book more useful. Please email opsforensics@gmail.com.

Guide for the Reader

Part 1 is an introduction to how financial statements provide useful but incomplete insights into the operations of a business. The remainder of the book is divided into three parts:

	Primary relevance			
	Period	Horizon	Sources	Audience
Operational indicators	Before investment	Future	Public information	Analysts
Operational due diligence	During investment	Now	Proprietary information	Private equity investors
Operational turnaround	After investment	Now	Proprietary information	Managers, consultants

I assume that readers have some basic familiarity with operations management—such as the concepts of capacity and queueing—but I provide some refresher material when these concepts are first used in the text. There is also a glossary at the end of the book.

I mark the more mathematical material as advanced topics, and these may be skipped without loss of continuity. The material in the earlier chapters can be addressed with less mathematics than that in the later chapters, so the reader will see a gradual increase in mathematical sophistication through the book. This, I hope, also makes it easier for the reader to get used to the material and style, before getting into the thick of equations and formulas.

Acknowledgments

We owe the material in this book to a large and productive academy of researchers—and many practitioners—primarily in the field of operations management. To reiterate, this is not a research but a pedagogical document. The intent is not to document the origins of the ideas—almost none of which are due to me—but primarily to provide a resource to students. Nevertheless, I would like to acknowledge the assistance of many students and colleagues.

I thank the many students who suffered through the birth pangs of this course. In particular, I am grateful to Aleksander Baranski, Monique Bell, Clayton Bischoff, Harris Brody, Casey Carey, Arthur Chamberlain, Christophe Defert, Michael Dreimann, Phillip Druce, Samuel Eskilden, Isaac Esseku, Fatima Faheemi, Gabriel Gerenstein, Mark Hanson, Uttam Jain, Jonathan Karmel, Salim Kassam, Noah Kaye, Sunny Kim, Brendy Lange, Dominic Lavalle, Julia Lee, Howard Levine, Patrick Mcbrearty, Andrew Nodes, Sean Nowak, Hichem Omezzine, Franz Paul, Tim Plain, Len Podolsky, Gabriel Reinstein, Matthew Schwab, Justin Serafini, Suchita Shah, Gavin Teo, Jean-Marie Truelle, Katherine White, and Tzyy-Ming Yeh.

I am also grateful for feedback from my Wharton colleagues, and for guidance and test runs of the materials from those outside Wharton (some of whom read the text cover to cover): John Birge of Chicago, Jan van Mieghem and Gad Allon from Kellogg, Hau Lee from Stanford, Marcelo Olivares from Columbia, Leon Zhu from the University of Southern California, and especially my mentors Ananth Raman of Harvard and Vishal Gaur of Cornell, who are the pioneers in this area. Their improvements to this material are many, so I have not credited them at every specific point of the text. Of course, I am responsible for any remaining faults.

Richard Lai
Philadelphia and New York, 2012

I INTRODUCTION

1 Operations Forensics

1.1 The Three Components of Operations Forensics

Operations forensics is comprised of operational indicators, operational due diligence, and operational turnarounds. Let's begin by briefly introducing these three key components.

1.1.1 Operational Indicators

In May 1998, Mark Gerson had just left Yale Law School when he met Thomas Lehrman, who had been working for two years at a major hedge fund, Tiger Management. Together they founded a business based on the proposition that financial analysts crave information beyond the scope of traditional financial models and statements.

By 2010, the Gerson-Lehrman Group operated a network of over 250,000 experts to provide detailed, operational models and information to blue-chip clients such as Credit Suisse, Salomon Smith Barney, and J. P. Morgan. It has been called the "most valuable NYC [New York City] company no one outside of Wall Street has ever heard of,"[1] with a valuation of $900 million.

What Gerson-Lehrman and many other similar firms—and their investment banking and private equity clients—represent is an emerging discipline that uses *operational* (not financial) models and data to better predict companies' performance. These *operational indicators* of performance represent one of three aspects of what we call *operations forensics*. Operational indicators can explain:

• how Texas Instruments could predict unit cost reductions so accurately that it could preemptively and precisely price its calculators to gain share from its competitors;

• how hedge fund manager David Berman uses operational—in additional to financial—leading indicators to predict retailers' fortunes;

• how IBM and CDC were driven out of the disk drive market, because they did not predict that the disruptive technologies were *incremental,* rather than radical.

1.1.2   Operational Due Diligence

On October 15, 2010, the *Financial Times* revealed that HSBC Bank had dropped its plan to buy Nedbank. The reason: "due diligence on the South African bank's operations had proved more complex than expected."[2] Among practitioners, there is considerable understanding of what constitutes financial or legal due diligence, but much less is known about the nature of operational due diligence. How do we verify companies' claims about operational excellence? How do we value their operational assets? This second aspect—*operational due diligence*—constitutes another part of the scope of operations forensics. For example, we will learn:

• how to assess the extent to which CompUSA moved from a brick-and-mortar to an e-commerce retailing model;

• how to evaluate[3] whether a General Motors plant is practicing lean manufacturing;

• how—without gaining access to a restaurant's kitchen (or a bank's back office, or a recycling plant)—we could estimate[4] the number of cooks (or bank officers, or garbage compaction lines) by making observations outside the facility.

1.1.3   Operational Turnaround

In the fall of 2008, the United States experienced one of the biggest financial crises since the Great Depression. In the resulting credit squeeze, potential investors found it difficult to promote and execute buyout strategies based on the tax advantages of increased leverage. Because of low interest rates, invested shareholders found little appeal in turnaround strategies based on debt reduction. As in many similar times before the 2008 crisis, many actual and potential investors looked to turnarounds based more on operational than on financial practices. This third aspect—*operational turnaround*—is the last component of operations forensics. Operational turnaround addresses questions like:

• what state-of-the-art research says about the likely success of turnarounds based on operations versus those based on organizational changes;

• how Ford reengineered its accounts payable process, leading to a 75% reduction in staff requirements;

• how Du Pont preemptively expanded its titanium dioxide capacity to become an industry leader.

In table 1.1, we see how the three aspects of operational forensics are related to each other. What table 1.1 shows, of course, is only their primary relevance. Turnaround, for example, is not only of interest to an investor after investing; indeed, an investor often considers how much value she can achieve with a turnaround before she invests. But it is still useful to associate turnaround with the core skills of, say, a private equity investor who has already taken positions in investee companies. Each of the following three parts

Table 1.1
Three Components of Operations Forensics

	Primary relevance			
	Period	Horizon	Sources	Audience
Operational indicators	Before investment	Future	Public information	Analysts
Operational due diligence	During investment	Now	Proprietary information	Private equity investors
Operational turnaround	After investment	Now	Proprietary information	Managers, consultants

of this book addresses one of the key components of operations forensics in table 1.1. But before we explore these parts, it is useful to step back and describe the unifying theme in operations forensics.

1.2 Operations Forensics as a Perspective

One theme you should already see is that operations forensics is operations management not from the traditional perspective of a manager, but from that of an investor—whether one seeking to invest in a company or one who already has a shareholding of the company. The investor's perspective differs from the manager's in at least these three ways:

1. *Incentives misalignment.*   Investors are primarily interested in the value of their share in a company. But managers may have divergent interests. For example, managers whose compensation is tied to keeping costs down may be overzealous in reducing the headcount for quality control—which is immediately visible in the income statement—even if the reduction is detrimental to the company's reputation for quality in the long term.

2. *Information asymmetry.*   The investor—whether a board member or a proxy such as a financial analyst—often has less information on a company's operations than a manager has. The information an investor receives may be dated, partial, costly to obtain, and perhaps even inaccurate.

3. *Rights asymmetry.*   While managers at various levels have a wide range of decision rights on how to run a company, an investor's decision rights are often limited to voting at board meetings. Operational decisions at the board level are often limited to strategic investments. Investors can also fire managers they deem unsuitable, but such decisions are after the fact.

To use a detective story analogy, managers often have the motive (incentives misalignment), opportunity (information asymmetry), and means (rights asymmetry) to run a company differently than an investor would.

Therefore, operations forensics is about diving into a firm's operations—beyond commonly used and publicly available financials—to better discern and influence its valuation.

In this book, "operations" means the mechanics of running a business that involve a system, a process, or a technology. We avoid areas that are already clearly addressed in other fields, such as pricing (addressed in marketing and strategy), leadership (in organizational behavior and entrepreneurship), financial leverage (in accounting and finance), or regulations (in public policy and strategy). What we mean by "forensics" matches the *American Heritage Dictionary* definition directly: "relating to the use of science or technology in the investigation and establishment of facts or evidence." Viewed this way, operations forensics has been around as long as anyone has considered investing in a business. Although our collective knowledge had been anecdotal, in the last few decades researchers have discovered regularities about and have developed tools for addressing the three aspects of indicators, due diligence, and turnaround. Most of this new knowledge resides in the research literature, and is known mostly within research specializations. It is not captured in contemporary texts. For example, many texts on finance and accounting focus on information available on financial statements. And most texts on operations management are for the manager. The goal of this book is to put together the diverse collection of knowledge under a unifying operations forensics perspective, so that it is useful not only to researchers but also to practitioners.

1.3   Operations Forensics in the Field

Operations forensics is already being used in the field, perhaps even unknowingly, by a variety of practitioners. We will now describe how some analysts, private equity firms, and managers and consultants actually use operations forensics.

1.3.1   Analysts

For many analysts, operational matters constitute a top concern. Table 1.2 shows how often operations-related word stems such as "stores" and "inventory" show up in analyst conferences. The analysis was done on 1,502 transcripts of 54 companies in the apparel industry, in the years 2003 through 2006.

Indeed, when we group the word stems by function, operations rank second only to marketing (see table 1.3).

Of course, the detail into which analysts will go depends on many factors, such as the industry in question. For example, on a day-to-day basis, retail analysts may go as far as physically checking stores to look at merchandising and report that "a few back tables and racks of clearance tees and tops [are] marked down at 20–40%," as in an actual report on Abercrombie and Fitch.

Table 1.2
Frequency Distribution of Word Stems in Analyst Conference Transcripts

Rank	Word stem	Frequency
1	**Stores**	**7.8%**
2	Sales	4.5%
3	Results	2.2%
4	Brand	1.9%
5	Customers	1.9%
6	Statements	1.8%
7	Comp(arative)	1.8%
8	Expectation	1.8%
9	Margins	1.8%
10	**Inventory**	**1.7%**
11	**Merchandising**	**1.6%**
12	Shares	1.6%
13	Products	1.5%
14	Growth	1.5%
15	Plans	1.4%
16	Expense	1.3%
17	Markets	1.2%
18	**Operations**	**1.2%**
19	Performance	1.2%
20	Improvements	1.1%

Boldface words are often associated with operations.

Table 1.3
Frequency Distribution of Word Stems, by Function, in Analyst Conference Transcripts

Rank	Function	Frequency
1	Marketing	43.9%
2	**Operations**	29.1%
3	Finance	26.7%
4	General	19.0%
5	Strategy	11.4%
6	Organization	2.7%
7	Geography	2.0%
8	Governance	1.2%
	Total	136%

The total exceeds 100% because some word stems are classified into multiple functions.

Table 1.4
Count of Word Stems per Page in Analyst Reports for Joseph A. Banks and Men's Wearhouse

Word stem	Joseph A. Banks	Men's Wearhouse
Inventory	0.55	0.24
Sales	2.28	1.95
Ratio of inventory to sales	0.24	0.12

Adapted from Fisher and Raman (2010). From analyst reports for June 2005 through December 2007.

In any case, analyst scrutiny intensifies when operational problems surface. For example, when *inventory turn*—defined as the ratio of cost of goods sold (COGS) to inventory—dropped at Joseph A. Bank, a men's wear retailer, in 2004–2005 even when sales and gross margin were increasing, analysts began to pose numerous operational questions to the company and increased their scrutiny, as reflected in their reports. A J. P. Morgan report of June 9, 2005, said: "JOSB's inventory days outstanding at 245 days (adjusting COGS for occupancy costs) are higher than any other retailer we follow. This puts margins and cash flows at risk given any slowdown in the business could lead to accelerated markdowns . . . we find it difficult to recommend the stock due to the potential volatility introduced by the company's high inventory model."

The number of mentions of the word stem "inventory" also increased relative to competing retailers. Table 1.4 shows that it is mentioned twice as intensely in reports for Joseph A. Banks as in reports for Men's Wearhouse, a competitor. This is observed whether on a raw basis (frequency of the word stem "inventory" per page) or relatively (ratio of the frequencies of "inventory" to "sales").

To sum up, there is some evidence that analysts do place emphasis on operational matters. Given how costly it is to get into operational matters, it also appears that analysts tend to stay at a high level, but dive into operations when companies' financial metrics deteriorate.

Goldman Sachs's Retail Analyst Group

It is instructive to look at one of the larger retail analyst groups, at Goldman Sachs, to see how they are organized and how they obtain information from businesses. Table 1.5 shows the size of the group and who works with whom to cover what. Senior analysts cover as many as ten to fifteen companies alone.

These analysts undertake the kind of activities described earlier: walk through stores, attend conference calls, model financials. To give a sense of their interests, box 1.1 shows the transcript of a conversation of Goldman analyst Adrianne Shapira with Kevin Mansell, CEO of Kohl's.

Notice the frequent probing of inventory management and, in particular, of the balance between gross margin and inventory turn[5] and the appropriate inventory level.[6]

Table 1.5
Goldman Sachs's Retail Analyst Group and Its Team and Individual Coverage

Analysts	Companies covered
Adrianne S.	BJ's Wholesale Club, Inc.
	Costco Wholesale
	Dollar Tree Stores, Inc.
	Family Dollar Stores, Inc.
	J.C. Penney Company
	Kohl's Corp.
	Macy's Inc.
	Nordstrom, Inc.
	Ross Stores, Inc.
	Saks Inc.
	Sears Holdings Corp.
	Target Corporation
	The TJX Companies, Inc.
	Tiffany & Company
	Wal-Mart Stores, Inc.
Adrianne S.; Benjamin H. R., CFA	Costco Wholesale
	J.C. Penney Company
	Macy's Inc.
	Nordstrom, Inc.
	Saks Inc.
	The TJX Companies, Inc.
	Tiffany & Company
Adrianne S.; Jonathan H.; Michelle T., CFA	J.C. Penney Company
	Kohl's Corp.
	Macy's Inc.
	Nordstrom, Inc.
Irma S.	Wal-Mart de Mexico
James M., CFA	Amazon.com Inc.
James M., CFA; Jennifer W., CFA	1-800-FLOWERS.COM, Inc.
	Amazon.com Inc.
Jennifer W., CFA; James M., CFA	1-800-FLOWERS.COM, Inc.
	GSI Commerce, Inc.
John H.	CVS Caremark Corp.
	Kroger Company
	Rite Aid Corp.
	Safeway Inc.
	SUPERVALU Inc.
	The Great A&P Tea Company
	The Pantry, Inc.
	Walgreen Company
	Weis Markets, Inc.
	Whole Foods Market, Inc.
John H.; Afua A.	The Pantry, Inc.
Joshua L.; Caroline L., CFA	China Nepstar Chain Drugstore
Matthew J. F.; Jonathan B.; Robert H., CFA; Mark-Andre S.	Dick's Sporting Goods
	Office Depot
	PETsMART, Inc.
	Staples, Inc.

Table 1.5
(continued)

Analysts	Companies covered
Kristina O.; Sarah F., CFA; Marc F.; Matthew J. F.; Lucy B.; Adrianne S.; Joshua L.; Sho K.; Paul H.; Andrew H.	Abercrombie & Fitch Bed Bath & Beyond, Inc. Best Buy Company, Inc. Costco Wholesale CVS Caremark Corp. Gap Inc. J.C. Penney Company Kohl's Corp. Kroger Company Lowe's Companies, Inc. Macy's Inc. Nordstrom, Inc. Safeway Inc. Sears Holdings Corp. Staples, Inc. Target Corporation The Home Depot, Inc. The TJX Companies, Inc. Tiffany & Company Walgreen Company Wal-Mart Stores, Inc.
Matthew J. F.; Mark-Andre S.; Robert H., CFA; Jonathan B.	Advance Auto Parts Inc. AutoNation, Inc. AutoZone Inc. CarMax Inc. Group 1 Automotive, Inc. O'Reilly Automotive, Inc. Penske Automotive Group, Inc. Sonic Automotive, Inc.
Matthew J. F.; Robert H., CFA; Mark-Andre S.; Jonathan B.	Advance Auto Parts Inc. Bed Bath & Beyond, Inc. Best Buy Company, Inc. Dick's Sporting Goods Lowe's Companies, Inc. Office Depot O'Reilly Automotive, Inc. RadioShack Corp. Staples, Inc. The Home Depot, Inc. Williams-Sonoma, Inc.
May-Kin H., Ph.D.; Jami R.; Randall S., CFA; Matthew B., CFA	Omnicare, Inc.
Michelle T., CFA	Abercrombie & Fitch Aeropostale American Eagle Outfitters Inc. Ann Taylor Stores Corp. Chico's FAS, Inc. Gap Inc. J. Crew Group, Inc. Limited Brands, Inc. lululemon athletica inc. Urban Outfitters Inc.
Randall S., CFA	Medco Health Solutions Omnicare, Inc.
Robert H., CFA; Matthew J. F.; Jonathan B.; Mark-Andre S.	GameStop Corp.
Robert H., CFA; Matthew J. F.; Mark-Andre S.; Jonathan B.	GameStop Corp. Lumber Liquidators, Inc. Tractor Supply Company
Stephen G.; Irma S.	Wal-Mart de Mexico

Source: Goldman Sachs, 2010.

Box 1.1
Portion of Q2 2009 earnings call transcript, between Adrianne S. of Goldman Sachs and Kevin M. of Kohl's

> *Adrianne S., Goldman Sachs*   Kevin, maybe just focusing a bit on **gross margin**—obviously tremendous performance in the first half and if you can kind of walk us through the three buckets of that performance, the **inventory management**, lower clearance levels, and higher private brands, if you were to prioritize what drove the upside and then perhaps help us think about as you kind of somewhat raise guidance in the back half as it relates to **margins**, where do you see the most opportunity coming from?
>
> *Kevin M., Kohl's*   I think it was a **balance**, actually. We kind of think about the **margin improvement all as inventory management** because the decisions we made to improve the opportunity for a customer to choose only a Kohl's brand in an increasing way. The inventory management has an impact not only on our regular-priced selling and the resulting mix but also the transitional level of inventory we have when we move to clearance, so I'd say between the obvious things of closer receipts to sales and the improved penetration, it's a pretty even **balance** and I think as we think about the second half, we're thinking about it the same way.
>
> *Adrianne S.*   Okay, great. And then as it relates to the better comps in the back half of the down 3 to down 5, how to think about **inventory, what's the right level of inventory**? We were saying sort of down mid-singles per store, it sounds like where you'd like to end in the third quarter but should we expect that to build as we are looking for better comps in the back half?
>
> *Kevin M.*   I mean, high-level, our focus is flowing receipts to sales and we think we've changed our business model sufficiently enough that if there is upside in the sales, we can flow additional receipts to support it. If the sales aren't as good, we will flow less receipts. We have an **opportunity to improve inventory, so we're going to continue to focus on improvement in inventory turn overall**. That's why we still think at the end of the third quarter, even with negative 3 to 5 comps, our **inventory would probably be down a little** more than that.

Note: **Boldface** represents author's emphasis.

Of course, even the best analysts do not obtain all the information they want in conversations with managers. Managers may not oblige because they may not be authorized to disclose many figures, or they may be wary that the information will be used to their disadvantage by competitors.

Box 1.2 illustrates such a situation, in which even one of Goldman's star analysts, Michelle Tan, can get only a cursory answer from Ann Taylor's CFO Michael J. Nicholson.

We bear in mind that analysts cannot legally get proprietary information direct from managers; the latter can release information only in public and not to individual analysts. This constraint, of course, does not apply to investors in private securities, a topic we turn to next.

Box 1.2
Portion of Q3 2008 earnings call transcript, between Michelle T. of Goldman Sachs and Michael J. N. of Ann Taylor

---

Michelle T., Goldman Sachs   If you look at the individual divisions at Ann Taylor you've got **inventory per foot** down 18% including beauty, right? And inventory at Loft down around 14% or 15%. So you know what else is in there?

Michael J. N., Ann Taylor   There's a couple of drivers. Within those business units, it's the **impact of in-transit** year on year as well as to your point, the incremental inventory in the current year period to **support the launch** of Loft Outlet as well as incremental inventory in the current year to support the Internet business.

Michelle T.   Okay. Can you give us a sense of how big those things are? And so **in-transit** is included in the total inventory per foot?

Michael J. N.   Correct.

Michelle T.   How big—do you know roughly how big the in-transit number is?

Michael J. N.   Okay. We don't provide a specific guidance on that.

Michelle T.   All right. Great. Thanks for the clarification.

Note: **Boldface** represents author's emphasis.

1.3.2   Private Equity Firms

"Buying cleverly and making money out of leverage or multiples isn't happening. The only way to make money is through improving businesses, so more firms are putting effort into it than before," so writes a news report.[7] As Henry Kravis of the private equity firm Kohlberg Kravis & Roberts (KKR) says, "to be successful, the real work in a private equity transaction begins on the first day of owning a company. Buying a company is easy. Just pay enough and you will own a company. The hard part is making changes in the way a company operates so as to increase shareholder value."[8]

Further, operational improvements are a constant over different stages of the economic cycle. Kravis remarks: "The reason [operations] is so important is that 33 years of investing in all cycles has demonstrated that operational improvements create real value over the long term, even during difficult economic cycles."[9]

Many private equity firms either have in-house *operating partners* or recruit them when needed. For example, in 2009, British mid-market private equity firm Langholm Capital hired Steven Esom, the former managing director of Waitrose and executive director of food for Marks & Spencer. Esom oversaw portfolio companies such as Tyrrells Potato Chips, Dorset Cereals, and cosmetics company Lumene.

However, the role of an operating partner is not that of a CEO. As Esom said: "As a CEO, you have a lot of direct influence over decision making, strategy, and resources. As an operating partner you work with portfolio companies, through the management team. You provide challenge and support rather than getting hands on."[10]

Table 1.6
Four Examples of Private Equity Firms and Their Operating Partners

Investment firm	Example operating partners	Role
Langholm Capital	Steven Esom, former managing director of Waitrose; executive director of food for Marks & Spencer	"Work with portfolio companies, through the management team. You provide challenge and support rather than getting hands on."
Index Ventures	Mike Volpi, former chief executive of online video company Joost and chief strategy officer of Cisco Systems	"We are extremely close with our portfolio companies and spend lots of time with them, but we let them manage. We back up existing management by helping on strategy, recruitment, etc."
Advent International	Paolo Cantarella, former chief executive of Fiat; former director of Polaroid Bob Wigley, former Merrill Lynch chairman in Europe, the Middle East, and Africa Jayendra Nayak, who helped build Axis Bank, India's third largest private bank	"We appoint operating partners without specific portfolio companies in mind . . ." Deal sourcing with industry knowledge
KKR	KKR Capstone: "We have more than 50 executives worldwide with experience and seniority. . . . Most are generalist with a mix of industry and consulting experience, and most have specific knowledge of a particular industry sector. We also have functional specialists in areas such as IT, purchasing, and manufacturing."	"Work on due diligence, a 100-day plan and execution, which typically lasts for about 18 months. . . . About 60% of the value creation at the firm's portfolio companies comes from EBITDA growth."

Source: P. Hodkinson, "Delicate Operations: Partners Differ on How to Manage Their Firms' Investments," *Financial News*, July 27, 2009.

Table 1.6 shows examples of private equity firms and their operating partners. In these cases, the operating partners are in-house standing members of the firms. In other private equity firms, such as AEA Investors, operating partners are hired as needed.

Below, we briefly describe two such private equity investors with strong operating partners.

KKR's Capstone Group

The Capstone Group was formed by Dean Nelson, a former senior partner at the Boston Consulting Group's Chicago office. Some of the portfolio companies Capstone has worked on include Toys 'R' Us, Dollar General, Sealy, and Primedia. Capstone has expertise in many operational areas, such as IT, procurement, and Six Sigma. As Nelson has explained: "Our goal at Capstone is to help our portfolio companies with key, operational-specific action plans. We don't do the monitoring; the deal guys do that. We don't do the managing; the management team does that. We're there to help them fix two or three things and then we move on." Indeed, the Group has been such an integral part of KKR that "for a while now we have shied away from assets where we did not think we could improve them operationally. If we can't improve the business, we probably shouldn't buy it."[11] As Henry

Kravis said, "A key KKR resource for strengthening operations is our in-house consulting business, called Capstone. . . . In fact, our biggest problem is getting the Capstone personnel back from the company where they are working, because managements want to keep them engaged since they are truly value added."[12]

Broadly, KKR and the Capstone Group "began implementing a '100-day plan' that is agreed upon by management and ourselves. This way we ring-fence the management and have an agreed upon plan to immediately improve the operations of the company. This plan is a detailed agreement on the steps necessary to achieve strategic and operational goals—for example, what are you going to do to improve margins and productivity? How can we shorten the supply chain? It is a very detailed, line-by-line, person-by-person review and strategy." The operating mode is to put "two to three people in a portfolio company . . . in the US we can productively work with 10 to 12 companies at any given time. . . . Normally, it's as soon as possible—it could be before the close or it could be right at the close. At that point, we would have already established a 100-day plan with the management team and determined the two, three, or four major objectives."[13]

For Capstone, the priority improvement areas are threefold: renegotiating procurement, gaining market share, and reducing costs. As an example, the Group worked on Dollar General, "where we were able to go in and improve the quality of store standards and help out on the merchandising front. The numbers of new Dollar Generals are now outpacing Family Dollar, Wal-Mart and other big retailers."

Bain Capital

Bain Capital was started in 1984 by Mitt Romney, who raised $36 million to invest in private equity deals. The angle Bain Capital took was "wringing more profit from the operation" of its portfolio companies. At many private equity firms, "the staff often comes largely from the realm of investment bankers—highflying deal makers with expertise on the financial aspect of a deal, but less hands-on business experience. By contrast, Bain people tend to come from a background in industry or corporate management, or from a consulting firm. Often, that consulting firm is Bain & Company, the company that spun off Bain Capital; today the two are separate entities. And unlike other private-equity firms, Bain Capital eschews a star culture."[14]

The firm has been so successful that it is one of the few to insist on taking 30% of the profits on its investments, compared to the industry average of 20%.

Among the major Bain investments are Baxter's diagnostic division, Burger King, Domino's, Dunkin' Brands, Gartner Group, Michaels Stores, Staples, and Toys 'R' Us. Like many investment firms, it also has its investment losses, such as Dade Behring Inc. and KB Toys.

Bain Capital's mode is to undertake in-depth research and implementation. In the HCA deal, for example, it had "eight people poring over the books for two months. For other deals, it assigns twice that number of analysts—a figure larger than the entire investment staff of some competitors. As a result, in deals where it joins with other buyout firms, Bain usually does most of the research beforehand into the company's strategies and business soundness and tends to focus on the strategy for expanding the company's businesses by analyzing customers, expenses and competition. Meanwhile, the other buyout firms are more likely to come up with financing plans."[15]

1.3.3 Managers and Consultants

Operations forensics is also relevant to corporate managers and management consultants. The motivation for this is obvious: to increase the company's valuation. But like analysts or investors, even managers and consultants sometimes do not get all the information they need at the time they want it.[16] For example, the chief operating officer might be so high up in the organizational hierarchy that she or he gets only biased information that underlings want to pass up. A consultant might find that, despite a directive from the chief executive officer to the rest of the company to cooperate, many departments jealously guard their information from outsiders.

1.4 Takeaways

Operations forensics has been around as long as anyone has considered investing in a business. With recent advances in our knowledge in several disciplines, and especially in operations management, it is helpful to put together various tools and frameworks under operations forensics as a perspective. Investors and managers use various forms of operations forensics, perhaps without using that term. Therefore, learning about operations forensics can help distinguish ourselves in a crowded field of analysts, private equity investors, corporate managers, and consultants, whose traditional training often emphasizes just accounting and finance.

Before we proceed to the three main parts of the book, we motivate operations forensics by considering where financial statements might be useful in revealing the operations of a company, and where they might fall short. That is the goal of the next chapter.

1.5 Further Reading

Cachon, G., and C. Terwiesch. 2006. *Matching Supply with Demand: An Introduction to Operations Management*. New York: McGraw-Hill.

Fisher, M. L., and A. Raman. 2010. Introduction to M. L. Fisher and A. Raman, eds., *The New Science of Retailing: How Analytics Are Transforming the Supply Chain and Improving Performance*. Boston: Harvard Business Review Press.

van Mieghem, J. A. 2008. *Operations Strategy: Principles and Practice*. Belmont, MA: Dynamic Ideas.

2 What Financial Statements May or May Not Reveal

In 1955, Anthony "Tino" De Angelis formed the Allied Crude Vegetable Oil Refining Corporation to sell shortening and other vegetable oils to Europe (*Time*, 1963).[1] His company operated out of Bayonne, New Jersey, where he constructed a farm of oil tanks to store oil. By 1962, De Angelis was borrowing heavily from American Express's (Amex's) Field Warehousing subsidiary and other banks, using the oil in the Bayonne tanks as collateral. With the loans, De Angelis became a major player in the salad oil market. But judging from his balance sheet, Amex should have been curious: the assets entry showed that the tanks contained more oil than the monthly consumption in the entire United States.

It was not easy for Amex to discover anything untoward. When its auditors went to one oil tank and dipped in their measuring stick, they would find the tank full. Little did they know that sometimes the tanks were simply filled with water, except for the layer of oil on top. At other times, as the auditors proceeded from one tank to another, De Angelis's men would pump oil from the first tank to the second. Attempted briberies and delivery mistakes eventually gave the game away, and by 1963, Allied Crude contributed to the crash of the futures market. Amex's stock dived from $60 to $41 a share.

This episode illustrates two points we address in this chapter. First, financial statements do reveal something about operations, as Allied Crude's asset line did even if Amex seemed not to follow through on the information. Second, outright fraud is hard to detect when a company is determined to hide information.

Outright fraud is also difficult to detect when auditors or investors themselves have a stake in perpetuating the scam. The urban myth of the "Hong Kong sardine dodge" illustrates this. During the famine in China in the 1960s, a Hong Kong merchant sold cans of "sardines" that were really filled only with mud. A second merchant bought these cans and resold them for a profit, and a third merchant did likewise. When the fourth merchant bought the cans and opened them to his horror, the third merchant dismissed his outrage saying: "But why did you open the cans?"

As these events illustrate, financial statements can both disclose and disguise important operational information. Specifically, in this chapter, we ask:

• *What financial statements reveal.* Can we discern a company's operational model from its financial statements? We give four useful guidelines that can help us answer this question in a surprising number of cases.

• *What financial statements do not reveal.* One of the running themes in this book is that, with limited time and resources, we need to prioritize what we can do to maximize our understanding of a firm's business operations. So:

> *Where might financial statements be less complete?* Because no financial statement can or is intended to fully capture every aspect of a business's operations, what might be missing from the picture they portray?

> *When might financial statements be less accurate?* When and how could items in financial statements misrepresent the true state of operations? Do managers have an incentive to manipulate these items?

2.1   What Financial Statements Reveal

The ability to determine what financial statements reveal is a powerful tool in answering questions such as:

• To what extent has CompUSA moved from brick-and-mortar to e-commerce retailing?

• To what extent has IBM's much-touted strategy of moving from manufacturing to services been truly implemented?

• How do we verify Dell's claim that it sells as much to business customers as it does to more finicky retail customers?

• To what extent is Archer Daniels Midland (ADM) a conglomerate of foods, beverages, industrials, animal feed, and logistics businesses? ADM has sometimes been criticized for being overly diversified. The hiring of Patricia Woertz as CEO in 2006 was expected to get ADM more focused on developing biofuels. Has Woertz succeeded?

These are essentially questions about what business model a business runs. We'll next describe rules of thumb to answer such questions, using information in financial statements.

2.1.1   Inferring Business Model from Asset Intensity

Different business models often require different asset holdings. Some are asset-intensive and some not. And we could distinguish among the asset-intensive businesses by the type of assets, such as physical versus financial.

Asset-Intensive Business Models

Table 2.1 compares some asset-related ratios for three companies. Two of Cisco's ratios are considerably larger than those of American Airlines and J. P. Morgan Chase, due to

Table 2.1
Examples of "Regular" and Asset-Intensive Business Models

	Cisco	American Airlines	J. P. Morgan Chase
Income/assets (ROA)	11.3%	1.9%	1.1%
PPE/assets	7.1%	56.3%	0.04%
Equity/assets	83.3%	15.6%	8.2%

Source: Capital IQ. In billions of dollars; data is for 2007.

Table 2.2
Examples of Asset-Light Business Models

	LSE Group	Accenture	Yahoo!	Troc de l'Ile
Income/assets (ROA)	31.6%	16.4%	2.9%	3.8%
PPE/assets	17.5%	7.0%	12%	19.2%
Inventory/assets	0%	0%	0%	6.2%

Source: Capital IQ. In billions of dollars; data is for 2008 except for LSE Group, which is for 2006.

Cisco's relatively low level of assets. For some asset-intensive business models, such as that for airlines (American Airlines), the dominant asset is plant, property, and equipment (PPE). For financial services firms, the dominant asset class is financial, such as loans for J. P. Morgan Chase.

There are at least two distinguishing features between physical- and financial-asset businesses. Financial models tend to use enormous liabilities (deposits) to support enormous assets (loans). Not surprisingly, we should expect that financial services firms have very low ROA. There is even a "1% ROA rule" in the lore of commercial banking: banks making more than 1% ROA are considered high-performing.

Another distinguishing feature between physical- and financial-asset businesses is in their core competence in managing these assets. While both types of businesses require excellence in achieving high utilization of their assets,[2] financial businesses also need to carefully manage the risks involved in their enormous balance sheets. One particularly important risk is in the mismatch between the maturities of the assets and the liabilities. Many banks operate an explicit "assets-liabilities management" (ALM) function at senior management levels.

Asset-Light Business Models

At the opposite extreme are business models that are light on assets. Table 2.2 shows examples of four such asset-light business models. These companies represent different operating models:

• *The brokerage model.* In this model, value is added by connecting supplier and customer without holding on to proprietary assets. Table 2.2 shows some figures for the London Stock Exchange (LSE) Group plc. Being a financial institution, the LSE does have some cash assets, although these, with PPE (such as exchange-related technology) and negligible inventory, still constitute a low asset base. Not surprisingly, the LSE has a high ROA, at 31.6%.

· *The professional services firm.*   Although such a firm has scant physical assets, it often has vast human assets—whether they be architects, lawyers, management consultants, or accountants. Table 2.2 shows the figures for Accenture, the consulting firm. It is similar to the LSE in following an asset-light model; the main difference is that, compared with a stock exchange, it owns even less PPE.

· *The online business model.*   This model takes a different route to boosting ROA, replacing an intensive type of PPE—storefronts and distribution facilities—with a lighter form—websites and drop shipping, in which goods are shipped directly from suppliers to customers. Table 2.2 shows Yahoo! as a representative online firm. We see that Yahoo!— with its server farms—has approximately the same PPE/assets ratio as the LSE. But its ROA is considerably lower, suggesting that light assets are no guarantee of a high ROA when income is also small.

· *The consignment business model.*   This model is similar to the online model in that it reduces a particular type of assets: inventory. Bookstores and some grocery stores use this model, in which they "sell" shelf space but do not take suppliers' inventory onto their books. Table 2.2 shows data for Troc de l'Ile, based in France with stores throughout much of Europe. It is a consignment sales chain for secondhand electric household appliances.

We should mention that ROA comparisons should be made with great caution. It would not be sensible to conclude that high ROA businesses are good ones: if that were the case, all funding would have flown to these businesses with little for others. In particular, high ROA can be achieved by stripping assets or financial leverage. This, of course, increases the risk of the business as a tradeoff.

An analysis of asset intensity allows us to answer one of the questions posed at the beginning of this section: to what extent has CompUSA moved from brick-and-mortar to e-commerce retailing? Table 2.3 shows some asset intensity measures for CompUSA and PC Connection. While both companies have similar asset intensity in terms of their ROAs, CompUSA has a higher portion of its assets in PPE. This suggests that CompUSA is substantially more of a brick-and-mortar outfit than PC Connection. Of course, asset

Table 2.3
Asset Intensity Measures for CompUSA and PC Connection

	CompUSA	PC Connection
Income/assets (ROA)	5.3%	6.2%
PPE/assets	27.4	19.3

Source: Capital IQ (CompUSA, 1998; the company went private later) and Google (PC Connection, 2009). In billions of dollars.

Table 2.4
Comparison of Days of Inventory

	Cisco	McDonald's	Accenture
Average inventory	1.2	0.1	0
Annual COGS	14.2	14.9	18.1
Days of inventory = inventory/(COGS/365)	30.8	2.4	0

Source: Google Finance. The first two lines are in billions of dollars; data is for 2008.

intensity measures are not the only lens through which we can see this point. In subsequent sections, especially in the discussion on days of working capital (see section 2.1.4), we see more evidence of the same point.

2.1.2   Inferring Product Mix from Days of Inventory

A special type of assets is inventory. One common measure of inventory is days of inventory, which is average inventory level divided by daily cost of goods sold (COGS).[3] We bear in mind that we divide by COGS rather than by revenues: inventory is valued at cost, so the denominator should be valued likewise. Table 2.4 shows three examples.

A company's days of inventory provides us with three clues about its operations. First, having little inventory often points to the company's being a service provider. Indeed, pure service providers have no inventory. Table 2.4 shows that Cisco, a manufacturer, has considerably more inventory than McDonald's, more of a services firm. Accenture, a pure services firm providing consulting advice, has no inventory.

Note that this first inference about whether a company is a service provider is one that we cannot obtain by looking at assets in general. While many asset-light businesses are indeed service providers, many asset-intensive businesses—such as airlines and utilities—also provide services.

The measure of days of inventory also suggests how perishable are the goods carried by a company. For example, we expect that restaurants and computer makers generally have lower inventory than appliance retailers and furniture makers. This is reflected in table 2.4, in which Cisco's longer days of inventory, compared with McDonald's, reflects the former's dealing with goods that are generally less perishable.

Finally, shorter days of inventory could be explained by the company's having a focused product mix. Consider two grocers with the same sales volume in perishable goods. If one has a narrower mix of products, each of its stock-keeping units (SKU, or "type of product") must have large sales volume. Greater volume enhances the scale of inventory management, and so leads to shorter days of inventory.

We should also bear in mind an asymmetry in the inferences above: while shorter days of inventory often implies either a services model, more perishable goods, or lower product diversity, longer days may *not* imply the opposite. Specifically, longer days of inventory could be a result of poor inventory management. If we are comparing two companies that

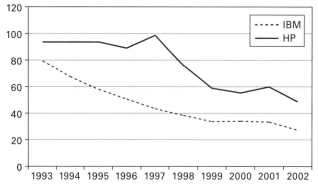

Figure 2.1
Days of inventory for IBM and HP. Source: Capital IQ.

we know a priori to have similar inventory management capabilities, then days of inventory is a good indicator of service model or product shelf life. If we are comparing two companies that we know a priori to have the same service model or product shelf life, then days of inventory is better thought of as an indicator of inventory management capability.

Now we are in a position to answer another question posed at the beginning of this section: to what extent has IBM's much-touted strategy of moving from manufacturing to services been truly implemented?

Figure 2.1 shows days of inventory for IBM from 1993 through 2002, when Louis Gerstner was CEO and steered the company toward services. The figure shows that IBM's days of inventory indeed dropped, consistent with a shift toward services. What about the absolute level: what do we make of IBM's 27 days of inventory by 2002? One benchmark is to consider all-services technology consulting firms such as Accenture and Perot Systems. These have negligible inventory, suggesting that IBM is, not surprisingly, far from being a services firm as represented by Accenture or Perot. Another benchmark is to consider Hewlett-Packard, which to our knowledge does not have a stated strategy of turning to services. Its days of inventory are substantially higher than IBM's, suggesting that IBM indeed has gone much more toward services.

2.1.3   Inferring Customer Type from Days of Receivables

In the US, sales to customers often involve receivables. Many companies that sell to business customers offer trade credit, often of 30- to 90-day durations. Of course, in many situations, companies also offer a discount should a business customer pay earlier. But for most companies selling to business customers, the measure of *days of receivables*— average accounts receivables (average of the year beginning and year end levels) divided by daily revenues—is a few weeks.

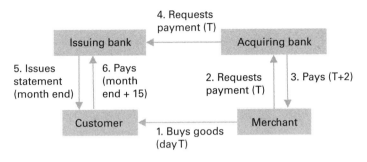

Figure 2.2
Flow of payments when a credit card is used.

Table 2.5
Comparison of Days of Receivables

	CompUSA	Ingram Micro	Dell
Average accounts receivables (AR)	0.2	4.1	6.7
Annual revenues	6.2	35.0	61.1
Days of receivables = AR/(rev/365)	12.6	38.6	41.5

Source: Capital IQ. The first two lines are in billions of dollars; data is for 2007 except for CompUSA, which is for 1998.

In contrast, companies selling to retail customers have much shorter days of receivables. Retail customers typically pay in cash (as at a newspaper stand) or with credit cards (as in a restaurant). When a credit card is used, the flow of payments is as shown in figure 2.2. In step 1, a customer buys something from a merchant on day T. In step 2, the merchant immediately sends a request for payment from her acquiring bank, the bank which works with her to validate and process credit card transactions. Importantly, the merchant receives payments within days (step 3 shows an illustrative 2 days after T, the day of transaction). This means that a merchant who sells to retail customers has days of receivables shorter than a week, even if customers pay their issuing bank much later (steps 5 and 6).

Table 2.5 shows the days of receivables for three computer sellers. CompUSA is mostly a retailer and Ingram Micro a wholesaler. The days of receivables are in line with our prediction: retailers tend to have receivables in days; wholesalers in weeks, if not months.

Now we can again answer a question from the start of this section: how do we verify Dell's claim that it sells as much to business customers as it does to retail customers? We see that the days of receivables for Dell is comparable to that for Ingram Micro, amounting to several weeks. Therefore, even though Dell is commonly thought of as a retailer, this data suggests that a substantial amount of its revenue comes from businesses rather than individual customers.

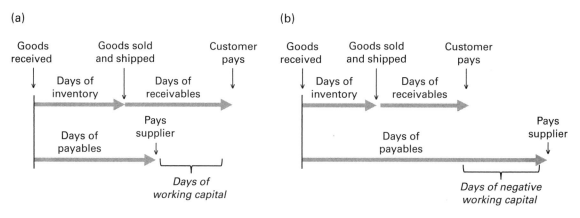

Figure 2.3
Positive working capital (a); negative working capital (b).

2.1.4   Inferring the Cash Conversion Cycle from Receivables, Payables, and Inventory

A particularly important way in which operations affects the economics of a business is through the cash conversion cycle. Consider figure 2.3, panel (a). Start with the top time arrows. The time between when we receive our goods and when the goods are sold and shipped is the *days of inventory*. The time from then to when we get paid is the *days of receivables*. Next we introduce *days of payables*, which is accounts payables divided by daily COGS. Notice that we use COGS as the divisor—as in the formulas for days of inventory but not that for days of receivables—because like days of inventory, payables are valued at cost.

The time between paying our suppliers and getting paid by our customers is the *days of working capital*. Put another way, every dollar of goods that we purchase and sell needs to be supported by this many days of dollars in working capital. This is especially onerous when trying to grow a business. Each dollar of additional sales over last year's sales needs an additional day of dollars in working capital over last year's days of working capital. This is why some firms are constrained in their growth. They cannot get additional capital to finance the growing working capital.

In figure 2.3, panel (b), we see what happens when customers pay us so quickly that we have negative working capital. Now, every dollar of additional sales over last year's sales volume generates a dollar of capital over the (negative) days of working capital. We can put such capital to other uses or even return it to shareholders if the growth can be expected to continue.

Table 2.6
Comparison of Days of Working Capital

	CompUSA	Ingram Micro	Dell
Days of inventory	39.9	29.9	6.8
Days of receivables	12.6	38.6	41.5
Days of payables	38.3	44.6	79.8
Days of working capital	14.2	23.9	−31.5

Source: Capital IQ. Data is for 2007 except for CompUSA, which is for 1998.

Table 2.6 shows the same companies as table 2.5. We see that even though CompUSA has the highest days of inventory among the three companies, its very low days of receivables helps to keep the overall days of working capital down. In contrast, Ingram Micro's high days of receivables pushes its days of working capital up. Dell's days of receivables is even higher, since like Ingram it sells mostly to businesses. But operationally, Dell has managed to keep its days of inventory so low that its days of working capital are even negative.

This analysis raises the important point that there are different possible sources for a company's low working capital. Generally speaking, one source is operational, through low inventory, and another is marketing power, through low days of receivables or high days of payables.

While the above describes cash conversion in managing material inputs, we can of course extend the analysis to investigate cash conversion for other types of inputs. Consider, for example, labor input in which we pay wages at every month end. The days of payables will vary. For a unit that is produced at month beginning, its days of payables will be the full month. For a unit that is produced at month end, its days of payables will be zero.

2.1.5   Inferring Margin from Inventory Turn and Vice Versa

Some analysts measure inventory using not days of inventory but its reciprocal, *inventory turn*. Recall that this is the ratio of cost of goods sold to inventory.[4] Just as we should not blindly go for high ROAs, we should also not blindly go for high inventory turns. In particular, there is a tradeoff between gross margin and inventory turn. For example, groceries might have thin margins but high inventory turn. Jewelers might have high margins but low turn.

This tradeoff can also exist within the same industry. Figure 2.4 shows this for four computer makers, with each data point representing a year. We see that HP tends to have higher margins but lower turns, with Lenovo at the opposite extreme, and Acer in the middle. Apple appears to travel on a higher plane altogether, suggesting that its business model is somewhat distinct from those of the Wintel (Windows-Intel) manufacturers Acer, HP, and Lenovo. This also suggests that a useful construct is the multiple of gross margin

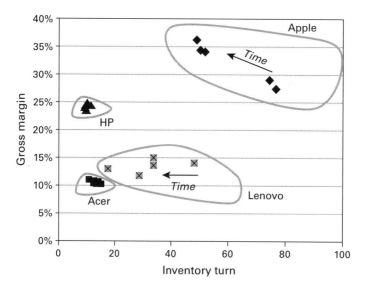

Figure 2.4
Gross margin versus inventory turn. The different points for each company represent different years, between 2004 and 2008. Source: Capital IQ.

and turn. Indeed, the research literature proposes just such a measure, called *gross margin return on inventory*, or GMROI.[5] A higher GMROI contributes to higher valuation, other things being equal. So Apple is more valuable than the Wintel companies.

Once GMROI is determined, we can infer for a firm its appropriate gross margin from its inventory turn or, conversely, its appropriate inventory turn from its gross margin. For example, Apple experienced a reduction in turn during these years, but this was accompanied by rising margins (see figure 2.4). Lenovo's case is interesting: it seems to have had deteriorating turn without a corresponding increase in margin. In short, its GMROI decreased over time. This could help explain why its share price remained stagnant between 2004 and 2008, while the overall industry's valuation was increasing. For example, Apple's share price increased from about $15 in 2004 to about $181 in mid-2008.

2.1.6 Inferring the Business Mix

So far we have mostly analyzed businesses as if they are pure plays, such as whether a business carries perishable products or is asset-light. Let's return to the last question we posed at the beginning: can we tell to what extent ADM is still a conglomerate of foods, beverages, industrials, animal feed, and logistics businesses? By considering different weights on the financials of pure plays, we can get a sense—even if an imperfect one—of the component businesses of a conglomerate.

There could be different sets of weights on pure plays that can produce the same financials of a given conglomerate. But the point here is to check whether a company is a pure play or not; so as long as a business has nonzero weights on various business models, we can conclude that it is not a pure play.

2.1.7 Exercise: From Financial Statements to Operations

Consider the balance sheets and associated financial ratios in table 2.7, for four unidentified companies A through D. For the sake of distilling the lessons from this exercise, we assume that these are pure plays. Can we tell which of these firms is an online media company, a commercial bank, a direct marketer, and a brick-and-mortar retail chain? Yes, we can using the above rules of thumb.

The first rule of thumb (section 2.1.1, regarding asset intensity) suggests that the online media and direct marketing companies would be asset-light, while the bank would be heavy on financial assets and the retailer heavy on physical assets. Looking at ROA alone, it seems that the bank is either B or C, with enormous assets that drive ROA to the low single digits. But a look at the components of assets suggest that B is the bank—it has large "long-term investments" or deposits—and D is the retailer—it has large inventory and PPE.

The second rule of thumb (section 2.1.2) suggests that, between A and C, C with some inventory is the direct marketer. It also suggests that, between B and D, B without inventory is confirmed as the bank, a pure services company. D, with the positive days of inventory, is likely to be the retailer.

Just to be sure, we also revisit the third rule of thumb (section 2.1.3). D's days of receivables is shorter than 30 days, suggesting again that it is the retailer, since the other companies could have a mix of retail and business customers. B's very long days of receivables and payables suggest that it is a bank, with long maturity dates of its loans and deposits.

The fourth rule of thumb (section 2.1.4) also suggests that D, with positive days of working capital, is the retailer. It is plausible that the online media firm and direct marketer get paid before they pay.

The fifth rule of thumb (section 2.1.5) is more useful in discerning companies within the same industry, and is less applicable here.

Taken together, the above analysis suggests that A is the online media company; B, the bank; C, the direct marketer; and D, the retailer. Indeed, these four are Google, J. P. Morgan Chase, PC Connection, and Abercrombie & Fitch, respectively.

We close by noting that the above type of analysis also allows us to see that seemingly similar companies in the "same" industry—such as CompUSA versus Dell, or Apple versus HP—may have really different operations (e.g., brick-and-mortar versus online, brand versus scale), while seemingly different companies—such as the various asset-light companies like real estate brokers and advertising firms—may have really similar operational drivers of success.

Table 2.7
Balance Sheets and Selected Ratios, 2009

Company	A	B	C	D
Assets	**100.0%**	**100.0%**	**100.0%**	**100.0%**
Current assets	72.0%	17.3%	84.5%	43.8%
Cash and cash equivalent	25.2%	14.0%	11.5%	24.1%
Short-term investments	35.3%	0.0%	0.0%	1.1%
Net receivables	9.5%	3.3%	55.5%	4.8%
Inventory	0.0%	0.0%	16.8%	11.0%
Other current assets	2.1%	0.0%	0.7%	2.7%
Long-term investments	0.3%	73.5%	0.0%	5.0%
Property, plant, and equipment	12.0%	0.5%	3.1%	44.1%
Goodwill	12.1%	2.4%	12.0%	0.0%
Intangible assets	1.9%	1.0%	0.3%	0.0%
Other assets	1.0%	5.3%	0.1%	7.1%
Deferred charges	0.6%	0.0%	0.0%	0.0%
Liabilities	**11.1%**	**91.9%**	**41.3%**	**35.2%**
Current liabilities	6.8%	0.0%	38.7%	15.9%
Accounts payable	6.1%	8.0%	38.5%	13.0%
Short-term debt	0.0%	14.9%	0.2%	0.0%
Others	0.7%	46.2%	0.0%	3.0%
Long-term debt	0.0%	19.3%	0.7%	2.5%
Other liabilities	4.2%	2.7%	1.0%	7.6%
Deferred charges	0.1%	0.0%	1.0%	9.2%
Minority interest	0.0%	0.7%	0.0%	0.0%
Stockholders' equity	**88.9%**	**8.1%**	**58.7%**	**64.8%**
Preferred stock	0.0%	0.4%	0.0%	0.0%
Common stock	0.0%	0.2%	0.1%	0.0%
Retained earnings	49.6%	3.1%	35.2%	77.4%
Treasury stock	0.0%	−0.4%	−0.8%	−24.4%
Capital surplus	39.1%	4.8%	24.2%	12.0%
Others	0.3%	0.0%	0.0%	−0.3%
Net tangible assets	**74.9%**	**4.8%**	**46.4%**	**64.8%**
Selected ratios				
Return on assets	16.1%	0.6%	−0.3%	18.5%
Inventory turn (per yr)	N/A	N/A	21	3
Days of inventory	0	0	18	108
Days of receivables	59	245	52	47
Days of payables	102	591	41	46
Days of working cap.	−42	−346	29	110
Gross margin	62.6%	N/A	11.8%	64.3%

Source: Yahoo! Finance.

2.2 What Financial Statements Do Not Reveal

We now turn to what financial statements might not be revealing, either by omission or by misrepresentation. The Financial Accounting and Standards Board (FASB) has put tremendous thought into what financial statements should include. Still, some aspects of operations are not captured in these statements.

2.2.1 Risks

There are many financial risks not explicit in financial statements. Some examples include risks from currency positions, credit, maturity mismatches between assets and liabilities, and litigation. Then there are business risks. Some of these—such as the correlation of sales with costs or the ratio of fixed to total costs (both indicating how a business's costs can be flexibly managed)—may be partially gleaned from financial statements.

There are, however, many important business risks that are almost impossible to quantify in simple statistics and are missing in financial statements. These may include risks stemming from information technology systems used, processes of all types, competition, or changes in regulation. Sometimes, the risks are not involved in the processes themselves but in the governance structure. Examples of these are in the setting of thresholds such as authorization limits, or in the organization of who checks whom in approvals.

2.2.2 Contingent Claims

Many options and insurance are not reflected on balance sheets and are called "off-balance-sheet items." Likewise, some aspects of pension claims or insurance claims that are not on the insurer's balance sheet are fully reflected on company balance sheets. Even if some of these practices are not permitted for listed companies, they may be permissible for private firms.

2.2.3 Covenants and Rights

A bank loan may come with restrictions on what can or cannot be done with the collateral. Other kinds of liabilities may have their own covenants and rights. For example, some debt may be convertible to equity. Some equities may have preferred cash flow and voting rights. All these impact the valuation of the business.

2.2.4 Reserves

In a sense, these are the opposite of contingent claims: they are hidden assets rather than claims. In many countries, such as some in Europe and Asia, banks can accumulate hidden reserves to tide them over fluctuations in loan profits and losses. These are sometimes called "cookie jar accounting" practices. Also, some kinds of provisions for debt, taxes, and other kinds of liabilities might not be evident from financial statements.

2.2.5   Intangible Assets

Examples of these include human capital, patents, trade secrets, research and development pipelines, goodwill and relationships with regulators, the strength of and bargaining power with suppliers and customers, and structural advantages such as monopoly charters and loyalty programs. The special difficulties with these assets are that they are difficult to value, their value can be fleeting, and their value can also depend on interactions—e.g., they work only when other assets are present, or they work better with some owners than with others.

2.2.6   Static and Backward-Looking View

Finally, financial statements give only a snapshot of a company's performance. Some investors, such as Henry Kravis of the private equity firm KKR, even argue that "financial statements, as valuable as they are, give you a rearview look at performance."[6] Therefore, the statements need to be supplemented if we wish to have a forward-looking perspective on a business.

2.3   When Might Financial Statements Be Less Accurate?

One way to begin is to address the three considerations in a good mystery novel: opportunity, means, and motive. But *unlike* in a mystery novel, the last of these—motive—is not a necessary condition in our analysis; we are interested in inaccuracies that arise not only from ill intent, but also from sources such as cognitive biases, system failures, or even just accidents.

2.3.1   Opportunity

The opportunity to misstate financials can be found both in what is stated in balance sheets and income statements, and what is not.

When it comes to the balance sheet, auditors have developed a useful framework to inspect what is stated. They stress the auditing of assets for their:

• *Existence.*   For example, does the inventory level stated on a balance sheet reflect the true level found in warehouses? Shrinkage (a euphemism for losses resulting from theft) and misplaced items can be very significant for some businesses such as retailers.

• *Ownership.*   For example, is the inventory in the warehouse really owned by the business, or is it on consignment from a supplier? Or has it been sold but not yet delivered? Are some of the sales returned, and has ownership reverted to the business in question?

• *Value.*   For example, are marketable securities marked to market, and should they be? Are the receivables all collectible? Is the inventory really as valuable as stated on the balance sheet? Sometimes there is incentive to say that inventory is worse than it really is. A new CEO, or one in a bad year, might take a "big bath" to clean out the cumulative doubtful assets and inflate liabilities, so as to get all the negativism out at one time or to set a low bar for future performance benchmarking.

From an operational point of view, there are several other aspects of an asset that make it valuable. First, the more flexible an asset, the more valuable it is. Second, the marginal value of an asset may be dictated by how close it is to becoming a bottleneck. At the extreme, a bottleneck asset is extremely valuable, since to produce an extra unit of one product, we may have to produce one fewer unit of another product that uses the same asset. Third, the value may need to be risk-adjusted, as in financial assets. For example, a workstation may be able to produce at a higher rate but with more stoppages, or may have the same effective production rate as a second workstation that produces at a lower rate with fewer stoppages. Since variability can cause disruptions to other workstations, the value of the first workstation might have to be adjusted down relative to that of the second.

When it comes to the income and cash flow statements, we can also examine the revenues and expenses for:

• *Timing.*   In 1967, a manager at the British cotton company Thomas Gerrard & Son postdated purchases and antedated sales around the year end, so as to show higher year-end earnings. Another thing to look for is delaying of expenses arising from writeoffs of obsolete inventory. In 2001, Xerox had to reclassify its revenues because it booked as revenues maintenance payments that should have been booked over the duration of the maintenance contracts rather than at one time.

• *Inflation and deflation.*   A popular example is artificially inflating sales to improve sales bonuses or short-term earnings. In channel stuffing, goods are sold and delivered to customers at discounts or on generous return terms, just in time so that revenues from these sales can be recognized at year end. The result of bringing revenues forward is that customers buy less in the future. Another example is inflating the amortization period of a capital expenditure, thereby reducing the expense reported in each year.

• *Tunneling.*   The idea here is that revenues that might accrue to one business are "tunneled" to another, in a "related-party transaction." This benefits an owner who has a smaller share in the first business than in the second. Consider SARL Peronnet, a home construction firm in France whose majority owner is the Peronnet family. In 1999, the family was accused of setting up SCI, a warehouse company owned 100% by the family, and structuring contracts between SARL Peronnet and SCI to the advantage of SCI. The courts eventually ruled in favor of the family against minority shareholders of SARL, because it viewed the latter as not having suffered an actual loss. In general, civil law countries, even developed ones such as France, tend to have narrower interpretations of minority oppression than common law countries such as the US.

• *Reclassification.* For example, one-time extraordinary revenues—say from the sale of an asset—might be reclassified as if they were recurrent. Conversely, a recurring expense might be classified as a one-time extraordinary expense. Another kind of reclassification is in the cash flow statement. Operating cash flows are generally viewed as more recurrent than investment cash flows, so a firm could reclassify a greater portion of an investment revenue stream as operating, or a greater portion of an operating expense—such as software development expense—as investment.

• *Transfer pricing.* Firms use discretion in how transactions between related companies are priced. In principle, it should be straightforward: price at market rates. But all sorts of adjustments can be employed, using arguments that the goods and services are of different quality, transacted at a different time, and so on.

Finally, there are some things that publicly traded firms can (illegally) do, such as "ghosting" or a "wash sale," in which trading volume and prices are artificially inflated by buying and selling one's own stock, possibly through different brokers to hide the trail. Sometimes the objective is to reduce taxes. For example, "crystallization" means selling securities at a capital loss (to reduce taxes) and immediately buying them back. Because there are tax regulations against these practices, they may involve tax risks.

Many of the above opportunities arise from areas of discretion permissible in accounting principles, although many also arise with the intent not to abide by the letter or the spirit of the principles.

2.3.2   Means

Consider a firm's manager. Using an analogy from forensic science, the manager might be said to have the means to produce inaccurate financial statements if she has control over what decisions to take and these decisions are not transparent to the investor:

• *The manager has decision rights.* For example, a manager might have the authority to decide on what inventory levels to carry or what investments to make. Importantly, the manager has the authority to manipulate not only accounting figures but also real operations. It is also worth clarifying that wrong decisions need not stem from a manager attending to her private interests at the expense of the company's. They could also be made out of incompetence, irrationality, cognitive biases, or just plain accidents.

• *The investor has less information than the manager (information asymmetry).* The ideal modern corporation is set up with many checks and balances. For example, major decisions can only be made with approval of the board of directors, and really major ones—such as the sale of a company—may even need votes by all shareholders. Within the business, lower managers are overseen by upper managers, and so on. But the key is that a supervisee (or "agent," in economic parlance) often has more information than the supervisor ("principal"). Therefore, it is difficult for the supervisor to micromanage or second-guess a supervisee. To the extent that such information asymmetry is costly to remedy, agents have means that can lead to inaccurate financial statements.

The above two conditions make it possible for managers to produce inaccurate statements. We now turn to the issue of managers' incentives to exploit the opportunity.

2.3.3 Motive

Managers sometimes have a motive to create misleading financial statements. Clear motive often arise from three sources:

• *The benefits are high enough.* Managers often hold some equity of their firms or their compensation may be tied to share prices, so they have direct incentives to keep their firms' share prices high. They may also want to keep share prices high because low prices invite takeovers that threaten their careers, and low prices reduce the managers' marketability when they are looking for their next jobs. Managerial compensation may also be tied to revenues or earnings, so there are also incentives to manipulate these.

Often, these incentives may provide for short-term gains to managers at the expense of long-term gains to shareholders. For example, sales bonuses might be a function of sales at a particular point—the end of the fiscal year—so managers may manipulate sales figures to show higher sales just before the fiscal year end. Managers also may cater to the equity market, which prefers smooth and short-term earnings.

From the debt perspective, managers may also face pressure to maintain covenant metrics—such as minimum interest cover ratios, current ratios, or leverage ratios—imposed by lenders. Failure to maintain these ratios may lead to bankruptcy and an end to the managers' careers.

Some economists also suggest that managers prefer a "quiet life" or may shirk their duties, so that, without proper monitoring, they might not care enough about keeping financial statements accurate. There are also arguments that managers receive private benefits when they run bigger companies—perhaps because their perks and compensation are tied to company size—giving them an incentive to make the balance sheet larger than it ought to be.

Finally, we note that some companies have an incentive to show lower performance— such as lower earnings—to avoid taxes, reduce regulatory scrutiny, or reduce public interest in their profitability. So managers' bias in inflating results may also diverge from companies' in these respects.

· *The probability of detection is low enough.*   There could be insufficient checks and balances. At the highest level, the board of directors could be too busy or unfamiliar with the business to ask the right questions, or they could be beholden to managers who have the incentive to manipulate. Other monitors—auditors, regulators, analysts—could also be biased in favor of managers. There could also be a lack of oversight at the transactional level, as in the case that led to the demise of Barings Bank, where a trader was allowed to be both front-end trader and back-end settlements clerk, so that he was able to process trades without checks by another party.

· *The penalty is low or not vivid enough.*   In chapter 4, we will see that there is practically no penalty for a manager who inflates inventory so as to send investors false signals of upcoming boosts in sales. Even when the manager is asked to explain the inventory situation, he or she can easily defend the move as the outcome of a well-intentioned but inaccurate sales forecast.

The penalty for other types of transgressions could be large but not visible. For example, the average drop in share price is about 9% in the two days after an announcement of a restatement of financials. For the worst offenders, the drop can be even larger (see table 2.8). However, on a day-to-day basis these possibilities are just not vivid enough to keep a lid on deviant behavior.

To reiterate, our discussion in this section is not meant to suggest that the misstating of a company's true financial situation always stems from managers acting on their private intentions. Unintended actions, arising from incompetence, irrationality, cognitive biases, or just plain accidents, could also be a cause. The lure of high benefits is often a motive for private intentions, while low detection probability and low penalty are often the motives for unintended actions.

Table 2.8
Market Reaction to Restatement of Financial Statements

Company	Approximate drop in share price in two days after announcement
Sybase	20%
Nine West Group	18%
MicroStrategy, Inc.	62%
California Micro Devices Corp.	40%
Cendant Corp.	47%
Banker Hughes, Inc.	15%

Source: Mulford and Comiskey (2002).

2.4 Takeaways

This chapter shows us that:

• Financial statements can tell us a surprising amount about the operations of a business. For example, we can tell whether a business serves retail or business customers, the shelf life of its product, its inventory management capability, what industry it is likely to be in, how likely it is to run out of cash, and whether its growth will be constrained.

• Nevertheless, financial statements can be incomplete, because there are critical elements of a business that are not reflected in the statements.

• They can also be inaccurate, because managers have the opportunity, means, and motive to produce inaccurate statements.

These points motivate the rest of this book, in which we show how tools and frameworks that probe into the operations of a firm might help complement publicly available information in financial statements.

2.5 Survey of Prior Research in One Paragraph

The innovative pedagogical technique of uncovering business models from financial statements is due to William Fruhan. The implicit question in this chapter is: What operational factors drive performance? At the highest level, some of the factors are:

• economy-specific—e.g., institutions and infrastructure;
• industry-specific—e.g., barriers to entry, concentration of players;
• firm-specific—e.g., investments, business model, governance;
• others, such as executive-specific—e.g., training, work experience—or just noise.

While there is no doubt that economy- and executive-specific drivers might have some influence on firm performance, scholars have framed the debate as a battle between the dominance of industry-specific and firm-specific drivers. Michael Porter and Anita McGahan (their writings are in "Further Reading" below) have argued forcefully that industry-specific drivers are dominant, but the consensus is moving toward firm-specific drivers as dominant. One of the earliest advocates for the latter view is Edith Penrose. Since industry-specific drivers still play a role, they form the underpinning of why firms in the same industry have similar characteristics. But as the research shows, firm-specific characteristics are just as important. It is these firm-specific characteristics that we study in subsequent chapters. Some of these include business models. Raffi Amit, Richard Lai, Tom Malone, Peter Weill, and Chris Zott all have studied business models and their economic drivers. Sergei Netessine and Nils Rudi are experts on the Internet drop shipping model, which significantly reduces inventory for an e-commerce firm. Vishal Gaur, Ananth Raman, and Marshall Fisher study the relationship between gross margin and inventory turns. On the inadequacies of reported information, Paul Healy is one of the first researchers on earnings management. Eli Amir, Bob Holthausen, Baruch Lev, and others have written about earnings manipulation and the value relevance of financial statements. The tunneling case of Peronnet is from Simon Johnson, Rafael La Porta, Florencio Lopez-de-Silanes, and Andrei Shleifer. Some of the material in this chapter also coincides with textbooks on auditing and in particular on forensic accounting. The Generally Accepted Auditing Standards (GAAS) of the American Institute of Certified Public Accountants is a useful reference. There are also some specialized areas such as information technology audit.

2.6   Further Reading

Amir, E., and B. Lev. 1996. "Value-Relevance of Nonfinancial Information: The Wireless Communications Industry." *Journal of Accounting and Economics* 22 (1–3): 3–30.

Anonymous. 1963. "Wall Street: Boiling in Oil." *Time*, December 13.

Barney, J. B. 1986. "Types of Competition and the Theory of Strategy: Toward an Integrative Framework." *Academy of Management Review* 11 (4): 791–800.

Barth, M. E., W. H. Beaver, and W. R. Landsman. 2001. "The Relevance of the Value Relevance Literature for Financial Accounting Standard Setting: Another View." *Journal of Accounting and Economics* 31 (1–3): 77–104.

Beneish, M. D. 1999. "The Detection of Earnings Manipulation." *Financial Analysts Journal* 55 (5): 24–36.

Collins, D. W., E. L. Maydew, and I. S. Weiss. 1997. "Changes in the Value-Relevance of Earnings and Book Values over the Past Forty Years." *Journal of Accounting and Economics* 24 (1): 39–67.

Fruhan, W. E. 2006. "The Case of the Unidentified Industries." Harvard Business School, Boston, MA, Case 207-096.

Gaur, V., M. L. Fisher, and A. Raman. 2005. "An Econometric Analysis of Inventory Turnover Performance in Retail Services." *Management Science* 51 (2): 181–194.

Healy, P. 1985. "The Effect of Bonus Schemes on Accounting Decisions." *Journal of Accounting and Economics* 7 (1–3): 85–107.

Healy, P. M., and J. M. Wahlen. 1999. "A Review of the Earnings Management Literature and Its Implications for Standard Setting." *Accounting Horizons* 13 (4): 365–383.

Holthausen, R. W., and R. L. Watts. 2001. "The Relevance of the Value Relevance Literature for Financial Accounting Standard Setting." *Journal of Accounting and Economics* 31 (1–3): 3–75.

Johnson, S., R. La Porta, F. Lopez-de-Silanes, and A. Shleifer. 2000. "Tunneling." *American Economic Review* 90 (2): 22–27.

Malone, T. W., P. Weill, R. K. Lai, V. T. D'Urso, G. Herman, T. G. Apel, S. Woerner, and I. Author. 2007. "Do Some Business Models Perform Better Than Others?" MIT Sloan Research Paper, 4615-06.

McGahan, A. M., and M. E. Porter. 1997. "How Much Does Industry Matter, Really?" *Strategic Management Journal* 18 (Summer): 15–30.

McGahan, A. M., and M. E. Porter. 2002. "What Do We Know about Variance in Accounting Profitability?" *Management Science* 48 (7): 834–851.

Mulford, C. W., and E. E. Comiskey. 2002. *The Financial Numbers Game: Detecting Creative Accounting Practices*. New York: Wiley.

Netessine, S., and N. Rudi. 2006. "Supply Chain Choice on the Internet." *Management Science* 52 (6): 84.

Penrose, E. T. 1995. *The Theory of the Growth of the Firm*. New York: Oxford University Press.

Porter, M. E. *Competitive Strategy*. New York: Free Press, 1980.

Rumelt, R. P. 1991. "How Much Does Industry Matter?" *Strategic Management Journal* 12 (3): 167–185.

Wernerfelt, B. 1984. "A Resource-Based View of the Firm." *Strategic Management Journal* 5 (2): 171–180.

Zott, C., and R. Amit. 2008. "The Fit between Product Market Strategy and Business Model: Implications for Firm Performance." *Strategic Management Journal* 29 (1).

II OPERATIONAL INDICATORS

Now that we have acknowledged the usefulness of publicly available data, and its incompleteness, we look at several types of operational data that can predict performance:

1. ***Indicators of accounting performance.*** We first consider indicators of current accounting performance, as measured by return on assets (ROA). We do this by deriving ROA drivers in the form of an "ROA tree." We then look at leading indicators for measures of future performance, such as future sales, earnings, margins, unit costs, and capital efficiency.

2. ***Indicators of stock market performance.*** We move from accounting to a stock valuation-based measure of performance. We describe several indicators of stock market valuation, such as inventory turn. By knowing how the stock market considers these indicators, firms and managers may manipulate them.

3. ***Indicators of disruption.*** We next consider a negative performance metric, in which companies' fortunes are disrupted. What indicators can predict disruption?

4. ***Indicators of distress.*** Finally, we consider the worst-case scenario: indicators of bankruptcy.

3 Indicators of Accounting Performance

In this chapter, we focus on operational indicators of accounting-based performance—such as return on assets (ROA) and its drivers like sales and earnings. Specifically we ask:

• *What indicators drive current performance?*   If we were to decompose performance—say ROA—into its operational components, what would these be? Not surprisingly, the answer is industry-specific, and we construct "ROA trees" for some representative industries.

• *What leading indicators drive future performance?*   While ROA trees are useful, they mostly provide only a view of performance at a snapshot in time (e.g., today's ROA is, by definition, today's earnings divided by today's assets). But what drivers predict future performance?

3.1 Indicators of Current Performance: ROA Trees

ROA is a common measure of current accounting performance. It reflects how much money is made after putting a certain amount of funds into a business. To discover the indicators of ROA, we can decompose it. There are many approaches to doing this. One is to use what is sometimes called the DuPont formula:

$$\text{ROA} = \frac{\text{earnings}}{\text{COGS}} \times \frac{\text{COGS}}{\text{assets}},$$

where COGS is cost of goods sold.[1] The first term captures margin (reflecting factors such as market power and branding) and the second represents asset turn (reflecting operational efficiency).

Another way to break down ROA might look like figure 3.1. ROA is earnings divided by assets, and earnings are in turn sales minus expenses.

Whichever decomposition we use, we very quickly go from financial measures to operational measures. In the case of a manufacturer, sales is flow rate—how many units are

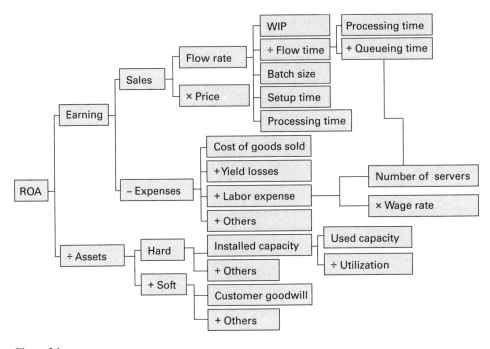

Figure 3.1
An ROA tree.

produced per year—times price. For simplicity, we assume that what is produced is sold, so flow rate is given as work-in-progress (WIP) inventory divided by flow time,[2] which is the duration starting from the arrival of raw materials and ending with the departure of produced units to customers. This decomposition is represented by the dashed lines at the top of the figure. Another way to break down flow rate is to consider how fast units are produced when we produce them in batches. Viewed this way, flow rate can also be recast as:

$$\text{flow rate} = \frac{\text{batch size}}{\text{setup time} + (\text{batch size} \times \text{unit processing time})}$$

This is obtained by considering each batch. In the numerator, we have the number of units produced in a batch. In the denominator we have the time taken to produce that batch, which is the sum of the setup time and the time to produce each of the units in the batch.

How do we know what financial or operational decompositions to use? Indeed, how does one build ROA trees in the first place?

3.1.1   Principles for Developing ROA Trees

We describe some general principles for developing ROA trees, often returning to figure 3.1 for illustration.

Begin with Industry Language

Since much of an ROA tree is likely to be industry-specific, it often helps to know the industry jargon. Once we know it, we may see that they are just using different words for what we already know—e.g., "par level" in the restaurant business is "finished goods inventory" in manufacturing.

Often, however, industry language is not just different terms for the same underlying concept, but rather an indicator of management intuition about how to run a business. For example, "block hours" in the airline industry could be relabeled "flow time" in standard operations management: it is the elapsed time in a process, between an aircraft's leaving a departure gate and arriving at the destination's arrival gate. But the term "block hours" also strongly suggests that scheduling and aircraft utilization are some of the important drivers of airline performance.

Use as Many Decompositions for a Measure as Is Useful

There may be different ways of decomposing a measure, and we are not limited to using only one decomposition if using more can illuminate the measure. In the example earlier in figure 3.1, flow rate can be usefully decomposed in different ways.

The key, however, is to use only decompositions that provide actionable levers. For example, flow rate can also be decomposed as flow rate per staff multiplied by the number of staff. If the number of staff is unchangeable because of strict union rules, then the actionable lever is flow rate per staff and not the number of staff.

Use a Driver for as Many Measures as Is Useful

In the breakdown for expenses, we write labor expense as the multiple of the number of servers and the wage rate. But the number of servers also determines queueing time. Therefore, a driver may determine more than one measure. Indeed, sometimes the driver may affect ROA positively via one measure and negatively via another.

Exploit Operational Principles in Decomposition

Some decompositions are "mere" arithmetic. For example, ROA is, by definition, return divided by assets, so it is natural to decompose ROA into return and assets.

But more useful decompositions exploit operational principles. For example, Little's Law (see the discussion in section A.2.4 in the appendix) says that inventory is flow rate times flow time, under generous conditions. Also, a batching law (see also section 3.1) says that the flow rate is batch size divided by the sum of setup time and batch size × processing time. These types of operational principles describe how the mechanisms work in a process, and therefore can be more useful to managers. For example, decomposing flow rate into setup and process times allows managers to see how improving these times can in turn improve flow rate.

Needless to say, we should use the appropriate operational principle. For example, flow time should be decomposed differently depending on whether customers can wait. If we are looking at a queueing system in which customers wait if they do not yet have a unit to purchase, then flow time is the sum of processing and queueing times. If customers cannot wait and no queue really forms, then we would use a different breakdown.

Use Different Trees for Different Roles

How wide and deep should an ROA tree be? That depends on who uses it and for what purpose. For example, a chief financial officer (CFO) might want the tree to be broad but not too deep, since a CFO's role rarely goes into details such as plant-level drivers.

At the other end of the scale, a plant mechanic might want a very narrow but deep ROA tree, since she has only a small role in areas outside her responsibilities, but she is interested in how direct actions she takes at the plant level would affect ROA.

It can also be helpful to use subtrees for lower-level staff, such as one that has "Units produced per year" rather than ROA as the root.

As this discussion suggests, one general principle is that the width (sometimes called the span) of the tree may be determined by the drivers for which the user has some control. Another principle is that the root should be whatever the goal is for the user.

Make Explicit Both Current and Full Potential

Consider assets. One component of hard assets is installed capacity, such as a plant. A critical aspect of operations is that the plant may be imperfectly run. Produced goods may not be sold, and the plant may not be fully utilized.

It is useful to make explicit both the full potential capacity as well as the utilized capacity. This provides a picture of how much we can improve without the need to install new capacity.

Make Intangibles Explicit

Finally, some drivers might be "soft," intangible, or hard to measure. An example is customer goodwill. Others might be less soft but still hard to measure, such as research and development. Nevertheless, it is helpful to codify these drivers, even if all we do is to note them rather than to measure them.

This also implies that our ROAs may not coincide with accounting ROAs, if we include more than just accounting assets on balance sheets.

We now return to our initial observation, that ROA trees can be most useful when we become as specific as is necessary and possible. Often, this means creating industry-specific ROA trees.

3.1.2 ROA Tree for Airlines

For an industry example, we will look at the principal indicators of ROA for an airline (figure 3.2), then discuss them in the context of the famously successful Southwest Airlines, and finally discuss them in the context of international airlines.

Major Operational Indicators of ROA Performance

We start with the revenue side. An important indicator is revenue passenger-miles, or RPM—the paid seats times the number of miles traveled. RPM considers revenue enplanements but excludes empty seats or seats obtained with frequent flyer program (FFP) redemptions or redemptions arising from compensating passengers bumped because of overbooking (we study this in section 15.4.2).

RPM can be considered a multiple of ASM—available seat-miles, or the number of seats multiplied by the number of miles flown—and the load factor. ASM is determined by the number of planes, how many seats in the average plane, how many departures the plane makes, and the average distance traveled for each departure (which is a function of route mix, the mix of long- and short-haul flights). Load factor captures utilization—that is, what percentage of the ASM is sold.

These three critical indicators—RPM, ASM, load factor—have their equivalents for cargo revenues. These use payload capacity rather than number of seats in their construction.

There are also variations of these passenger and cargo indicators. For example, one set of passenger indicators simply uses seats sold, without the adjustment for distance traveled. This produces revenue passenger seats, available seats, and a seat load factor. Another way is to weigh the indicators not only by distance traveled but also by dollar amounts. Finally, there is a variation that combines passenger and cargo businesses. The *overall load factor* combines passenger and cargo businesses using standard passenger and baggage weights (200 pounds together) to convert passengers to cargo-equivalent payload.

All these load factors in various forms may be benchmarked against a breakeven load factor (BELF): this is the load factor for which operating profits are zero.

Figure 3.2 also shows some major indicators of expenses. One of them is maintenance cost, which is in turn driven by—among other factors—the mix of aircraft types. A diverse mix increases maintenance cost because an airline cannot pool the use of parts for different aircraft types (see section 3.2.3). There also needs to be more training for maintenance staff on different types of parts. A variation on the mix of aircraft types is the age distribution of the fleet. A wide distribution by age also has a deleterious effect on maintenance cost.

Maintenance cost is also driven by block hours. An aircraft's block hours are the hours from when the aircraft leaves the blocks at its wheels on departure until its wheels get blocked on its arrival at destination. It is important to consider what drivers of costs are

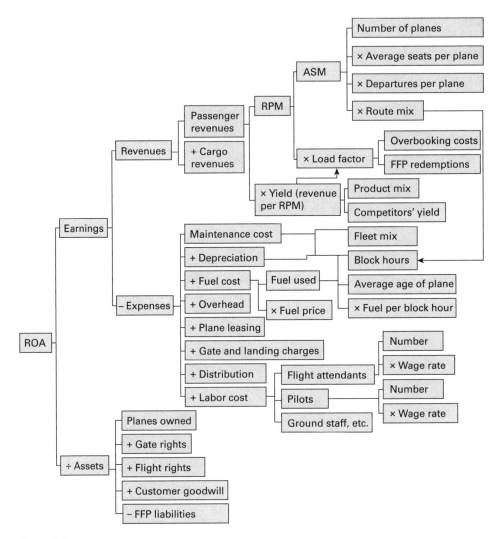

Figure 3.2
ROA tree for airlines. Note: ASM = available seat-miles, RPM = revenue passenger-miles, FFP = frequent flyer program.

more salient. Consider two planes that are of similar make but have very different seat configurations. Would maintenance cost be driven more by block hours or by ASM, which considers not just distance traveled (similar to block hours) but also the number of seats? Unless the two planes are very dissimilar in physical size, for the most part we can say that block hours is a more salient driver than ASM.

The other key cost components, as shown in the ROA tree, include depreciation, fuel cost, overhead, leasing costs, and so on. The tree also shows important components of assets, such as the fleet and various rights.

The revenue and cost components can also be normalized by their units. Yield is the price per RPM and CASM is the cost per ASM.

For a more interesting variation to the decomposition in figure 3.2, instead of separating revenue components by product line and cost components by type such as maintenance and fuel, we could frame the components as seen by passengers. This has the advantage of reminding ourselves of the costs and benefits that only customers care about.

To accomplish this, we can think through the process experience of a passenger. From the time the passenger ponders a trip and buys a ticket through some distribution channel, there is already a vast amount of operational work behind the scenes. This may include configuring an airline's route structure, optimizing the use of gates and landing rights, scheduling of personnel both in the air and on the ground, publishing the in-flight magazine, filing FAA (Federal Aviation Administration) reports, and so on. In some cases, these processes might be outsourced to third parties, and in other cases they might be the responsibility of airport authorities.

Many of these processes are on the *land side*—that is, even before departure immigration. On the day of departure, an airline may have to deal with anything from passenger requests for changes and complimentary limousine service for first-class passengers to manual and automatic check-in counters.

Once the passenger clears immigration, the airline continues to be involved on the *air side*, from lounges for premium passengers and gate control to cleaning arrival aircraft and preparing meals.

To sum up, our airline ROA reflects many of the guidelines mentioned in the previous section. It includes industry language (such as RPM), exploits operational concepts (such as utilization), and can even afford different decompositions (by product and cost component, or by the process as view by passengers).

Case: Southwest Airlines

Southwest Airlines started in 1967 by flying between three cities: Dallas, Houston, and San Antonio. In the years since, it has been celebrated as a highly successful operation. Its story is told in a children's book—*Gumwrappers and Goggles*—and in a musical—*Show Your Spirit*. According to Herb Kelleher, a cofounder of Southwest Airlines, "If you had invested $100,000 in 1972, it would have grown to $102 million by 2002."[3]

Table 3.1
Some ROA Drivers for Some Larger US Airlines

	Southwest	Continental	American	Delta	United	US Air
ROA (%)	1.2	−4.6	−11.2	−19.8	−27.0	−30.6
ASM (bil)	103	103	164	166	152	89
Block hours/day	5,853	3,950	6,365	4,797	4,772	3,538
Departures/day	3,267	1,065	2,016	1,455	1,398	1,359
Aircraft in service	537	350	664	1,023	409	458
Aircraft leased	91	201	296	339	200	343
Aircraft owned	446	149	368	684	209	115
Load factor	71	81	81	81	81	80
Revenue/ASM ($)	11	13	14	14	13	14
Passenger revenue per ASM ($)	10.2	11.1	11.2	11.8	11.3	12.4
Passenger revenue ($mil)	10,549	13,737	18,234	19,583	18,435	11,062
Passenger revenue per RPM ($)	14	14	14	15	15	15
Revenue passengers (mil)	89	49			63	82
RPM (bil)	73	83	132	135	122	71
Operating expenses per ASM ($)	10	12	14	19	16	16
Average aircraft age (years)	10.1	9.4	15.0	13.2	13.0	
Fuel expense ($mil)	3,713	4,905	8,154	7,346	8,979	4,755
Fuel price (¢/gal)	244	327	303	316	354	318
Fuel used (mil gal)	1.5	1.5	2.7	2.7	2.6	1.5
International % of ASM		50	38	44	43	22
Flight attendants	7,692	8,808	15,962	11,742	13,214	7,099
Pilots	5,588	4,578	8,306	6,391	6,337	4,234
Pilot wages ($000/yr)	173	136	139	126	119	114
Flight attendant wages ($000/yr)	53	49	50	37	40	40

Source: Capital IQ.

There are several popular conceptions of why Southwest succeeds, which we can verify with information from an ROA tree.

Table 3.1 shows the figures for some ROA indicators for Southwest and other large US airlines. Southwest is reputed to achieve quick turnarounds of its aircraft to maximize capacity. This seems to be borne out by the number of block hours and departures as shown in the table. Interestingly, this means more capacity and, all things being equal, would mean that Southwest has a lower load factor. Therefore, Southwest's strategy is both to have this increased capacity from quick turnarounds and to keep costs low to fill the capacity. "For [Kelleher], as always, the key is costs. 'Traffic depends on fare levels,' he said. 'And you can bribe passengers to fly.' In other words, if fares are low enough, more people will take to the air. Southwest saw that after it initiated service between Baltimore and Chicago. Since then, overall traffic between the two airports has increased by more than 2,000%."[4] The result is that while Southwest's load factor may be lower than that at other airlines, it has a lower breakeven load factor.

However, we also bear in mind that the ROA tree as constructed does not reveal the reasons behind Southwest's quick turnaround. To make it more useful, we would flesh out these reasons in the ROA tree (not shown in the figure). These include its using secondary airports that are less congested, having little in the way of amenities and food on board to clean up and resupply, training its ground staff as if they were in a car race pit stop, and most importantly, operating a point-to-point route structure rather than a hub-and-spoke structure in which planes have to wait for one another in order to transfer passengers among them.

We next turn our attention to revenues, and then to expenses.

Southwest's RPM is smaller than those for most other big airlines. This is driven by its relatively low passenger revenue per RPM, given the airline's focus on low pricing. It does have a higher number of revenue passengers, since each mile has more passengers given its shorter-haul flights. But the higher number of revenue passengers does not compensate enough for the lower pricing; hence the low total RPM.

Fortunately, the low pricing is sustained by low costs. In table 3.1, we see that Southwest keeps is fleet younger than most of its peers. Together with its using just Boeing 737s—possible because of its focus on short-haul flights—this keeps its maintenance cost low (not shown in the table).

Southwest also keeps its fuel cost low. Not shown in the table is how: this is achieved primarily through derivatives that bet in favor of rising fuel costs. For years, this has been advantageous to Southwest. Naturally, such bets can also work against the airline. In 2008, it suffered its first loss in seventeen years despite a general reduction in fuel costs, because of its bets on oil prices.

Finally, table 3.1 also shows that the Southwest staff is not necessarily low-paid, as is widely thought. Indeed, the wages are higher than those at its peers.

As we can see, the operational indicators point to areas for further research. How does Southwest have more block hours? Why are its fuel costs lower? Why are its wages higher? In getting the answers to these questions, one can uncover the key to Southwest's success and better value its performance in the market.

Non-US Airlines

We chose to describe the airline industry because this industry has the interesting characteristic that it went global long before globalization became a buzzword. This makes international comparisons more realistic. Table 3.2 shows non-US airlines, some with higher ROAs and some with lower. Both groups are ranked with the highest ROA at left and the lowest at right.

In some ways, the indicators for ROA performance mentioned in the previous two sections apply for non-US airlines. For example, the higher-ROA airlines tend to have higher load factors, a younger fleet (lower maintenance cost), and in general a lower cost per ASM.

But there are significant differences too. One distinguishing feature among non-US airlines is that their revenue per ASM tends to be higher; we could speculate that this is due to the higher degree of competition and shorter-haul routes among US airlines. While

Table 3.2
ROA Drivers for Some International Airlines

I: Higher ROAs

	Chile	Ireland	Britain	Canada	Germany
	LAN	Ryanair	BA	Westjet	Lufthansa
ROA (%)	6.8	6.2	6.1	5.4	2.7
ASM (bil)	22	41	93	17	121
Aircraft in service	96	163	245	76	524
ASM/aircraft (bil)	0.23	0.25	0.38	0.22	0.23
Aircraft leased	33			24	
Aircraft owned	63			52	
Average aircraft age (years)	5.2			4.0	
Load factor	77	82	76	80	79
Revenue/ASM ($)	21	10	19	15	29
Passenger revenue per ASM ($)	13	9	16	13	19
Passenger revenue ($mil)	2,859	3,518	14,973	2,301	23,459
Passenger revenue per RPM ($)	17	10	21	17	24
Revenue passengers (mil)	13,240	50,932	33,161	14,284	70,543
RPM (bil)	17	34	70	14	96
Operating expense per ASM ($)		8.1		13.2	
Fuel price (¢/gal)	320	265	245		
Fuel used (mil gal)	0.4			0.2	
Fuel expense ($mil)	1,424	1,251	4,080	803	7,484

II: Lower ROAs

	Canada	China	Canada	Brazil	China
	Jazz	Southern	Air	TAM, SA	Eastern
ROA (%)	−0.8	−5.8	−9.0	−10.3	−20.9
ASM (bil)	6	70	62	35	47
Aircraft in service	137	348	200	129	240
ASM/aircraft (bil)	0.04	0.20	0.31	0.27	0.20
Aircraft leased	89		129	129	
Aircraft owned	48		71	0	
Average aircraft age (years)	13.4	6.3	8.8	5.5	
Load factor	73	74	81	71	71
Revenue/ASM ($)	29	12	18	13	13
Passenger revenue per ASM ($)	29	11	16	11	11
Passenger revenue ($mil)	1,623	7,389	9,713	3,876	5,016
Passenger revenue per RPM ($)	40	14	19	15	15
Revenue passengers (mil)	9,718	58,237		30,144	37,232
RPM (bil)	4	52	51	25	33
Operating expense per ASM ($)	26.3		17.9	12.0	
Fuel price (¢/gal)					
Fuel used (mil gal)			1.0	0.5	
Fuel expense ($mil)	430	3,384	3,419	1,695	2,710

Source: Capital IQ.

Table 3.3
Scale of "Freedoms of the Air" for a US Airline

Freedom	Rights (incremental over rights of the lower degrees of freedom)
1st	Fly over foreign country
2nd	Stop at foreign country to refuel or undertake maintenance
3rd	Take passengers from US to foreign country
4th	Take passengers from foreign country to US
5th	Take passengers from foreign country A to foreign country B, as long as route begins from or ends in US
6th	Take passengers from A to US to B
7th	Take passengers directly from A to B
8th	Take passengers from one of A's airports A1 to another of A's airports A2, as long as route begins from or ends in US. Passenger transport within the same country (A in this case) is called cabotage.
9th	Take passengers directly from A1 to A2

US airlines rarely have more than $12 on that metric, many non-US ones do. The exceptions are Ryanair, which still does well—perhaps because it achieves an admirably high load factor—and the Chinese and Brazilian airlines—which do not do so well on ROA. Thus, even this simple set of data can provide us with fact-based hypotheses about the economics of airlines.

Another indicator that figures prominently among non-US airlines is the operational choice to focus on short- or long-haul flights or a mix of both. These have different implications. For example, Southwest's focus on short flights means that it can ignore the food and entertainment expectations customers have for longer flights. Many international flights, however, are long-haul, and these are subject to an additional consideration: government-to-government agreements called "freedoms of the air," signed at the 1944 Chicago Convention. Table 3.3 describes these freedoms.

The ability of governments to negotiate these freedoms and the ability of airlines to obtain "superior access" to these negotiated freedoms (a core competence often called "regulatory management") are highly critical to the operational economics of airlines.

To date, freedoms beyond the fourth are still rare, and some airlines collaborate with others through code-sharing arrangements so as to enlarge their freedoms. Furthermore, the cross-ownership of airlines to some extent, and open skies treaties to another, have also relaxed the constraints on routing. In short, any forensics into an airline must consider what network structure it has and what it might lose or gain.

3.2 Indicators of Future Performance

The ROA trees look at a contemporaneous connection between one current performance metric (ROA) and its drivers, financial or operational. For many investors, the more interesting question is whether these drivers can indicate not just this year's performance but also future years'. It is more difficult to predict aggregate measures such as ROA because—as we learn in the previous section—these are driven by many factors. Therefore, in this section we describe three examples of how to predict finer measures of performance: sales, costs, and capital efficiency.

3.2.1 Advanced Topic: Predicting Sales, Earnings, and Margins Using Inventory Information—the Bernard-Noel Model

The simple way to predict sales is to use past sales. Many analysts do just this. For example, Bernstein Research analyst Toni Sacconaghi reports: "An analysis based on *extrapolating* sales trajectories of [the iPhone, iPod Touch, and all netbooks] suggests that Apple could sell a staggering 25 million iPads or more in FY 11."[5] Forecasting by extrapolation runs the danger of assuming that past conditions are representative of future ones. In truth, Apple sold a staggering 32 million iPads in fiscal year 2011.[6]

Figure 3.3, panel (a), signals a more rigorous way of extrapolating from the past to predict Apple's sales in 2011:

1. We first specify the prediction model, in which $sales_t$ represents sales in year t. A simple approach could be as easy as finding α and β in this equation:

$$sales_{t+1} = \alpha + \beta \cdot sales_t,$$

which would allow us, given $sales_t$, to find $sales_{t+1}$.

2. We next collect Apple's sales for all years before 2011.

3. We run a regression of the data in step 2 using the model in step 1, to get α and β.

4. Finally, we predict Apple's 2011 sales as α plus β times its 2010 sales.

There are some ways to improve the above approach. For example, we can include data from similar companies to boost the accuracy of our prediction. We can also introduce some control variables, which would be especially important if we were to use data from other retailers.

But the fact remains that there is little evidence for past sales predicting future sales. What if we do some forensic work and dive into this black box of drivers of future sales? Victor Bernard and James Noel of the University of Michigan show how we can achieve better predictions. Below is an adaptation of their approach. We focus on sales here, but they also show similar models for predicting earnings and margins.

The key is to improve step 1 by incorporating a deeper understanding of how past sales drive future sales. Figure 3.3, panel (b), shows that there can be many relationships going on. The left three boxes indicate current—indexed by the subscript t—demand, inventory, and sales. The right three boxes are the same for the future, indexed by $t+1$. Of course, this depiction over just one year is a simplification, but it is still accurate to the first order and provides a foundation for creating multiyear models.

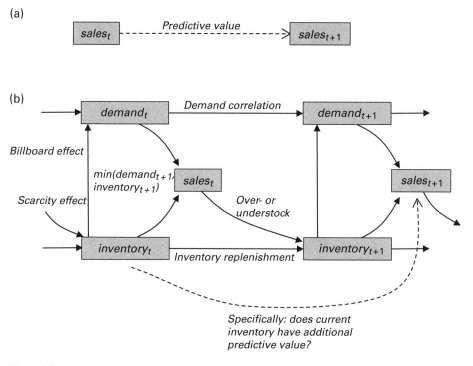

Figure 3.3
Simple and deeper approaches to predicting sales. Simple approach to predicting future sales (a); deeper theories of what predicts future sales (b). Solid arrows indicate causal relationships. The dash arrow indicates the relationship of interest.

Solid arrows in the diagram indicate causal relationships. Consider sales. It is the minimum of demand and inventory: if demand exceeds inventory, we can only sell the inventory; if inventory exceeds demand, then we sell to the demand. Now look at inventory. One component is the leftover, or overstock, from the previous year if inventory exceeded demand; if demand exceeded inventory, we would have understocking and nothing left over. Another component of inventory comes from management's decision on how to replenish the inventory. Finally, let us look at demand. It is also affected by two components. The first is a simple notion that current demand is (say positively) correlated with past demand.[7] The other component is that inventory could also affect demand. The billboard effect is that more inventory generates demand, in the way that having lots of Campbell Soup cans on a supermarket shelf provides an advertising billboard, or that having piles of a teenage accessory in a retail store suggests that other teenagers are wearing that accessory. But in other situations, inventory could have a scarcity effect, and hurt demand. For example, lots of accessory on shelves might suggest that few are buying them; many luxury houses such as LVMH keep their fashion pieces scarce to create the impression of exclusivity. At the extreme, some, like the Hermes Kelly bag, have long waiting lists of customers.

Given the above, we can now build a deeper prediction model. This modification of the previous step 1 involves:

1a. Writing out the effects just described. Specifically, we write out how $sales_{t+1}$, $demand_{t+1}$, and $inventory_{t+1}$ are determined. The equation for sales is simple:

$$sales_{t+1} = I(demand_{t+1} > inventory_{t+1}) \times inventory_{t+1} + I(demand_{t+1} < inventory_{t+1}) \times demand_{t+1},$$

where $inventory_{t+1}$ is the inventory level at the beginning of period $t+1$. $I(demand > inventory)$ is an indicator variable that is 1 if demand is above inventory and 0 otherwise. This equation effectively captures the relationship that sales are the minimum of inventory and demand.

For demand, the equation would depend on how demand correlates with past demand and on billboard/scarcity effects:

$$demand_{t+1} = \gamma \cdot demand_t + \delta \cdot inventory_{t+1},$$

where γ captures the demand correlation effect and δ the billboard/scarcity effect (if δ is positive, it would be a net billboard effect, and if it is negative, a net scarcity effect).

For inventory, Bernard and Noel write out the equation as:

$$inventory_{t+1} =$$

$$\zeta \cdot I(demand_t > inventory_t) \cdot (demand_t - inventory_t) + \eta \cdot I(demand_t < inventory_t) \cdot (inventory_t - demand_t) + \theta \cdot inventory_t.$$

What Bernard and Noel are saying is that $inventory_{t+1}$ depends on the three terms, which represent: (1) the cost of understocking, (2) the cost of overstocking, (3) some cost (say due to lead times) of adjusting from $inventory_t$.

1b. Substituting the $demand_{t+1}$ and $inventory_{t+1}$ equations into that for $sales_{t+1}$. Now we have a theoretically grounded prediction model of $sales_{t+1}$ that depends on $sales_t$, $demand_t$, and $inventory_t$, rather than the previous atheoretical reliance on a single black box $sales_t$. But there is one problem: this new model relies on $demand_t$, which outside investors cannot observe. In fact, even inside managers can only guess at this, since demand data is lost if managers do not track when a customer walks out of a store empty-handed. One way is to use some function of $sales_t$ as a proxy, based on an a priori estimate about stockouts. This is reasonable because $sales_t$ is an aggregate statistic that captures many theories of the dynamics of inventory and how inventory interacts with demand.

Table 3.4
The Bernard-Noel Results for How Inventory Predicts Sales, Earnings, and Margins

I: Next-quarter sales

Industry	Inventory Type		
	Raw Materials	Work-in-Progress	Finished Goods
Drugs	5.9%	4.3%	2.0%
Metals	4.5%*	3.5%*	4.8%*
Machinery	4.3%	4.9%*	−4.0%*
Electronics	4.4%*	7.3%*	4.2%
Computers	4.1%*	5.0%*	−0.9%
Transport	3.5%	1.0%	0.2%
Instruments	0.2%	3.2%*	1.5%
Retail			3.8%*

II: Next-year sales, earnings, margins

	Inventory Type		
	Raw Materials	Work-in-Progress	Finished Goods
Sales			
Manufacturing	2.6%*	3.6%*	0.9%
Retail			1.4%*
Earnings			
Manufacturing	−0.1%*	0.1%	−0.4%*
Retail			−0.3%*
Margins			
Manufacturing	−0.2%	−0.2%	−0.4%*
Retail			−0.2%*

Source: Bernard and Noel (1991). The coefficients show how much sales, earnings, or margins change with a 0.1 unexpected increase in inventory/sales.
* = Significant at the 5% level, two-tailed test.

To the extent that we understand when these theories apply for a specific business, we can better predict $sales_{t+1}$. As figure 3.3, panel (b), shows, $sales_{t+1}$ is affected by $sales_t$ in subtle ways—through $inventory_{t+1}$ and $demand_{t+1}$—and $inventory_{t+1}$ and $demand_{t+1}$ are themselves affected not just by $sales_t$ but also by $inventory_t$ and $demand_t$.

Table 3.4 shows the empirical predictive value of inventory on sales (and earnings and margins) according to Bernard and Noel. Actually, they make two further modifications that are not material here: they scale inventory by sales in the $inventory_{t+1}$ equation and use "unexpected inventory" in step 1b rather than just inventory. For example, the table shows that—in the retail industry—if a company's inventory/sales ratio unexpectedly increases by 0.1, its next-quarter sales can be predicted to increase by 3.8%.

3.2.2 Predicting Unit Costs Using the Experience Curve

In the early 1970s, a number of companies vied for the digital watches market. The major suppliers sold watches in the range of $40 to $75 apiece. But Texas Instruments (TI) suddenly introduced a watch at $20. By 1977, faced with shrinking market share and reduced profits, competitors such as Fairchild, Gillette, Litronix, and National Semiconductor all announced withdrawals from the market.

It is easy to dismiss TI's feat as just preemptive pricing: anticipating that costs would go down with volume, it reduced its price to garner market share. TI's true weapon, however, lay in its ability to accurately predict what unit costs would be when it did reach large volumes. Had it been unable to predict this, TI might have priced too low and risked losing too much profits (and customer goodwill, when it had to return to higher pricing) or priced too high and not been able to garner enough share (especially when competitors could more easily follow suit if the price reduction was small).

The analytical tool at TI's disposal was the experience curve.

For many products—especially high-volume commodity products—there is well-established research on how we can predict the unit cost of production, using the expected cumulative units a business has produced by then. By plotting unit cost and cumulative units using a log-log scale, we can more easily see this relationship as a straight line.[8] A familiar way to describe these "curves" is to say how much unit costs drop if we double cumulative units. Table 3.5 shows some examples. The drop also depends on the position

Table 3.5
Some Experience Curves by Industry

Industry	From	To	Drop in Unit Cost when Cumulative Units Double*
Microprocessors	1980	2005	60%
LCDs	1997	2003	60%
Brokerages	1990	2003	64%
Wireless services	1991	1995	66%
Butter	1970	2005	68%
VCRs	1993	2004	71%
Airlines	1988	2003	75%
Crushed stone	1940	2004	75%
Mobile phone services	1994	2000	76%
Personal computers	1988	2004	77%
DVD players/recorders	1997	2005	78%
Cable set-top boxes	1998	2003	80%
Cars**	1968	2004	81%
Milk bottles	1990	2004	81%
Plastics	1987	2004	81%
Color TVs	1955	2005	83%
DVDs	1997	2002	85%

Source: Gottfredson et al. (2008).
* Price drops are used as proxies for cost drops.
** Adjusted for changes in features and regulatory requirements.

Table 3.6
Some Experience Curves by Process Step in Semiconductor Diode Manufacturing

Process Step	Drop in Unit Cost when Cumulative Units Double
Photolithography	80%
Diffusion	85%
Contact plating	70%
Scribing	80%
Furnace sealing	85%

Source: Yelle (1976)

in the value chain. Table 3.6 shows these for different process steps in a semiconductor diode manufacturer.

Experience curves slope downward for three main reasons, and these imply that the curves are most definable only in circumstances where these reasons are salient:

1. *Learning*, resulting in improvements in process and product design. If learning is mostly within-firm, then it makes sense to have "cumulative units within firm" on the horizontal axis. If learning leaks and is mostly between firms, then it makes more sense to have "industry cumulative units" on the horizontal axis; "cumulative units within firm" may not really drive unit costs down.

2. *Scale*, arising from spreading fixed costs over more units (even if over time). This suggests that products more amenable to scaling—perhaps commoditized rather than differentiated products, and with high fixed costs—will exhibit curve behavior.

3. *Outside-firm time effects*, arising from general changes that are not specific to the product in question. Some, like inflation, are not interesting from a productivity viewpoint and should be factored out. Others, like general technological improvements such as computer technology, may filter into some companies that have greater "absorptive capacity" —a company's capacity to assimilate and use new information—and therefore could be firm-specific. More likely, this contributes to an experience curve for the industry—or even the economy—as a whole.

We should therefore be cautious about using the experience curve when the above factors are not salient. In particular, when there are significant technical changes (e.g., in auto assembly lines), the experience curve framework would not apply.

Suppose these considerations for an experience curve are met. The experience curve provides an indication of how unit costs may decrease with more cumulative units. To see this, consider the form of the experience curve given by:

$$unitCost_n = unitCost_1 \cdot n^{-\lambda} \tag{1}$$

where $unitCost_n$ is the unit cost of the nth cumulative unit and λ captures how much unit costs drop for a small percentage increase in n—that is, λ is the elasticity of unit cost with respect to n. For a large additional percent increase in n, we have to directly compare unit costs using equation (1). For example, if λ is 0.3, then when we double cumulative volume from $n = 100$ to 200 units, unit costs would have fallen by this fraction:

$$1 - \frac{unitCost_1 \, 200^{-\lambda}}{unitCost_1 \, 100^{-\lambda}} = 1 - \frac{1}{2^\lambda} = 1 - \frac{1}{2^{0.3}} = 0.188. \tag{2}$$

In other words, this is an 18.8% experience curve.

It is useful to go through an exercise to predict unit costs. Consider microprocessors. Table 3.5 shows that unit costs decline by 60% when cumulative production volume doubles. Suppose our cumulative production is now 1 million units, our unit cost is $2.50, and our annual production is 100,000 units growing at 5% a year. What does the experience curve predict our unit cost to be in 3 years?

In 3 years, our cumulative production will be $1 + 0.1 + (0.1 \times 1.05) + (0.1 \times 1.05^2) =$ 1.31525 million units. So we want:

$$unitCost_{1,315,250} = unitCost_1 \times (1,315,250)^{-\lambda}. \tag{3}$$

To find λ, we use equation (2):

$$1 - \frac{1}{2^\lambda} = 0.6.$$

With some alegbra (or a calculator), this means that λ is 1.322. To find $unitCost_1$, we use equation (1):

$$unitCost_{1,000,000} = unitCost_1 \times (1,000,000)^{-\lambda}$$

$$2.50 = unitCost_1 \times (1,000,000)^{-1.322}$$

$$unitCost_1 = 2.50 \times (1,000,000)^{1.322}.$$

Substituting these values of λ and $unitCost_1$ into equation (3) gives:

$$unitCost_{1,315,250} = 2.50 \times (1,000,000)^{1.322} \times (1,315,250)^{-1.322} = \$1.74.$$

3.2.3 Predicting Capital Efficiency

We now turn our attention to predicting capital costs. There are two ways in which capital costs could be reduced: risk pooling and scale.

Risk Pooling with the Square Root Rule

Often, machines that can be used for a common purpose can be pooled so as to provide redundancy or spare capacity in case any one machine breaks down or is busy. Warehouses storing inventory can be pooled to provide for one another's stockouts. Demand for many types of finished products can be filled from the same undifferentiated intermediate product, so delaying the final differentiation of the intermediate product is also a kind of risk pooling (see section 11.5.1).

Many types of risk pooling "save" capital. In the three examples above, pooling means fewer machines, less warehouse inventory, and less unsold finished goods inventory. The "saving" of capital occurs because, as the total volume of business doubles, the capital needed often increases only by the square root of 2, which is about 1.414.

Why? Consider the warehouse inventory example. For each warehouse, the amount of safety inventory needed to guard against stockouts is proportional to the standard deviation. Intuitively, if we want a given fill rate, then more variable demand means that we need to have more inventory, in case the demand shoots way up (we elaborate in section 12.4 and section 13.3.1).

Suppose we have two warehouses, each with:

individual standard deviation $= \sigma$.

So the inventory in each warehouse is proportional to σ, and, with two warehouses, the total inventory is proportional to 2σ.

Now suppose we pool the two warehouses. Together, they have:

pooled standard deviation $= \sigma\sqrt{[2(1+\rho)]}$,

where $-1 \leq \rho \leq 1$ is the correlation coefficient of the two warehouse demands. Suppose, as in many real-life cases, the two warehouse demands are independent, or $\rho = 0$. So the pooled coefficient of variation is $\sigma\sqrt{2}$: inventory increases by only the square root of 2.

Of course, at one extreme when $\rho = -1$, the pooled standard deviation is zero since any upward spike in demand at one warehouse is perfectly correlated with a downward spike in the other warehouse. At the other extreme, when $\rho = 1$, the pooled inventory needs to be same as the total unpooled inventory since an upward spike in one warehouse is correlated with an upward spike in the other. More often, ρ might be positive and less than 1. This happens, for example, with product proliferation and customization, in which demands for the various extensions and customizations are correlated with each other.

Scaling with the Square-Cube Rule

The cost of a piece of capital asset increases roughly with the square of the cube root of its capacity. Consider a spherical gas tank, such as might be seen in many gas plants. The cost of the tank increases with the amount of material for its surface area, which scales up at the rate of the square of its linear dimension—here, its radius.[9] But its capacity increases with the volume, which scales up at the rate of the cube of the linear dimension.

Hence the square-cube rule: when the costs of a capital asset go up by its square, capacity goes up by its cube. Suppose we wish to see how cost goes up if we were to increase capacity of a piece of equipment by, say, 8 times. Applying the square-cube rule, we first take the cube root of 8 (i.e., 2) and then square that (to get 4), and infer that costs will increase by approximately 4 times.

What happens when our capacity expansion is subject to both the square root and square-cube rules? The answer is that we would combine the two effects. For example, if we were to double expected capacity, our costs (say in terms of working capital, such as inventory) will increase by only $\sqrt{(2^{2/3})} = 1.26$, or equivalently, $(\sqrt{2})^{2/3} = 1.26$.

3.3   Takeaways and Toolkit

In this chapter, we have seen that:

• ROA trees can be a powerful tool for seeing what operational and financial metrics drive ROA. The exact tree requires some industry knowledge, and the appendix shows trees for many more industries.

• ROA trees provide a view of current performance: they only show how a current change on one metric affects the current ROA.

• To determine indicators of future performance, we explore indicators of sales (and to a lesser extent, of earnings and margins), unit cost, and capital costs.

We summarize the key steps in table 3.7.

Earlier in this chapter, we noted that while ROA is a good measure for current performance, there is not as good a single aggregate measure of future performance. That is why we dived deeper into finer measures of future performance, such as sales, costs, or capacities. Of course, these three are not the only main drivers of future performance. In later chapters, we look at other performance drivers—such as customer loyalty, supplier resilience, organizational capacities (such as lean management), options—

Table 3.7
Toolkit: What Can Investors Do?

Goal	Key Steps
Get contemporaneous drivers of business	Build ROA tree: • Begin with industry language • Use as many decompositions for a measure as is useful • Use a driver for as many measures as is useful • Exploit operational principles in decomposition • Use different trees for different roles • Make explicit both current and full potential • Make intangibles explicit
Get leading indicators of business	• Predicting sales, earnings, and margins: use the Bernard-Noel model, which relies on using past sales, earnings, and margins, as well as inventory information • Predicting costs: use the experience curve • Predicting capital efficiency: use the square root and square-cube roots

and other performance dampers such as risks and the inability to deal with market disruptions.

There is one single aggregate measure of future performance that is commonly used: stock market valuation. Although it is imperfect because it is subject to the vagaries of market sentiment, it is one that many investors and managers look at. Therefore, in the next chapter we consider indicators of stock market valuation.

3.4 Survey of Prior Research in One Paragraph

The ROA tree is a generic concept, although it has been popularized by management consultants such as Tom Copeland, Tim Koller, and Jack Murrin. Vishal Gaur is a leading scholar on using operational indicators for forecasting. Jeffery Abarbanell, Brian Bushee, and Chris Ittner conduct research on nonfinancial indicators and the broader rubric of fundamental analyses. Eric Bradlow, Peter Fader, and Sam Hui have a series of interesting studies on how operational information about the paths of customers—such as their paths through grocery stores or their eye movements over web pages—can be used to predict the propensity of sales. Gad Allon and Awi Federgruen extend the idea of risk pooling to increase capital efficiencies in service industries.

3.5 Further Reading

Abarbanell, J. S., and B. J. Bushee. 1997. "Fundamental Analysis, Future Earnings, and Stock Price." *Journal of Accounting Research*, 1–24.

Allon, G., and A. Federgruen. 2009. "Competition in Service Industries with Segmented Markets." *Management Science* 55 (4): 619–634.

Bernard, V. L., and J. Noel. 1991. "Do Inventory Disclosures Predict Sales and Earnings?" *Journal of Accounting, Auditing and Finance* 6: 145–181.

Copeland, T. E., T. Koller, and J. Murrin. 2000. *Valuation: Measuring and Managing the Value of Companies*. New York: Wiley.

Fruhan, W. E. 2006. "The Case of the Unidentified Industries." Harvard Business School, Boston, MA, Case 207-096.

Gottfredson, M., S. Schaubert, and H. Saenz. 2008. "The New Leader's Guide to Diagnosing the Business." *Harvard Business Review* 86 (2): 62.

Hieggelke, B. 2005. "Marketing ROI—Learn It, Love It, Act on It." *Industry Insights from Webtrends*.

Hui, S. K., P. S. Fader, and E. T. Bradlow. 2009. "Path Data in Marketing: An Integrative Framework and Prospectus for Model Building." *Marketing Science* 28 (2): 320–335.

Ittner, C. D., and D. F. Larcker. 1998. "Are Nonfinancial Measures Leading Indicators of Financial Performance? An Analysis of Customer Satisfaction." *Journal of Accounting Research* 36: 1–35.

Ittner, C. D., and D. F. Larcker. 1997. "The Performance Effects of Process Management Techniques." *Management Science*, 522–534.

Melnick, E. L., P. R. Nayyar, M. L. Pinedo, and S. Seshadri. 2000. *Creating Value in Financial Services: Strategies, Operations, and Technologies*. New York: Springer.

Yelle, L. E. 1976. "Estimating Learning Curves for Potential Products." *Industrial Marketing Management* 5 (2–3): 147–154.

4 Indicators of Stock Market Performance

While it is surely important for an investor to look at the accounting performance of a firm, as we have in the last chapter, it is also important to look at the firm's stock market performance, if the firm is publicly listed. After all, it is by buying and selling the stock of a firm that the investor participates in a firm's performance.

But one can ask the obvious question: doesn't accounting performance more or less track stock market performance, so why look at the latter when it is sufficient to look at just the former?

One important reason is that an accounting measure such as ROA captures only current performance, while stock prices incorporate the future potential of firms' performance. In addition, accounting figures, even when audited, might be less than complete (see section 2.2) or even inaccurate (section 2.3). Stock prices, on the other hand, seem less susceptible to these kinds of issues since they benefit from the "collective intelligence" of the stock market as a whole. Also, when looking at accounting performance we might debate endlessly about whether we should look at ROA or ROE or profit margin or all of these; but when looking at stock market performance, we primarily look at just the stock price. In short, stock market performance differs significantly from accounting performance: it is forward-looking, it benefits from more assessments by many investors, and is simpler with a single metric which is the stock price.

Of course, if it is just a simple story of looking at the stock price, we would end the chapter here. But there is now a growing body of research to suggest that firms can and often do manipulate their operations to "manage" their stock market performance, is the subject of this chapter.

Consider the case of David Berman, who runs Berman Capital. Berman Capital is a hedge fund that prides itself on how its deeper understanding of retail operations generates superior returns. For eight years since its founding in 1998, Berman Capital had a return of 17% a year, with only three negative months.[1] Big names like Robert Bishop of the Impala Fund invest their personal money with Berman.[2]

Berman's proposition is that retailers can and often do manipulate[3] their operational characteristics to generate short-term accounting earnings at the expense of long-term results. Further, most equity analysts do not pay enough attention to these manipulations. By carefully examining operational characteristics, Berman believes he can beat the market by going short or long on a retail stock.

Berman's pitch is not an isolated one. For example, Buckingham Capital, also based in New York, prides itself on excruciatingly detailed intelligence of its retail investments. "We literally check whether a shirt we saw last week is still there this week," said Costas Constantinides, a former Wharton student who worked at Buckingham.

The work of these investors raises important questions (the first two should be familiar to anyone who has read a detective mystery; see also section 2.3). In this chapter, we ask:

• *Why and how do businesses*—whether intentionally or otherwise, and whether legally or otherwise—make operational decisions to "manage" stock market valuation? We seek to understand the opportunity, the means (Can retailers really manipulate their operational characteristics? Why can't analysts and investors see through any manipulation?), and the motive.

• *How can we detect such manipulations*, should they occur? What can analysts and investors do? As a cautionary note, we hasten to add that if managers are determined to commit fraud, it is much harder to catch anything; recall the case of the Allied Crude Vegetable Oil Refining Corporation (see chapter 2).

To address these questions, we use a simple model of a retailer manipulating an operational metric (inventory) to boost stock market valuation. We look at inventory as the prototypical operational decision because: (1) many fund managers like Berman and Buckingham focus on that, and (2) inventory forms more than half (53%) of a typical retailer's working capital and more than a third (36%) of its total assets.

We bear in mind that the utility of the model lies in clarifying the questions posed earlier. What the model predicts (e.g., "a retailer will keep higher levels of inventory than is optimal") depends on what theories are fed into it. Therefore, as an analyst, you could develop your own theories and use the model just the same, to clarify who might do what.

4.1   A Perfect World

In a perfect world—in which a retailer's interest is aligned with her investors'—how much inventory should the retailer stock? Suppose this depends on two subdecisions:

• How much new stock to buy, to serve future demand,

• How much existing stock to mark down, to recycle working capital (recall that inventory is a form of working capital).

The more stock the retailer buys, the higher will its inventory be on its balance sheet. The more stock it marks down, the lower will inventory be on its balance sheet.

These two subdecisions in turn depend on two respective considerations:

· The expected future demand, and

· The quality of the current stock.

Let us summarize these two considerations (future demand, quality of current stock) as the "situation" today. A good situation is one in which demand and quality are high, and a bad one is one in which both are low.

Obviously, the higher the future demand, the more stock the retailer should buy.[4] Doing otherwise would lower the value of the business. Similarly, the higher the quality of the current stock, the less the retailer needs to mark down now. For example, if the current stock is mostly white shirts that will be staples through several forthcoming seasons, there is no need to rush to mark down the shirts. But if the current stock is mostly high fashion that might fetch less in the future, then there is urgency in marking down now. Doing otherwise would lower the value of the business.

For the sake of exposition, let us assign some valuation numbers to the retailer for the two situations (good vs. bad) and the two inventory decisions (high, by stocking up and marking down less; and low, by the reverse), as in figure 4.1.

The exact numbers are not important, but the order is. For example, we expect that the top left cell have the highest valuation. The bottom right is also relatively high because it is an optimal inventory decision, given the bad situation. The worst is the bottom left, in which the retailer stocks more when it expects low future sales and marks down less even though the inventory quality is low. The top right is middling.

		Inventory decision	
		H (stock more, mark down less)	L (stock less, mark down more)
Situation	Good (H future sales, H inventory quality)	5*	2
	Bad (L future sales, L inventory quality)	1	3*

* = Optimal inventory decisions for each situation.

Figure 4.1
Inventory decision for each situation.

We put asterisks in the top left and bottom right, which represent optimal inventory decisions for each situation.

Next, we see whether firms have opportunity, means, and motive—as in any good detective mystery—to manipulate inventory decisions.

4.2   Opportunity Arising from Information Asymmetry

There are at least two theories of how a retailer has the opportunity to manipulate inventory without being seriously challenged. Both rely on some kind of information asymmetry between an investor, as an outsider, and the retailer (and its manager, treated synonymously here) as an insider.

The first theory involves information asymmetry about whether a retailer is facing a good or bad situation. As an outsider, the investor does not really know as much as the manager about what the future holds, or what the true inventory quality is. However, the investor can observe the retailer's inventory level, since this is stated in its audited balance sheet. Therefore, a retailer can always hold high inventory levels and explain it away with a good situation, or hold low inventory and explain that away with a bad situation. This opportunity to manipulate inventory level arises because there is little an outside investor can do to verify or counter any explanation proffered by the insider-retailer.

The second theory of how a retailer can manipulate inventory also relies on information asymmetry. Here, the investor observes only short-term earnings but cannot tell how these are generated—e.g., whether they are generated at the expense of long-term earnings. Knowing this, a retailer has the opportunity to generate short-term earnings at the expense of long-term. In terms of our model, short-term earnings is a result of inventory decisions, since stocking more or marking down less impacts current accounting earnings. However, long-term earnings is a result of the optimality of today's inventory decisions with respect to the situation that arises.

While these two theories are different, they both explain why managers have the opportunity to manipulate inventory.

4.3   Means Arising from Managerial Decision Rights

We have seen that a retail manager can have the opportunity to manipulate inventory levels or reported earnings. But does she have the means to do so? In most cases, the answer is "yes" because managers often have sufficient decision rights to decide what inventory to carry, and what levers to pull (such as what expenses to defer, for example) that could affect earnings.

Indeed, a retailer can even manipulate inventory and earnings at the same time. Below are some ways in which a retailer can manage inventory to boost earnings, at least in the short term.

• *Deferring markdowns.*   Marking down inventory reduces margins and sales revenues, so deferring this to the future boosts short-term earnings at the expense of future results. This is Berman's main thesis.

• *Setting cost of goods sold at the level of older, cheaper inventory.*   If a retailer has a first-in-first-out inventory accounting policy in a period of inflation, she could keep more inventory and continuously use inventory bought early and cheaply to fund its current sales. In effect, she uses working capital to tackle inflation. If the physical amount of inventory is constant, then this manipulation increases the dollar amount of inventory over time.

• *Pushing past the optimal level of inventory.*   The familiar "newsvendor formula" in operations management provides a way for a retailer to determine her optimal inventory: given expected demand, she has to balance the expected cost from understocking (lost sales, lost goodwill, etc.) against that from overstocking (markdowns to get rid of extra inventory). If all retailers do stock at such an optimal level, then a retailer observed to have a high level of inventory must be one with higher expected demand: assuming the same unit understocking and overstocking costs, higher expected demand means that it is more costly to understock (more sales to lose if there is insufficient inventory) and less costly to overstock (chances are that greater demand will soak up inventory). But there is little to prevent a retailer from stocking higher than her optimal level of inventory, sending a false signal to the market that she expects high demand. If demand actually turns out to be low, she can always explain that away by saying: "Once in a while, we get lower than expected, and sometimes, we get higher than expected. That's statistics."

4.4   Motives Arising from Valuation-Based Compensation and Short-termism

Now we ask why a retail manager might bother taking up the opportunity and means to manipulate inventory.

One reason is that many companies base a portion of managerial compensation on stock price performance. A company's stock price performance in turn is a function of its earnings. In the previous section, one theme running through the different available means is that they all boost earnings, thus providing an incentive for a retail manager to undertake those manipulations.

We also note that these actions to boost earnings on the income statement involve the retailer holding higher inventory on the balance sheet. Of course, higher inventory could be interpreted by an outside investor as the result of poor management, but it could also be interpreted as a signal of expected high future sales (the top left cell of figure 4.1). In other words, there are occasions where high inventory is also interpreted favorably by investors.

There is another characteristic about the manipulations described in the previous section: while they boost earnings in the short term, this boost is at the expense of long-term earnings. For example, the marking down of inventory can only be deferred; eventually, bad inventory has to be marked down, or as Berman remarks, the "music has to stop."

Some retailer managers care about short-term benefits. This is well documented in both research and practitioner literatures. One reason is that a retail manager might want to do a secondary offering soon, so she wants to prop up her short-term share price. Another is that the manager holds shares in the retailers, and she wants to sell these in the short term. Further, the manager may also care about her option to switch careers in the near term, so the share price of the retailer she manages is an important signal in the recruiting market. Perhaps most important, the manager's compensation could be substantially tied to the retailer's short-term share price. For a broad section of 2,568 US firms in the years between 1992 and 2004, short-term executive options formed 85% to 95% of the total of these options plus long-term compensation (usually more than 3 years in horizon) benefits.

In short, there are many reasons why a manager might care about the short-term valuation of the retailer.

4.5 Implications for Inventory as Indicator for Valuation

Given the opportunity, means, and motives for inventory manipulation, what are the implications for inventory as an indicator for retailer valuation?

Consider figure 4.2. In the long term, we assume that the "music has to stop" as described above, so there is no information asymmetry: the investor gives the accurate valuation to a retailer, depending on its inventory level and situation. This is shown in the top part of the figure, which simply replicates our figure 4.1 earlier.

In the short term, however, we assume there is information asymmetry, so there is the opportunity, means, and motive to manipulate inventory. How would an investor value a retailer when the former can observe only the retailer inventory level (columns) but not the situation (rows)? Thinking like a retailer, an investor might presume that even a retailer in a bad situation might want to stock a high level of inventory to pretend to be in a good situation. Given that, the investor will need some prior belief about how many bad- versus good-situation retailers are out there.

Let us say there are equal numbers of each. In that case, the investor would assign a valuation of $\frac{1}{2}(5) + \frac{1}{2}(1) = 3$ to any retailer who is observed to have high inventory. Likewise, on observing a retailer with low inventory, the investor assigns a valuation of $\frac{1}{2}(2) + \frac{1}{2}(3) = 2\frac{1}{2}$.

	Inventory decision	
Long-term	H (stock more, mark down less)	L (stock less, mark down more)
Good (H future sales, H inventory quality)	5*	2
Bad (L future sales, L inventory quality)	1	3*
Short-term		
Situation cannot be distinguished	½ × 5 + ½ × 1 = 3	½ × 2 + ½ × 3 = 2½

(Situation)

* = Optimal inventory decisions for each situation.

Figure 4.2
Long- and short-term valuations.

Suppose a retail manager is short-term-oriented: her motive is to place a weight of 80% on the retailer's short-term valuation and 20% on its long-term valuation. What inventory level would this retailer hold if she were in a bad situation? This depends on the weighted valuation she gets:

· Hold high inventory: 80%(3) + 20%(1) = 2.6 , versus

· Hold low inventory: 80%(2½) + 20%(3) = 2.6.

Put another way, if the retailer puts any more than 80% weight on short-term results, she would hold high levels of inventory, even though in the long term it would have been optimal for her to hold low levels of inventory. In other words, the picture is complete: investors believe that retailers always hold high inventory, and retailers, knowing that, always do. Because the long-term valuation of holding high inventory is 1 and that for holding low inventory is 3, bad-situation retailers destroy 3 − 1 = 2 units of value.

There is some empirical support for this idea that, with information asymmetry and sufficient weight on short-term valuation, retailers tend to cluster around high levels of inventory and the valuation of the average retailer is some average between those of a

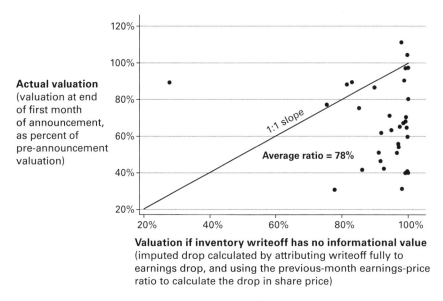

Figure 4.3
The informational role of inventory writeoffs.

"good retailer" and a "bad retailer." This theory predicts that if the actual situation of a retailer is revealed—such as when the retailer can hold bad inventory no longer and has to announce a writeoff—then the announcement not only reduces the valuation of the retailer by the size of the writeoff, but also has informational value: it tells an outsider-investor that the retailer is indeed in a bad situation. This revelation will drag the retailer's previously averaged valuation to the lower bad-situation retailer valuation.

Figure 4.3 shows the valuation of thirty-four manufacturers and retailers after they announce inventory writeoffs. These are all firms whose announcements are not confounded by other announcements (e.g., about earnings). The figure shows that the actual valuation is only about 78% of the valuation if inventory writeoffs have no informational role.

4.6 Detecting Deviations

Up to now, we have argued that it is possible that investors, as outsiders, cannot tell what operational deviations mean; hence the model. We now turn to the more practical step of how we are going to know whether there are deviations in the first place. Even if we do not always know what the deviations mean, we can at least start asking questions.

More generally, beyond the case of Berman's inventory, how do we know whether operations have deviated? For example, has inventory increased "too much"? Or earnings dropped "too much"? In determining what is "too much"—that is, an abnormal deviation—we evidently need some benchmark. Once we have determined that an abnormal deviation has occurred, we can then determine its cause. Perhaps an inventory increase is needed to anticipate future sales? Or perhaps it is a sign of slackening management? Or perhaps there is really nothing wrong, since any process tends to deviate (perhaps because of an occasional wrong forecast) once in a while, by the law of large numbers.

Our first task, nevertheless, is to determine whether there is a deviation. To do that, we can employ several tools. Statistical process control is more amenable to detecting deviations of a single measure arising from a stable process (e.g., the capacity of a production line). But sometimes we are given aggregated measures that are expected to vary (e.g., revenues, aggregated from volume of units and prices, and varying over time). In the latter case, we can exploit Benford's Law. Finally, we can use a regression model to detect deviations. We discuss these techniques below.

4.6.1 Statistical Process Control

Suppose we are interested in tracking the production capacity of a machine that makes smartphone bodies. We can use historical data to establish a benchmark. For example, we might find that the average production rate is 1,200 bodies per day, with a standard deviation of 100 bodies per day.

The basic idea of statistical process control is to form a benchmark with an upper bound—say the average plus three standard deviations—and a lower bound—say the average minus three standard deviations. If a future production rate falls outside these bounds, then we say the process deviates with a certain probability: the larger the number of standard deviations, the greater the probability. For example, standard statistics tells us that if we form the bounds with three standard deviations to the upper bound and three to the lower one, we have a 99.7% confidence that a deviation is a true deviation and not a false positive.

4.6.2 Benford's Law

In 1938, physicist Frank Benford discovered that many sets of numbers—from the drainage area of rivers to the numbers appearing in *Reader's Digest* articles—have the most numbers beginning with 1 and the fewest beginning with 9. This is curious, since we might expect the initial digits to be evenly distributed. Today, researchers rely on the following as the frequency distribution of the first digit of these numbers:

frequency(first digit = d) = $\log_{10}[1 + 1/d]$.

Likewise, the distribution of the second digit is:

Table 4.1
Frequency Distribution of Numbers in Various Digit Positions According to Benford's Law

Digit	First	Second	Third	Fourth
0		0.11968	0.10178	0.10018
1	0.30103	0.11389	0.10138	0.10014
2	0.17609	0.10882	0.10097	0.10010
3	0.12494	0.10433	0.10057	0.10006
4	0.09691	0.10031	0.10018	0.10002

Source: Nigrini and Mittermaier (1997).

frequency(second digit $= e) = \sum_d \log_{10}[1 + 1/(de)]$,

where $\sum_d$ means that we sum up all the log expressions for d, the first digit, from 1 through 9. Table 4.1 shows these frequencies for the first through the fourth digits.

There are many explanations for what is now called Benford's Law. One intuitive explanation is that in many (but not all) cases, smaller numbers are more frequent than larger ones. For example, there are very many smaller river basins and very few really enormous ones. More rigorously, mathematicians have proven that Benford's law holds up best when the numbers are aggregated from combinations of other sets of numbers, no matter the distribution of these latter sets of numbers. For example, if sales is a multiple of the volume of various products and the prices of these products, then a set of sales figures is likely to follow Benford's Law, with the first digit more likely to be 1 than 9.

Using this insight, we can test whether a set of numbers—say the monthly sales for various retails stores—conform to Benford's Law. For example, at a large medical center in the western United States, auditors found that the insurance refund checks had amounts that deviated from Benford's Law (figure 4.4). The officer involved, on questioning, explained that many checks whose amounts where below $1,000 were combined into larger checks so as to reduce the number of checks written. But it was subsequently found that the officer had opened bogus shell companies to which she fraudulently wrote many refund checks.

4.6.3   The Beneish Model for Detecting Earnings Manipulation

Messod Beneish of Indiana University has carefully constructed a "treatment set" of firms that were either found by the SEC or reported by the media to have manipulated earnings. These he then compared with a "control set" of firms that are assumed not to have manipulated earnings.

Table 4.2 shows five indicators that can produce a score for earnings manipulation (and three indicators that are statistically insignificant). The t is the year manipulation happens; the average manipulation is discovered 19 months from its occurrence, so these indicators provide detection of manipulation ahead of its general discovery. For example, if the "days

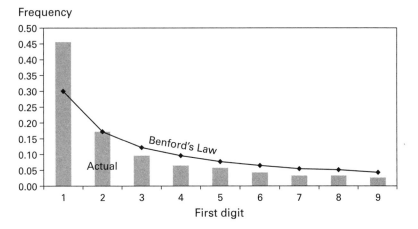

Frequency

Figure 4.4
Comparison of actual check amounts against amounts predicted with Benford's Law. Source: Durtschi et al. (2004).

Table 4.2
Indicators in the Beneish Model for Earnings Manipulation

Indicator	Definition	Coefficient
Days receivables growth	$\dfrac{\text{Receivables}_t / \text{Sales}_t}{\text{Receivables}_{t-1} / \text{Sales}_{t-1}}$	0.92*
Gross margin "reverse growth"	$\dfrac{1 - \text{COGS}_{t-1} / \text{Sales}_{t-1}}{1 - \text{COGS}_t / \text{Sales}_t}$	0.528*
Asset quality growth	$\dfrac{(1 - \text{CurrentAssets}_t + \text{PPE}_t) / \text{TotalAssets}_t}{(1 - \text{CurrentAssets}_{t-1} + \text{PPE}_{t-1}) / \text{TotalAssets}_{t-1}}$	0.404*
Sales growth	$\dfrac{\text{Sales}_t}{\text{Sales}_{t-1}}$	0.892*
Depreciation index	$\dfrac{\text{Depreciation}_{t-1} / (\text{Depreciation}_{t-1} + \text{PPE}_{t-1})}{\text{Depreciation}_t / (\text{Depreciation}_t + \text{PPE}_t)}$	0.115
SGA growth	$\dfrac{\text{SGA}_t / \text{Sales}_t}{\text{SGA}_{t-1} / \text{Sales}_{t-1}}$	−0.172
Total accruals to total assets	$\dfrac{\Delta\text{CurrentAssets}_t - \Delta\text{Cash}_t - \Delta\text{CurrentLiabilities}_t - \Delta\text{CurrentMaturitiesOfLTD}_t - \Delta\text{IncomeTaxPayable}_t - \text{DepreciationAndAmortization}_t}{\text{TotalAssets}_t}$	4.679*
Leverage growth	$\dfrac{(\text{LTD}_t + \text{CurrentLiabilities}_t) / \text{TotalAssets}_t}{(\text{LTD}_{t-1} + \text{CurrentLiabilities}_{t-1}) / \text{TotalAssets}_{t-1}}$	−0.327

Source: Beneish (1999). COGS = cost of goods sold; PPE = plant, property, equipment; LTD = long-term debt.
* Statistically significant at the 1% level; coefficients without asterisks are not statistically significant.

receivable growth" is 0.09, we multiply this by 0.92; and so on for the other indicators; then we add all the multiples to form a score.

Beneish finds that a score that is more positive than −1.89 is indicative of earnings manipulation. The predictability is reasonable: the probability of detecting earnings manipulation is more than 76%. The probability of a false alarm (also called a Type 1 error) is 24% and that of a missed problem (also called a Type 2 error) is 17.5%.

4.7 Takeaways and Toolkit

This chapter suggests that:

• Analysts and investors should be aware of how companies could manage their operations with a view to managers' private incentives, including their concern for short-term share price performance.

• Investors who understand how managers manipulate indicators of stock valuation are better placed to exploit opportunities (e.g., when a retailer writes off inventory). Some like Berman even claim that they can use public and proprietary information to penetrate the veil of information asymmetry. They do not have to completely understand what managers do, only to understand more than other investors do. They also argue that few other investors currently take the extra step of *using* the public information that is available.

• There are several techniques for identifying deviations from benchmarks. Statistical process analysis works best for measures of stable processes. For aggregated measures, we can compare actual data with predictions from Benford's Law. The Beneish model could be a useful tool to detect earnings manipulation using public data.

We summarize the key steps in table 4.3.

In the next chapter, we move from indicators of misvaluation to indicators of a more fundamental change: the entire disruption of a company's business model.

4.8 Survey of Prior Research in One Paragraph

Michael Jensen and William Meckling are most associated with emphasizing the importance of agency issues—i.e., that managers' private interests may not fully align with investors'. Jeremy Stein is one of the leading scholars in showing that agency, with information asymmetry and short-termism, can lead managers to deviate from investing optimally. Jeffery Abarbanell, John Birge (who pointed out Benford's Law to me), Brian Bushee, Marshall Fisher, Vishal Gaur, Chris Ittner, David Larcker, and Ananth Raman are among the leaders in showing how this deviation can occur in specific operational parameters, such as inventory or R&D management. Kevin Hendricks and Vinod Singhal have

Table 4.3
Toolkit: What Can Investors Do?

Goal	Key Steps
Get superior understanding of retailer	Some indicators that might be useful include: • *Inventory growth minus sales growth.* Berman calls this his DB (for David Berman) Index. The idea is that retailers whose inventory growth exceeds sales growth are more likely to be retailers in the kind of bad situations described. • *GMROI.* This stands for gross margin return on inventory, with the following equivalent definitions: GMROI = markup / inventory turn = (sales − COGS)/COGS × COGS/inventory = (gross profit)/inventory. Berman uses only inventory turn, but research suggests that two retailers with the same future performance could have high turn and low margin (e.g., grocery) or low turn and high margin (e.g., luxury jewelry). • *Accounts payables / inventory.* This provides a sense of the age of the stock. Accounts payables is that part of inventory that is purchased recently and is still unpaid (usually under 30, 60, or 90 days terms of credit), and is therefore likely to comprise fresher stock. • *Fieldwork*—such as interviews with management and store visits—to better assess retailers. In particular, this work seeks to obtain information on the underlying reason for inventory levels: Store changes, both in number and format; Product mix, and additions and elimination of product lines; Merchandising at the store level, and the upkeep of stock at stores and distribution centers; Training and experience of staff, as well as their deployment; Systems in place, including incentive systems and technology systems; Competitive positioning.
Detect deviations from operational benchmarks	• *Deviations in stable processes* (e.g., productivity should be unchanging, unless new technologies are introduced): use statistical process control. • *Deviations of aggregated measures* (e.g., revenue is a product of volume and price) *in nonstable processes* (e.g., revenues can go up or down): compare actual data to predictions from Benford's Law. • *Deviations in earnings.* Use the Beneish Model to detect earnings manipulation.

an influential set of studies showing how such operational deviations could affect market valuations. Messod Beneish has proposed a model to detecting earnings manipulation.

4.9 Further Reading

Abarbanell, J. S., and B. J. Bushee. 1997. "Fundamental Analysis, Future Earnings, and Stock Price." *Journal of Accounting Research*: 1–24.

Beneish, M. D. 1999. "The Detection of Earnings Manipulation." *Financial Analysts Journal* 55 (5): 24–36.

Durtschi, C., W. Hillison, and C. Pacini. 2004. "The Effective Use of Benford's Law to Assist in Detecting Fraud in Accounting Data." *Journal of Forensic Accounting* 5 (1): 17–43.

Gaur, V., M. L. Fisher, and A. Raman. 2005. "An Econometric Analysis of Inventory Turnover Performance in Retail Services." *Management Science* 51 (2): 181–194.

Hendricks, K. B., and V. R. Singhal. 2003. "The Effect of Supply Chain Glitches on Shareholder Wealth." *Journal of Operations Management* 21 (5): 501–522.

Ittner, C. D., and D. F. Larcker. 1998. "Are Nonfinancial Measures Leading Indicators of Financial Performance? An Analysis of Customer Satisfaction." *Journal of Accounting Research* 36: 1–35.

Jensen, M. C., and W. Meckling. 1976. "Theory of the Firm: Managerial Behavior, Agency Costs, and Capital Structure." *Journal of Financial Economics* 3 (4): 305–360.

Lai, R. 2006. "Inventory Signals." MSOM Conference, Atlanta, GA.

Nigrini, M. J., and L. J. Mittermaier. 1997. "The Use of Benford's Law as an Aid in Analytical Procedures." *Auditing* 16 (2): 52–67.

Stein, J. C. 1988. "Takeover Threats and Managerial Myopia." *Journal of Political Economy* 96 (1): 61–80.

Xu, X., and J. R. Birge. 2004. *Operational Decisions, Capital Structure, and Managerial Compensation: A Newsvendor Perspective.*

5 Indicators of Disruption

The *Encyclopaedia Britannica* was started in 1768 as a compendium of human knowledge. Through the years, its contributors have included luminaries such as Marie Curie, Albert Einstein, Benjamin Franklin, George Bernard Shaw, and Leon Trotsky. Its ownership has changed from the founding Scottish entrepreneurs to American hands, variously the Benton Foundation of Chicago and the Sears Roebuck Company. By 1989, its sales were at a record high of $627 million, and growing at 8.1% a year.

But the introduction of the compact disk (CD) clipped Britannica's wings. In a space of seven years, sales plunged by more than 50% to $325 million, losses were piling up, and Britannica the company was on sale.

What happened to Britannica represents a common pattern. Xerox was displaced by Canon's tabletop printers. IBM's mainframes were overtaken by DEC's minicomputers, which were in turn overtaken by IBM's microcomputers. In each case, technological innovation made for serious business disruption.

All the incumbents had been well-established companies with talented executives. In this chapter, we explore these questions:

• What are the types of technological innovations and why are some harder to manage than others?

• Why have established companies not foreseen technological disruptions?

• What can investors and managers do to develop indicators of such disruptions, so as to better anticipate and manage them?

5.1 Types of Technological Innovations

In thinking about changes, it can be helpful to consider them in various dimensions:

• **Product innovation.**   For example, Britannica added the *Propaedia*, an index to its encyclopedia. This addition facilitates searches for entries under multiple topics and enhances the value of the product.

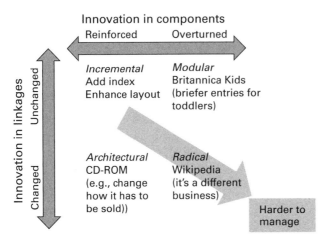

Figure 5.1
A typology of technological innovation.

• *Functional innovation.* An oft-cited example is how Beecham's "repurposed" Luco-zade, a glucose-based beverage originally developed to help the sick, became a fitness drink for the health-conscious.

• *Process innovation.* A positive change in how the product or service is made or delivered. Two important examples are the use of interchangeable parts for the manufacture of muskets in the early 1800s and Henry Ford's assembly line in the early 1900s.

There are, of course, many other types of innovation, such as innovation in business models or organizational development. Here we focus on the types that speak directly to operations. But even our typology misses an important consideration: what is the implication for managerial action?

Henderson and Clark proposed a typology of technological innovations; see figure 5.1. One dimension considers whether the innovation reinforces or overturns the components of the existing technology, and the other considers whether the innovation changes how the components are linked.

The important takeaway from the Henderson-Clark model is that managers will find it harder to cope with some types of innovations than others, and must therefore be aware of and learn about how to deal with such innovations.

5.1.1 Incremental Innovation

When the innovation reinforces the components but leaves their linkages unchanged, we have incremental innovation. For example, Britannica added the *Propaedia*, an index to its encyclopedia. This addition facilitates searches for entries under multiple topics, reinforcing the value of the entries. But the link between the indexed encyclopedia and other components of the encyclopedia value chain—such as editing, production, sales—were mostly unchanged. Another example is the layout, with pictures and different fonts, to reinforce the entries without changing their linkages. In the Henderson-Clark model, these are the easiest type of innovations for companies to develop and introduce into the marketplace.

5.1.2   Radical Innovation

At the opposite extreme, radical innovation involves tectonic shifts in business. For example, Wikipedia is different from Britannica on so many fronts that it is practically in a completely different business. The entries are developed not by appointed and salaried professionals but by volunteer experts. The entries can be easily edited, but edits can be easily rolled back, creating a dynamism. There are also considerably more entries, connected with hyperlinks to each other and to web pages outside of Wikipedia. The linkages between Wikipedia and other parts of the value chain are also radically changed. Contributors' incentives come more from social recognition than from financial considerations, there is no door-to-door sales force, there is a donor base to be cultivated and maintained, etc. Not surprisingly, such radical innovations are the hardest to introduce as a new entrant into a business field, or to cope with as an incumbent.

5.1.3   Modular Innovation

This type of innovation involves large changes in individual components, with relatively small changes in the linkages among them. For example, Britannica Kids radically overhauled many of the original entries into something that toddlers can absorb. However, many of the linkages are unchanged: editing, producing, and selling the Britannica lite may involve different skills, but the processes, incentives, and systems can be borrowed from those for the encyclopedia proper. Modular innovation can be managed by focusing attention only on the changed component.

5.1.4   Architectural Innovation

Henderson and Clark argue that the most important type of innovation involves simple component innovations that are intricately interlinked, so that the linkages need to be overhauled. These are the innovations most often underestimated by management. Individually, the innovation of switching from print to CDs seems innocuous for an established encyclopedia: the CDs enhance storage capacity and allow new ways of connecting the entries in the encyclopedia. But it has been difficult for Britannica to make a clean transition from the analog to the digital world. For example, it is incongruous for its door-to-door salespeople to be selling encyclopedias on CDs that have margins a fraction of those for encyclopedias in print. Then there are issues of production costs, piracy, competition from Microsoft's Encarta, software search engines, hyperlinks between entries, etc. Conversely, the difficulty that Britannica faces in managing the innovation also makes the innovation easier to introduce for new players, such as Grolier's and Microsoft. Some observers contend that Britannica's bankruptcy had much to do with its inability to cope with these new entrants and their technologies.

5.2 Sustaining and Disruptive Innovations

Clay Christensen's research is most associated with explaining a peculiar puzzle: many well-established companies have fallen prey not to the more complex types of innovation in the Henderson-Clark typology, but to much "simpler" incremental innovations.

Consider the hard disk drive industry studied by Christensen. In that industry, the performance characteristic is storage capacity. In 1974, the mainstream technology was the 14-inch Winchester drive; the main makers were IBM and CDC. This technology catered to mainframe computer makers, primarily IBM and the "Seven Dwarfs" (Burroughs, UNIVAC, NCR, CDC, Honeywell, GE, and RCA).[1] At that time, the 8-inch hard disk drive was an emerging technology. Shugart was one of the pioneers of that technology. The 8-inch drives simply did not have a storage capacity suitable for mainframe computers, even if they were cheaper on a dollar per MB basis. They could only be used for the emerging market for minicomputers (see figure 5.2).

In 1974, if a Winchester maker were to assess the attractiveness of investing in the emerging 8-inch drive technology, it would have hit a brick wall. First, it was clear that the emerging technology was not even capable of being used by the mainstream market

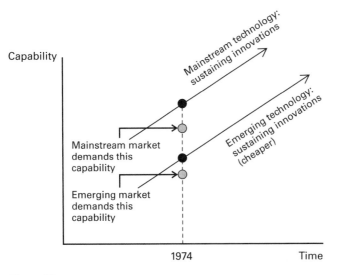

Figure 5.2
Performance of hard disk drive technology in 1974.

of mainframe manufacturers. It probably did not help that the primary makers of Winchester drives—IBM and CDC—did not need to listen to anyone but themselves: when it came to drives, they were their own customers. Christensen's main point here is that if mainstream companies ask their lead mainstream customers what the latter want, the answer will probably be "better mainstream technology."

Second, the market for the emerging technology was small and its margins were much thinner than those for the mainstream technology. Therefore, there was seemingly no urgency to serve the emerging market.

Third, in many cases the emerging technology only progresses at about the same rate as the mainstream technology, so it seems unlikely that the performance trajectory of the emerging technology will surpass that of the mainstream technology. Figure 5.3 shows almost parallel performance improvements in each generation of hard disk drive

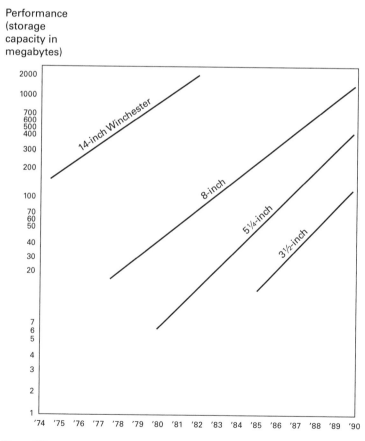

Figure 5.3
Performance trajectories of hard disk drive technologies.

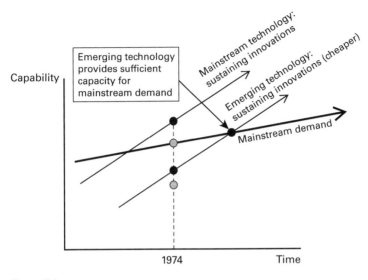

Figure 5.4
Emerging technology eventually can serve the mainstream market, where their trajectories intersect.

technologies. In effect, *both* mainstream and emerging technologies have highly effective incremental innovations. Christensen calls these forms of innovations along the performance trajectories *sustaining innovations*.

For all these reasons, it seems inevitable that, for mainstream technology producers, the obvious allocation of research and commercialization investments is to develop mainstream technology.

But Christensen argues that whether the emerging technology will surpass the mainstream technology is the wrong question to ask. The right question is: When will the emerging technology surpass mainstream customers' demand for performance? Figure 5.4 shows what happens. As explained earlier, the performance trajectories of mainstream and emerging technologies—indicated by the northeast arrows—are generally in parallel. However, the demand trajectory of the mainstream market tends to be slower. At a crucial point of intersection, the emerging technology can serve the mainstream market. Furthermore, it is also more cost-effective, since the emerging technology is less expensive than the mainstream technology. At that point, the emerging technology becomes a *disruptive innovation*.

Furthermore, the demand trajectory of the emerging market tends to rise faster than that of the mainstream market (see figure 5.5). So the disruptive innovation can now serve not only the mainstream market, but an emerging market that might even become mainstream as time passes.

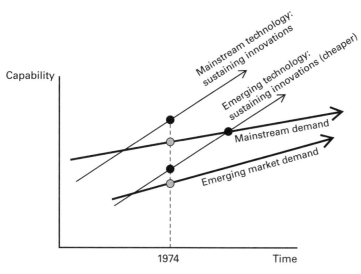

Figure 5.5
The rising demand trajectory of the emerging market.

5.3   Takeaways and Toolkit

This chapter describes how companies can be disrupted by innovations:

• There are four types of technological innovations, of which architectural innovation is the most frequently underestimated by management, in terms of what is required to manage it.

• Still, research shows that most disruptive innovations are not architectural but innocuously incremental. The disruptions come when incremental innovations in an emerging technology finally reach the ability to serve not just the emerging market, but also the mainstream market.

• Companies can map out the disruption point of potentially disruptive innovations, find the right information (unlikely to come from their lead customers) to estimate the size of the emerging market, and allocate resources to the emerging technology.

The Christensen analysis suggests several implications for companies that could face disruptive innovation; see table 5.1.

In the next chapter, we move from indicators of disruption to indicators of a more fatal change: bankruptcy.

Table 5.1
Toolkit: What Can Investors and Managers Do?

Goal	Key Steps
Identify the disruption point	Mainstream technology players tend to ask when emerging technologies can be as good as mainstream technologies. Instead, they should ask when mainstream demand will be met by emerging technologies—i.e., the disruption point. This requires a change in mindset, from asking a technological to asking a marketing question.
Project emerging market demand	To their credit, mainstream companies typically invest in emerging technologies, but their investments tend to be half-hearted. One reason mentioned is that companies seldom have a clear idea of the size and margin of this emerging market, because they ask their lead customers, who are in the mainstream market. By seeking out information from emerging customers, they can better assess the demand trajectory of this market.
Allocate resources based on the disruption point and the demand trajectory of the emerging market	Having the important pieces of information in the two previous steps, it becomes considerably easier—and more internally defensible—for even mainstream companies to invest in emerging technologies. It is critical to ring-fence the investment so that the investment does not get sucked back into the mainstream organization.

5.4   Survey of Prior Research in One Paragraph

Management scholars have developed many theories and empirical evidence on the issue of technological innovations and disruptions. The most famous work on the effect of innovation is arguably that of Joseph Schumpeter, whose idea of creative destruction has entered common parlance. Philip Anderson, Kim Clark, Rebecca Henderson, and Michael Tushman are some of the pioneering scholars who have developed theories of different types of innovations and how they come about. The major research on management of innovation is pioneered by Tom Burns and the psychologist G. M. Stalker. The material in this chapter is most closely associated with the research of Clayton Christensen.

5.5   Further Reading

Burns, T., and G. M. Stalker. 1994. *The Management of Innovation.* New York: Oxford University Press.

Christensen, C. M. 1999. *The Innovator's Dilemma.* Boston: Harvard Business School Press.

Henderson, R. M., and K. B. Clark. 1990. "Architectural Innovation: The Reconfiguration of Existing Product Technologies and the Failure of Established Firm." *Administrative Science Quarterly* 35 (1).

Schumpeter, J. A. 1994. *Capitalism, Socialism, and Democracy.* 5th ed. London: Routledge.

Tushman, M. L., and P. Anderson. 1986. "Technological Discontinuities and Organizational Environment." *Administrative Science Quarterly* 31: 439–465.

6 Indicators of Distress

As we discussed in the last chapter, in 1989 Encyclopaedia Britannica was at the top of its game. Sales were at a record high of $627 million and growing at 8.1% a year. In 1996, it declared bankruptcy.

In 1997, Amazon was also at the top of its game following its founding just three years before. Its initial public offering valued the company at $438 million. But by 2000 it had cumulative losses of over $550 million and accumulated a number of derogatory monikers: Amazon.toast, Amazon.bomb, and founder Jeff Bezos's favorite, Amazon.org, since "it was clearly a not-for-profit."

Lehman analysts Ravi Suria and C. Stan Oh predicted that Amazon would run out of cash in the next four quarters. The company had "the financial characteristics that have driven innumerable retailers to disaster through history." Jeff Bezos blasted the analysts thus: "On Friday there was a single analyst who wrote a report which isn't correct, without even calling us. . . . We actually expect to generate cash flow from operations through the rest of this year, not use cash [from our] operations. So it's wrong." Unlike Encyclopaedia Britannica, Amazon not only did not go bankrupt but also went on to become a household name.

Obviously, analysts, investors, and managers all would like to get a clearer idea of how close companies are to financial distress. In this chapter, we describe two ways to do this:

• **The Altman Z score.** This is an indicator of how close a company is to bankruptcy. It is statistically rigorous, but its theoretical foundation is limited—it is more of an empirical regularity. It is also very well tested, since it was first proposed in 1968.

• **The "runway."** This is an indicator for how long a company can burn cash before it takes off with positive cash flow. This approach is more fundamental because, by repeatedly "exploding" the indicator's components, one eventually reaches operational characteristics. It is currently popular in the venture capital industry, but could be very useful for established companies, too.

6.1   A Short Note on Terminology and Definition

Some writers use "bankruptcy" to denote distress for individuals and "insolvency" for corporations. Then there are those who identify two kinds of distress: (1) when an entity fails to meet interest payments and the debt covenant allows debt holders to take over the entity, or (2) when assets are valued less than liabilities (excluding shareholders' worth).

In lay use, these terms and definitions have been clouded, even if they can be very precise in certain parts of the bankruptcy code. We suggest that students clarify what is meant when they use the terms. In this chapter, we will use "bankruptcy" only to mean "when an entity fails to meet interest payments."

6.2   The Altman Z Score

The original conception of the Z score comes from separating manufacturing companies that have gone bankrupt from those that have not and using discriminant analysis to identify the factors—and their loadings—that predict bankruptcy.

6.2.1   Manufacturing Companies

Altman's Z score for manufacturing companies is calculated as:

$$Z_{manufacturing} = 1.2a + 1.4b + 3.3c + 0.6d + 0.999e,$$

where:

- a = (working capital) / (total assets). This captures liquidity.

- b = (retained earnings) / (total assets). This captures the cumulative profitability of the company. It also reflects an aspect of leverage: a high b means low leverage, since retained earnings is a portion of shareholders' equity.

- c = (earnings before interest and taxes) / (total assets). This is a form of return on assets. Altman suggests that it measures the "true productivity" of a company's assets and recognizes long-term viability.

- d = (market value of equity) / (book value of total liabilities). This reflects an external market validation of the company's prospects. Higher market value indicates a greater debt capacity. The numerator also captures future growth and risks. Altman also explains that this shows "how much the firm's assets can decline in value (measured by market value of equity plus debt) before the liabilities exceed the assets and the firm becomes insolvent. For example, a company with a market value of its equity of $1,000 and debt of $500 could experience a two-thirds drop in asset value before insolvency. However, the same firm with $250 in equity will be insolvent if its drop is only one-third in value."[1]

Table 6.1
Altman $Z_{manufacturing}$ Score Error Rates

Year Prior to Bankruptcy	Type 1 (False Positive)	Type 2 (False Negative)
1	6%	3%
2	18%	6%
3	52%	Not available
4	71%	Not available

• e = (sales) / (total assets). This measures sales turnover, which captures a form of operating efficiency.

It should be noted that the five components of the Z score are cast as ratios, not percentages.[2] Because Altman's dependent variable is a 0–1 measure (either bankrupt or not) and is not a probability, his prediction is also deterministic: a company with a $Z_{manufacturing}$ score below 1.8 is predicted to go into bankruptcy, one above 2.99 is not, and one in between is indeterminate.

Two kinds of error are possible in this sort of prediction. A false positive, or Type 1 error, is one in which a company is predicted to go bankrupt but does not do so. Conversely, a false negative, or Type 2 error, is one in which a company goes bankrupt but the $Z_{manufacturing}$ score fails to predict it.

Table 6.1 shows the error rates for the Altman $Z_{manufacturing}$ score. These rather impressive rates—at least for near-term predictions—are why the basic methodology of the Z score has endured through the decades, even though the score itself has undergone numerous transformations.

6.2.2 Service and Distribution Companies

Another variation of the model is developed for service and distribution companies:

$$Z_{service} = 6.56a + 3.26b + 6.72c + 1.05d,$$

where the factors are the same as before, without e.

In this variant, a company with a $Z_{service}$ score below 1.1 is predicted to go into bankruptcy, one with a score above 2.6 is predicted not to do so, and one with a score in between is indeterminate.

For example, the $Z_{service}$ for Amazon at the end of 2000 may be calculated as in table 6.2, resulting in a score of 3.5, well above the 2.6 threshold for nonbankruptcy.

Although it appears that the scoring mechanism worked in this case (since Amazon did not go into bankruptcy), the uniqueness of the situation raises questions that should be asked whenever we use a Z score. In this case, we may ask about:

Table 6.2
Z Score for Amazon, 2000

Item	$ Millions		
Working capital	386		
Total assets	2,135		
Retained earnings	(2,293)		
EBIT	1,321		
Market value of equity	5,000		
Total liabilities	3,102		

Factor	Coefficient	Ratio	Multiple
a	6.56	0.2	= 1.31
b	3.26	−1.1	= −3.59
c	6.72	0.6	= 4.03
d	1.05	1.6	= 1.68
$Z_{service}$ = sum of multiples			= 3.5

- **Path dependence.**   Since Amazon had just borrowed $680 million in 2000, what access to additional debt financing did it have in the near future? In general, the score may not reflect the path a company has taken to get to where it is, and this path can critically differentiate companies with the same score.

- **Off-balance-sheet items.**   In the year before—in 1999—Amazon exercised some options to generate $318 million. The score also does not fully capture items such as these, which are off the balance sheet.

- **Quality of assets and liabilities.**   Two companies may have the same inventory levels on their accounting books, but wildly different inventory quality (see section 4.2). The Z score does not account for such variations at a level below "working capital," for instance.

6.2.3   Private Companies

One important variation of the model is developed for private companies:

$$Z_{private} = 0.72a + 0.85b + 3.11c + 0.42d + 0.998e,$$

where the factors are the same as before, except that for d we use book value rather than market value of equity.

In this variant, a company with a $Z_{private}$ score below 1.23 is predicted to go into bankruptcy, one with a score above 2.9 is predicted not to do so, and one with a score in between is indeterminate.

6.3   The "Runway"

The concept of the runway provides a sense of how long a company can burn cash before it must take off with positive cash flow. It is defined as:

runway = cash / burn rate,

where burn rate is the rate at which cash and marketable securities are reduced over time. For example, United Airlines had a burn rate of about $7 million a day in the period before it sought bankruptcy protection. General Motors burned about $113 million a day as it spiraled into distress in 2009. An alternative and less conservative measure is not the runway but just the burn rate, in which one counts the reduction in all current assets, and not just cash and marketable securities.

In many ways, the runway provides a different view than the Z score. Recall that all the factors in the Z score have assets or liabilities in their denominators. In other words, the Z score measures how the balance sheet supports items such as working capital or generates other items such as sales.

The runway, on the other hand, captures how long a company has before it goes to a position of zero cash. Importantly, the runway considers only operating cash inflow and outflow, and does not consider cash changes that arise from investments or financing.[3] The Z score, through items such as market value of equity and total liabilities, accounts not just for the operating aspect of a company but also for its financing dimension.

The runway can be "exploded" into its components, driving down to operational characteristics. Figure 6.1 shows an example. Here cash and marketable securities have been usefully categorized by the degree to which these assets can be liquidated to feed the burn rate. For example, marketable securities are divided into those that can be immediately converted to cash without penalty, and others that carry some penalty if converted before their maturity dates.

Inventory is also categorized as fresh, stale, and "to be written off," with an adjustment to be made for marking the fresh and stale inventory to market prices.

The figure shows that burn rate comprises a number of items that eventually lead to operational characteristics. For example, managing days of payables, receivables, and inventory can reduce working capital needed to support sales growth. Changing labor hours worked or the number of stores in place affects the burn rate. A particularly important point is that an operational lever may hurt and improve the burn rate at the same time. For example, increasing sales naturally improves gross income, which reduces the burn rate. But if days of working capital is positive, increasing sales also increases working capital required to support growth, increasing burn rate. These sorts of mechanisms highlighted by the "exploding tree" can be useful, reflecting the actual tradeoffs companies face.

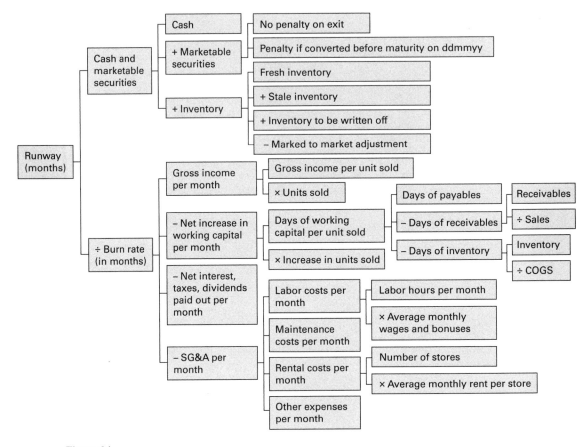

Figure 6.1
A runway tree.

In the case of Amazon in 2000, its burn rate was about $130 million a year, and it had cash and marketable securities of about $1,100 million, so the runway was 8.5 years, another indication that Amazon did not seem to be on the brink of bankruptcy. However, as with the Z score, it is important to consider the many other factors that could impact Amazon's viability, beyond just the runway.

6.4   Altman Z's Marriage to the Runway

A particularly useful undertaking may be to combine the attributes of the factors in the Altman Z score—such as ROI and sales turnover—with the "tree explosion" technique used for the runway. These sort of trees can expose many managerial tradeoffs, such as that inherent in managing fast growth in a cash-tight situation.

Table 6.3
Determining Distress Indicators

Goal	Key Steps
Determine Altman Z score for a publicly listed manufacturer	$Z_{manufacturing} = 1.2a + 1.4b + 3.3c + 0.6d + 0.999e$, a = working capital / total assets b = retained earnings / total assets c = earnings before interest and taxes / total assets d = market value of equity / book value of total liabilities e = sales / total assets
Determine Altman Z score for a publicly listed service and distribution business	$Z_{service} = 6.56a + 3.26b + 6.72c + 1.05d$, where a through d are as above
Determine Altman Z score for a private business	$Z_{private} = 0.72a + 0.85b + 3.11c + 0.42d + 0.998e$, where a through e are as above
Determine how long a business can burn cash before it must take off with positive cash flow	Runway = cash / burn rate

6.5   Takeaways and Toolkit

In this chapter, we have seen that:

• The Altman Z score has been surprisingly accurate and has endured a number of critiques over the years.

• The runway is an alternative measure, providing a temporal measure of how long a company has before it runs out of cash, assuming it does not have access to additional financing.

• "Tree explosions" of the factors used in the Z score can provide additional insight into how operational characteristics can affect those factors, and therefore the Z score.

In table 6.3, we summarize the distress indicators for the Altman Z score and the runway.

6.6   Survey of Prior Research in One Paragraph

William Beaver and Edward Altman are arguably the most famous researchers in this area. Altman's name is associated with his Z score to predict bankruptcy. Over the years, researchers have developed many variations of the original Altman model, which was designed for manufacturing companies. Not surprisingly, there are also some critiques, especially on the stability of the coefficients. Contemporary scholars include Dean Foster and Robert Stine. Those who study distress from operational and organizational perspectives include Raphael Amit, Marshall Fisher, Vishal Gaur, and Ananth Raman. There seems to be no rigorous study of runways yet.

6.7   Further Reading

Altman, E. I. 1968. "Financial Ratios, Discriminant Analysis and the Prediction of Corporate Bankruptcy." *Journal of Finance*: 589–609.

Beaver, W. H. 1966. "Financial Ratios as Predictors of Failure." *Journal of Accounting Research*: 71–111.

Foster, D. P., and R. A. Stine. 2001. "Variable Selection in Data Mining: Building a Predictive Model for Bankruptcy." Department of Statistics, Wharton School of the University of Pennsylvania, Working Paper 01-05.

Gaur, V., M. Fisher, and A. Raman. 2005. "What Explains Superior Retail Performance." New York University, Working Paper OM-2005-03.

Thornhill, S., and R. Amit. 2003. "Learning about Failure: Bankruptcy, Firm Age, and the Resource-Based Vie." *Organization Science* 14 (5): 497–509.

III OPERATIONAL DUE DILIGENCE

The first chapter in this part considers the nuts and bolts of doing operational due diligence. In subsequent chapters, we look at specifics, such as how to value customer bases, how to verify a company's processes—especially if it claims that it implemented the famous Toyota production system—and how to assess risks and options.

7 The Many Facets of Due Diligence

The most common types of due diligence deal with legal and financial aspects of a business. Operational due diligence focuses on understanding the efficiency and effectiveness of the business and is complementary to other aspects of due diligence. In this chapter, we address these issues:

- *Why* do we do due diligence?
- *What* should due diligence seek?
- *When* should it be done?
- *How* and *by whom*?

In subsequent chapters, we dive into specific "how" questions that are particularly important:

- *How* can we verify that a company has implemented "lean management" programs such as the Toyota production system?
- *How* do we value customers and products?
- *How* do we value intangibles, such as risks and research and development?

7.1 Why Do We Do Due Diligence?

We perform due diligence—operational or otherwise—to achieve these objectives:

1. get information,
2. verify information obtained,
3. develop a plan to enhance the value of the company, and
4. make actionable decisions.

The first objective of getting information circles back to the issue of information asymmetry in chapter 4. A main objective of due diligence is to overcome this asymmetry. Of course, even without information asymmetry, financial information is often outdated, presenting only a lagged picture of a company's health. Further, financial information is often aggregated, masking risks, problems, and areas for improvement that are only evident when we go beneath these financial figures.

The second objective of due diligence is really more common, but less acknowledged. In many cases, the parties that undertake due diligence—such as financial analysts and private equity investors—will already have obtained tremendous amounts of information from their target company. The issue is not whether the information is there, but whether the information is truly reflective of the target's fortunes. One important implication of this objective is that resources for due diligence should be allocated less to obtaining more information than to using the obtained information to craft investment theses—and the antitheses (why we should *not* invest). Only with these theses and antitheses can the information gathering and verification steps be effective and efficient.

For active investors, the third objective of due diligence is to develop a plan to enhance the value of a company. This object is often underestimated, but is particularly important in turnaround situations. In this case, the lens with which one does the due diligence is specific to turnarounds. For example, an important issue is the investee's willingness and capacity for change *relative* to the investor's capability and aspired degree of change.

Finally, the most important objective of due diligence is to make actionable decisions, such as whether to invest in a business. Suppose, given what we already know, we are faced with the following possibilities for a business:

- Pessimistic scenario: net present value (NPV) = \$−1 billion.
- Optimistic scenario: NPV = \$2 billion.

There are many plausible ways to decide whether to invest. One approach: we invest if the expected NPV is positive. Suppose the probabilities associated with the scenarios depend on the likelihood that a technology can lower production costs. If we denote the probability of the pessimistic scenario as p and that of the optimistic as $1 - p$, then the expected NPV is $-1p + 2(1 - p)$. This value is positive if[1] p is less than 2/3. So if we have an a priori belief that p is significantly less than 2/3, then it seems that due diligence on the technology need not be a high priority.

Of course, there is a caveat that we do not know what we don't know (the unknown unknowns), but the point of this discussion is that we have to be explicit about whether due diligence is going to make a difference in our decisions. If it will not, then we should think twice about what the due diligence is going to deliver.

These four objectives for due diligence are neither mutually exclusive nor collectively exhaustive. For example, a private equity investor certainly wants both to value a potential investee and to turn it around. And due diligence might support other objectives, such as obtaining intelligence about competitive firms, customers, or suppliers. The key point, however, is that without making explicit the objectives of a due diligence exercise, it is most difficult to flesh out what due diligence should seek to provide.

7.2   What Should Due Diligence Seek?

Due diligence needs to collect evidence for the above objectives. This evidence may be collected along different dimensions:

• *Strategic.*   This includes the size and growth of the addressable market, the value proposition, customer acquisition and retention costs, switching costs, unaddressed opportunities (including mergers and acquisitions, research and development pipeline), foreseeable technological disruptions, competition and expected competitive responses, and alternate ownership structures.

• *Organizational.*   Examples include six of the seven S's popularized by McKinsey: systems (training and incentive systems), staffing (strength, deployment, verification of background of key executives), skills, shared values (ethical), structure (governance, informal and formal), and style. The seventh S, strategy, is mentioned in the previous point.

• *Financial and accounting.*   This includes compliance with standards, explanations of budget departures, inventory and asset valuations, audits, and off-balance-sheet items.

• *Governance.*   This concerns issues of responsibility, accountability, and incentives. For example, at the board level, this might include questions such as how independent, knowledgeable, and involved board members are. But one could and should ask about governance at many other levels and on various issues, such as supply chains, information technology, labor practices, or management succession.

• *Tax.*   This includes liabilities and the possibility of restructuring that can achieve a reduced tax burden.

• *Legal.*   This includes intellectual property, all sorts of contracts (with employees, franchisees, suppliers, customers, debt holders and other financiers, outsourcing partners), regulatory compliance, upcoming regulatory issues, and outstanding litigation.

• *Risk management.*   This includes insurance coverage, consolidated exposures both financial and operational (e.g., to a single source of supply, environmental destruction, product liability), threats to information systems, disaster recovery plans, and the organization's ability and readiness to adhere to these plans.

• *Operational.*   This, of course, is the focus of this text. In the following subsections, we show how we can use basic principles in operations management to describe what we should look for in due diligence. (In the chapters following this, we will zoom in to more specific aspects, such as what to look for in a company's customer base or its research and development efforts.)

Broadly, we can think of operational due diligence as a process of determining how a company measures up in terms of various performance metrics. The specific metrics that would be relevant depend on the goals of our due diligence. Nevertheless, broadly there are several categories of metrics to consider.

7.2.1   Operational Metrics That Drive Financial Measures

One useful framework for deriving such metrics is the "exploding tree," like the ones in chapter 6. For example, we might draw a tree starting from the runway measure, which could be a reasonable objective for a due diligence exercise. As we saw in figure 6.1, we might want to ascertain operational metrics such as days of receivables, number of stores, or the age distribution of inventory.

Another possible—and probably more important—objective of due diligence is to start with the return on assets (ROA) of a business. We described these at length in chapter 3.

Here we remind ourselves that the tree eventually leads to operational metrics such as processing time (the time it takes to do value-added work), queueing time (the time during which no value-added work is done), the number of servers, and the location of bottlenecks. This tree technique allows us to connect what we need to know financially to what we need to know operationally. The technique can also be used in reverse. On observing operational metrics, the tree provides a means for us to ascertain what the financials are.

7.2.2   Operational Metrics That Address Strategic Concerns

We can also connect strategic concerns to operational metrics. For many manufacturers, productivity, efficiency, and utilization are strategic concerns, in that these have to be done well for manufacturers to distinguish themselves in the market. For others, flexibility and quality might be strategic concerns. Below are some examples of how these strategic concerns translate to operational metrics.

• *Productivity.*   This translates to flow rate—that is, how many outputs can be produced in a unit time.

• *Efficiency.*   This translates to some ratio of output to input or capital. For example, sales/COGS (margin), sales/assets (asset turn), and COGS/inventory (inventory turn) are all measures of efficiency. A particularly important aspect of improving efficiency is to de-bottleneck processes. To do this, we would calculate the implied utilization of each station in a process:

• *Implied utilization.*   This is

$$\frac{demand\ rate}{capacity}.$$

That is, implied utilization is the ratio of how fast the market wants units to be produced to how fast our business can produce them. Investment priority should go to the unit with the highest implied utilization.

• *Flexibility.*   This is perhaps less obvious, but the question of flexibility can be operationalized as how to produce smaller batches. At the extreme, a flexible process can economically switch between producing just one widget during one period and another widget of a different type in the next period. The key, then, is to look for setup costs or time, because these will determine the optimal batch size that can be produced after each setup.

• *Quality.*   Yield loss is a natural metric for quality. Another particularly important one is flow time—i.e., the end-to-end elapsed time that customers experience. This involves both the processing time that adds value to the customer and the queueing time that does not add value.

Two themes emerge from the above. First, we should focus on operational metrics that are externally (e.g., from the perspective of customers or suppliers) rather than internally driven. For example, instead of considering just processing time (top right of the ROA tree in figure 3.1), we should ascertain flow time, which captures a customer's experience from the first contact to the last. It is the externally oriented metrics that can better direct the resources of the company to executing a successful strategy.

Second, we can use operations management concepts to verify claims. Consider this case: a manufacturing plant claims that it practices "flexible manufacturing" and is "very responsive to changes in market conditions." "Flexibility" and "responsiveness" are vague but can be operationalized as the capability of the plant to use small batch sizes, so that the plant can easily switch from producing one type of stock-keeping unit (SKU) to another.

Suppose machines in the manufacturing plant need a setup time of one hour per SKU batch. After setup, the machines can make 50 units of an SKU every hour. The plant's demand across all SKUs is 1,000 units every 24 hours, and the plant operates round the clock.

How can we, undertaking due diligence on the plant, verify a claim such as "we are flexible because our SKU batch size can be as small as 100 units"?

To verify this flexibility—or small-batch-size—claim, we return to a simple formula for batching, which is:

batch size = flow rate × flow time.

One approach is to ask: can the claimed 100-unit batch size really meet the demand rate of 1,000 units (of all types of SKUs) every 24 hours? From the formula, we get:

100 = flow rate × (1 hour setup + 2 hours for the batch's 100 units).

This gives a flow rate of 100/3 = 33.3 units per hour, or 800 units every 24 hours. This is much slower than the desired demand rate of 1,000 units every 24 hours.

Another approach is to ask: what is the optimal batch size to meet the demand rate? We assume that all SKUs will follow the same batch size. So for any SKU:

batch size $b = 1,000/24 \times (1$ hour setup $+ b/50$ hours to make b units).

This gives $b = 250$ units per batch, which is considerably larger than the claimed 100 units per batch.

In short, the manufacturing plant must either sacrifice production rate if it wishes to use small 100-unit batches, or use a larger 250-unit batch size if it wishes to satisfy the demand rate. If it wishes to attain both small batch size and high production rate, it would have to have shorter setup times or make units faster than the 50 units per hour after setup.

7.2.3 Operational Metrics to Deduce Other Metrics

There are also operational metrics used to deduce other metrics that are difficult to observe or obtain directly. Some examples include:

• *Flow time.* Bankers are often hard pressed to say how long the end-to-end customer experience is in their mortgage processes, since these processes often involve multiple stations, each of which knows only its own timing and its own waiting times. But we know from Little's Law that:

$$flow\ time = \frac{work\ in\ progress\ inventory}{flow\ rate}.$$

Therefore, we only need to observe how much work-in-progress inventory there is (the total number of mortgages being processed or waiting to be processed in various parts of the mortgage process) and the flow rate (number of mortgages processed per week, say), which bankers are often more able to determine and willing to disclose. Similarly, while a hospital executive might be hard pressed to tell us how long the average patient spends in the hospital, we can derive that important information by observing how many patients there are at any time and how many enter or leave the hospital. What is particularly impressive about Little's Law is that it assumes very little, such as how randomly patients arrive and whether patients maintain the same order in the hospital upon arrival. A key assumption is that the arrival and departure rates are the same, which is reasonably true for a hospital over some period of time.

• *Number of servers.* As another example, someone doing due diligence might not be able to directly observe how many servers there are in a production unit. For example, how do we infer the number of stone crushers in a competitor's factory? The number of chefs in the kitchen of a potential investee restaurant? Again, we can employ standard operations management techniques to estimate these. For example, the formula for queueing[2] allows us to deduce the number of servers if we know: (1) the average processing time (e.g., how long does a stone crusher need to crush a ton of stone?), (2) the average interarrival time (e.g., how long between the arrival of the last ton and the arrival of this one), and (3) the average queue waiting time (e.g., how long does the average ton of stone have to wait before being processed). These three pieces of information would allow us to estimate the number of stone crushers in the factory.

The basic point is that with a solid understanding of operations management principles, we can use some metrics as inputs to derive other metrics. In the stone-crusher queueing example above, we could also solve a different problem: how long does a ton of stone needs to wait, on average, before it is processed? We can work this out if we can find out: (1) the number of stone crushers, (2) the average crusher's capacity, and (3) how fast tons of stone arrive at the crushers.

We should also point out that the above is at an abstract level that applies to most firms. Clearly, the nuances and labels of the metrics differ by industry. Appendix A provides salient metrics by industry.

Finally, we should mention an important metric that drives very many other operational metrics. This is variability, which may arise from demand (e.g., customer arrivals) or supply (e.g., different production rates, yield losses). Without variability, much of operations management would be easier: it would be considerably easier to match supply with demand, or to diagnose and fix yield problems. Indeed, the reduction of variability is central to the Toyota production system, which we discuss in the next chapter.

7.3   When Should It Be Done?

The obvious answer is that operational due diligence should be done only when we want to take a deeper look into the business of a company. But the real issue is a question of priority: when do we know we have to invest more in operational due diligence?

At the highest level, we should invest more when we believe financial statements may be less accurate. As we discussed in section 2.3, this is the case when we determine that executives in the firm to be investigated have three characteristics:

• *Opportunity.*   Do managers have leeway to run operations in ways that are not aligned with investors' interests, and in ways not noticeable by investors? In chapter 4 we gave an example of how this might arise because of information asymmetry: investors cannot and do not observe everything that a retailer does.

• *Means.*   Does the business in question have the ability to manage (or "manipulate," if egregious matters are involved) operations? For example, in section 4.3 we refer to the case of a retailer with the *decision rights* on operations at a day-to-day level. Such a retailer evidently has the means to manipulate its inventory.

• **Motive.**   Does the business have an incentive to manipulate operations? In the example in chapter 4, a retailer that places some weight on *short-term* misvaluation of its business has the incentive to manage operations so as to produce this misvaluation.

Often we may not even have enough information to determine whether these three characteristics apply. In such a case, there are two approaches available. One is to employ an empirically tested statistical approach to modeling earnings manipulation. We have already discussed this in section 4.6.3. The second is to employ an experienced-based set of rules of thumb. David Hawkins of Harvard lists some that are enormously useful in detecting the possibility of manipulation (edited here):

• Reported profit is significantly larger than respective cash flow measures. Specifically, net income is much greater than cash flow from operations, or earnings before interest, tax, depreciation, and amortization (EBITDA) is much greater than free cash flow.

• Reported performance—in profits, margins, or sales—significantly better than industry benchmarks.

• Managers prefer to be judged by non-GAAP measures such as EBITDA rather than by net income.

• Accounting improprieties or reporting mistakes have been revealed by other firms in the industry.

• Material events—such as large contracts or debt covenants—are about to be negatively impacted.

• The company delays financial announcements, such as regulatory filings or conference calls with analysts.

• There is notable turnover in key management, accounting, or financial positions and among auditors.

• The company's audit or legal fees are significantly out of line with industry benchmarks.

• There are unusually large corrections to provisions, accounting methods, or receivables.

• There are previous sanctions by regulators or current rumors of sanctions in the media or among employees.

Conversely, we might lighten our operational due diligence if we see positive signs. Examples of these include voluntary and extensive disclosures, or a significant portion of managerial compensation held for the very long term.

7.4 How and By Whom?

Due diligence, and especially operational due diligence, represents an enormous investment, and many companies have honed their due diligence processes to very effective and efficient levels.

One important process characteristic adopted by the best investment firms is to structure the due diligence according to two fundamental investment approaches:

• *Portfolio approach.* In this approach, the key is to contain risk through diversification over many small investments. Typically, such investors have small "bite size" or small "checks written," large assets under management (AUM), many employees, small AUM per employee, and minority equity positions. Typically, the portfolio approach also relies on public information, since it would have been costly to dedicate resources to obtaining private information for each deal in the portfolio.

• *Relationship approach.* In this approach, the investor contains risks by getting to know the investee in great detail, through constant monitoring and through deep relationships that could overcome information asymmetry problems. The economically viable way to adopt this approach is to have major equity positions, which involves large bite sizes and large AUM per employee. Not surprisingly, this approach typically relies on private information.

Table 7.1 shows some examples of investors and their bite sizes and AUM per employee. The ones at the top of the table tend to be early-stage players, with characteristics amenable to the portfolio approach: small bite sizes and small AUM per employee. The ones toward

Table 7.1
Investment Firms: Their Bite Sizes for Equity Investments and Assets under Management (AUM) per Employee

Company Name	Bite Size, Minimum ($mm)	Bite Size, Maximum ($mm)	AUM ($mm)	Employees	AUM ($mm/ employee)
Charles River Ventures	0.03	20	450	60	7.50
Dome Capital LLC	0.5	3	20	50	0.40
Ziff Brothers Investments	2	20	150	80	1.88
InterWest Partners	7	15	650	36	18.06
Key Principal Partners Corp.	10	40	520	243	2.14
American Capital, Ltd.	10	400	1,001	360	2.78
CIVC Partners, L.P.	15	85	649	220	2.95
Kohlberg & Company, L.L.C.	30	125	1,500	750	2.00
The Yucaipa Companies, LLC	50	300	1,527	50	30.54
Littlejohn & Co. LLC	50	100	850	17	50.00
Apollo Management	300	1,000	14,900	350	42.57

Source: Capital IQ, 2009.

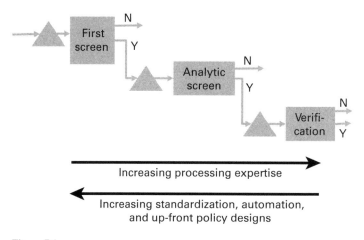

Figure 7.1
Staging in the due diligence process.

the bottom of the table are at the opposite extreme, with characteristics appropriate for a relationship approach to investing.

These different approaches have their natural implications for how much due diligence should be done on potential investees. The due diligence process typically has several screens, as shown in figure 7.1.

The first screen involves screening on the basis of the firm's investment charter. For example, a firm might look only for deals that are in the northeastern US, early stage, a $5 million investment quantum for a minority position, in the biotechnology sector.

This stage is often underestimated in its value in identifying investment theses and antitheses, which can focus the next stage in a most effective and efficient manner. An example of an investment thesis is that the potential investee has a bottleneck in the approval station in its mortgage handling process, and that suitable staffing of this station could substantially improve the productivity of the process. An example of an antithesis is that the potential investee does not have the kind of production flexibility that allows it to cope with a market in which product diversity is about to explode.

Once we have investment theses and antitheses, the subsequent stages—analytic screen and verification—can be very focused. In short, the due diligence process is a staged process, in that candidate deals have to go through different stages and may drop out at any stage. Of course, this does not mean that we blind ourselves to other issues outside the initial theses and antitheses in the subsequent stages.

The utility of staging is that it allows for differentiated staffing: for example, less experienced associates or even automation can be employed in the first screen. Staging also allocates the scarcest resources to where they are most needed, and only when they are needed. Finally, staging facilitates the development of specialized skills. Of course, with staging comes the possibility that one stage might starve because a prior stage is busy or might be blocked by a subsequent stage that is busy. A lack of accountability for the entire process might also set in.

To mitigate these possibilities, the best investment firms often deploy another structural form in their due diligence process: roving senior supervisory resources. These are often their managing directors, who de-bottleneck stages and assume overall responsibility for the process. This arrangement resembles a practice under the Toyota production system, which we study in the next chapter. The senior roving resource not only de-bottlenecks the due diligence process, but mentors less experienced staff and learns at first hand whether the process is executed in line with policy.

Yet another process arrangement that is useful in due diligence is to triage the cases. As in a hospital emergency room, some cases might need urgent attention, perhaps because competing investment firms are keen to bid on the potential investee. The best due diligence processes provide for such triage at each of the three stages of the process.

An important consideration in penetrating the fog shrouding the operations of a company is to triangulate—to countercheck whether different sources point to the same claim. One especially powerful kind of due diligence is to examine the target investee's suppliers, customers, and competitors. When the target investee claims it has a one-year lead on its market, its competitors might also be claiming the same for themselves.

Finally, in terms of staff deployment, the later stages normally utilize the most experienced staff; see figure 7.1. The earlier stages are more standardized, and perhaps even automated. What is needed there is up-front effort in designing the screening policies.

7.5 Takeaways and Toolkit

In this chapter, we have seen that:

• It is vital to clarify the objectives of a due diligence process, since its objectives have implications for its design.

• Operational due diligence should seek to ascertain performance on a number of metrics, which can be based on financial or strategic outcomes and concerns. Some metrics are not directly observable, but we can use operations management principles to derive them from other metrics.

• There are two major ways to structure due diligence: a portfolio versus a relationship approach.

For ease of reference, we summarize some due diligence guidelines in table 7.2. For completeness, we also enumerate some tactical issues, such as who we should try to talk to and when are the best times to undertake due diligence.

Table 7.2
Toolkit: Due Diligence Checklist

Area	Key Steps
Why do we undertake due diligence	• Get information, • Verify information obtained, • Develop a plan for realizing more value in the company, • Make actionable decisions.
What due diligence should find	• Operational metrics that drive financial measures: use an exploding tree from ROA or runway to get these metrics, • Operational metrics that speak to strategic concerns, such as productivity, efficiency, flexibility, quality: remember to exploit operations management principles to address the concerns; use externally oriented metrics, rather than internal ones, • Operational metrics to deduce other metrics: for example, use inventory and flow rate to find flow time. Variability is an import metric that drives other metrics.
When due diligence should be done, how, and by whom	• Stage so that the most important cases get the most due diligence, • Triage so that the urgent cases get attention, • Use a roving senior resource to de-bottleneck, mentor, and enhance learning among staff.
Some tactical guidelines	• Look not only for what is there, but for what is not there, • Look for "process creep," extensions and band-aids to broken processes that are opportunities for improvement, • Take a climate survey of staff morale (in one bank, the CEO was surprised that the most demoralized staff were senior executives, not the rank and file), • Talk to information brokers, those to whom others turn, • Watch out for those eager to please the due diligence staff—not all actions are necessarily selfless, • Look especially carefully at handoffs, departmental interfaces, cross-functional processes—that is often where things wait or get lost.

7.6   Survey of Prior Research in One Paragraph

There has not been much scientific study of the due diligence process, or of related topics such as business plans. William Sahlman and Howard Stevenson pioneered some of the early analyses. Raffi Amit, David Hsu, Paul Gompers, Steven Kaplan, Josh Lerner, and Andrew Metrick are some of the leading scholars in the related areas of private equity and venture capital. It is also worthwhile to revisit the key texts in operations management to recall what operating characteristics to look for in due diligence. The leading texts include those by Gerard Cachon and Christian Terwiesch, Wally Hopp and Mark Spearman, and Jan van Mieghem.

7.7 Further Reading

Cachon, G., and C. Terwiesch. 2006. *Matching Supply with Demand: An Introduction to Operations Management*. New York: McGraw-Hill.

Gompers, P. A., and J. Lerner. 2004. *The Venture Capital Cycle*. Cambridge, MA: MIT Press.

Hawkins, D. F. 1968. "Controversial Accounting Changes." *Harvard Business Review* (March-April): 20–41.

Hopp, W. J., and M. L. Spearman. 2001. *Factory Physics*. Boston: Irwin McGraw-Hill.

Hsu, D. H. 2008. "Technology-Based Entrepreneurship." In S. Shane, ed., *Handbook of Technology and Innovation Management*. Chichester, UK: Wiley.

Kaplan, S. N., B. A. Sensoy, and P. Stromberg. 2009. "Should Investors Bet on the Jockey or the Horse? Evidence from the Evolution of Firms from Early Business Plans to Public Companies." *Journal of Finance* 64 (1): 75–115.

Metrick, A. 2007. *Venture Capital and the Finance of Innovation*. New York: Wiley.

Sahlman, W. A., H. H. Stevenson, A. Bhide, and M. J. Roberts. 1999. *The Entrepreneurial Venture*. Boston: Harvard Business School Press.

Van Mieghem, J. A. 2008. *Operations Strategy: Principles and Practice*. Belmont, MA: Dynamic Ideas.

Zott, C., and R. Amit. 2008. "The Fit between Product Market Strategy and Business Model: Implications for Firm Performance." *Strategic Management Journal* 29 (1).

8 Assessing the Customer Base

For one retail bank, 80% of its customers make up 125% of its profits; the other customers are loss-making. For an auto dealership, reducing defection from 10% to 5% improved the net present value of its customer base by 81%.

Not surprisingly, many due diligence programs have assessing the value of the customer base as their core. The media is filled with headlines such as: "TelePacific to acquire SMB customer base and network of O1," "Direct Energy acquires Entergy's ERCOT customer base," or "Dieringer Research acquires Lein/Spiegelhoff customer base."

Yet the pertinent aspects about a company's customer base are not easily discernible from financial statements. How do we value a company's customer base? How can we improve that valuation? To do this, we need to dive below the financial statements.

In this chapter, we elaborate on these issues in the context of a retail bank. Retail banks offer a particularly suitable setting to discuss these because they have issues that many retailers and service companies share. They also face rapid and short episodes of technological changes, such as Internet banking. These short episodes allow us to examine these issues in the context of several life cycles of banking (the introduction of ATMs, globalization, Internet banking, etc.), making them the equivalent of a geneticist's fruit flies in the study of customer valuation.

In what follows, our description is at the customer level. This detailed level of analysis may not always be possible if we do not have customer-level data. Nevertheless, much of the discussion holds for analysis at the segment level, for which data is often more readily available.

8.1 How Much of Customer Valuation Is Revealed in Financial Statements?

The most obvious indication of customer valuation in financial statements is the revenue item. Other subitems, such as revenue growth, returns, and warranty reserves, give some indirect indication of the quality of products and services delivered, and therefore of customers' likelihood of retention. But financial statements are missing a few critical pieces of information: (1) how customer profitability differs by segment, and therefore the managerial implication of what to do with each segment, (2) the lifetime profitability of each segment, and (3) importantly, to what extent we can lift the profitability of low-profitability segments. For this last point, we focus on channels as a lever, given its importance in retail banking. In short, we need to get at these other types of information not readily apparent in financial statements, and we have to go deeper.

8.1.1   How Much of Customer Valuation Is Revealed in Satisfaction Surveys?

While financial statements may not capture an operational item such as customer value, what about satisfaction surveys? Indeed, many businesses link satisfaction scores to staff compensation, assuming that higher scores mean higher customer valuations.

But it turns out that in practice, the link between satisfaction scores and the true measure of customer valuation—the lifetime profitability of customers—is often tenuous. Reichheld and Teal note that, over the years, businesses across many industries have reached scores indicating that more than 90% of customers are satisfied. Yet only 40–50% of customers actually make repurchases. It is not uncommon for businesses to report that 60–80% of their customers are satisfied, only to find that they soon defect to the competition.

What could account for this discrepancy between satisfaction scores and customer profitability? Some of this may be due to customers' reluctance to be antagonistic, reporting greater satisfaction than they actually felt. There could also be a reporting bias, in which only satisfied customers complete survey forms. On the business end, salespeople often game the system to obtain higher satisfaction scores, especially if the scores are closely tied to compensation. Reichheld and Teal describe how a Toyota dealer offers a "Free Auto Detail" to customers who agreed to mark "Very Satisfied" on survey forms. The dealer even provides prefilled forms to show customers how to enter scores. Sometimes the gaming is more subtle. For example, businesses often survey customers right after purchases, because that is when customers are more likely to indicate satisfaction.

One final issue with satisfaction scores is that it is unclear how to quantify their value. How much more should we invest to move from 4.6 to 4.9? To measure customer profitability, we need a quantification of key aspects of customer behavior.

8.2   Measuring Customer Profitability

We begin with a simple, natural way to measure profitability: use a tree beginning with the profitability of a single customer. To illustrate, we use an example from retail banking, shown in figure 8.1, which is reproduced from a portion of figure A.1. The fact that one is a portion of the other makes clear that customer profitability drives overall bank profitability.

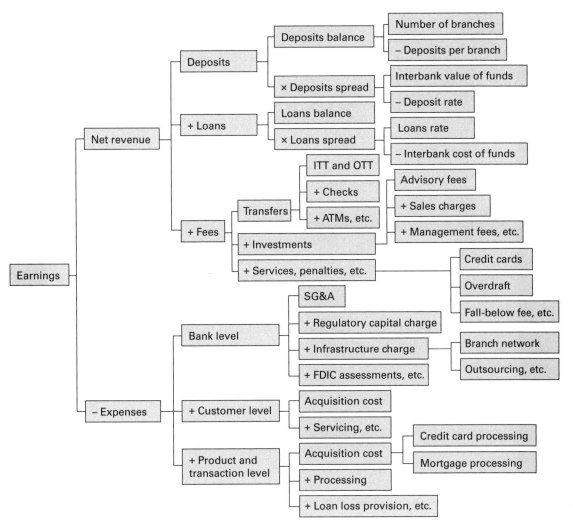

Figure 8.1
Profit tree for a bank customer (detail of figure A.1).

Box 8.1
The profitability of bank products

It is tempting to say that a bank's net revenues are its deposit and loan balances multiplied by the spread between loan and deposit rates. But this confounds the net revenues of the loans and deposits. Also, loan and deposit balances are rarely the same, so it is not clear which balance to use. Third, this does not yield market-priced net revenues. A better approach is to get net revenues from deposits by multiplying deposit balances by the market-priced spread, which is the difference between what the bank pays depositors and what it gets by placing the collected funds in the interbank market; and then similarly for loans.

Recall that retail banks have several sources of revenues: deposits, loans, transfers, investments, services, and penalty charges. The expenses may be categorized by level: bank, customer, and transaction level. Even this simple case shows the complexity of the measure.

First, a typical due diligence effort will find that many banks do not readily possess data on the profitability of a customer across all products. So although figure 8.1 shows an appealing picture of a customer's total profitability, the information is rarely easily accessible in practice.

Second, measures of profitability are often not robust to different ways of allocating costs. For example, a bank might take the easy approach of dividing bank-level expenses equally among all customers. To the extent that it is economically feasible, it would be more accurate to allocate based on customer behavior (e.g., transactions used, services used, sales cost incurred). Conversely, some transaction-level expenses should not be allocated to transactions or customers if these expenses are not going to be easily removed after an improvement program. For example, a small branch with just one teller may not want to allocate the teller's time to individual transactions if we cannot have half a teller by removing some transactions (though we can have "half a teller" if we can redeploy the teller's time).

Third, the profitability distribution of customers often has a profile like that in figure 8.2. This immediately suggests some actions that can boost profitability: keeping the top deciles satisfied, migrating lower deciles higher, and gently nudging out the unprofitable deciles.

However, the figure also misses an important consideration. A customer may be only moderately profitable to our bank and yet very profitable to competing banks. In other words, the picture does not account for the fact that our bank has only a share of the customer's wallet.

Fourth, simple versions of pictures like ROA trees or customer profitability distributions are snapshots in time. A more accurate picture would account for the lifetime value of a customer. Otherwise, we may nudge out what seem to be unprofitable customers in the short term who could be very profitable ones in the longer term (e.g., some MBA students).

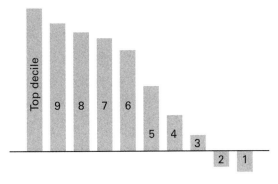

Figure 8.2
Customer base by profitability deciles (illustrative).

Box 8.2
Cohort analyses

A common error in customer profitability analysis is to look at a cross section of customers. Since different cohorts of customers tend to be different, it is better to track cohorts of customers instead.

Finally, it is easy to underestimate the strategic impact of the management of sales and service channels on profitability. One northeast bank sought to boost profitability by capping service expenses. It minimized the duration and frequency of customer interactions at teller windows, ATMs, and other channels. It measured its call center staff on "service rate," which purportedly captured how quickly customer calls could be closed. Within a year, it found that its sales had dropped 18%. At the call center, for example, instead of resolving customer calls, staff sought to direct customers away as quickly as possible. Sales that might have arisen when tellers referred opportunities to sales staff were dramatically reduced. It turned out that the connection between service and sales was a lot more intertwined.

The last two considerations—customer retention and channel management—are so critical that we dedicate the next two sections to these topics.

8.3   Impact of Customer Defections on Valuation

Frederick Reichheld probably has done the most to articulate the idea that reducing customer defections has a significant impact on the net present value (NPV) of a customer base.

Box 8.3
Steady-state analyses

> Another common error in customer analysis is to start with non-steady states. For example, what is the average tenure when the defection rate is 10%? We might think (erroneously) that with 10% defection, our customers in a base year would all defect in the course of 10 years, so the average tenure is 5 years. But this calculation ignores steady state. Instead, we should assume that the tenure is n, and solve this equation: $n = 90\%(n + 1) + 10\%(1)$. That is, in the next year, the tenures of loyal and new customers are $n + 1$ and 1, respectively. We see that $n = 1/(10\%)$ or 10 years. In general, $n = 1/(\text{defection rate})$.

There are five reasons why a company with more loyal customers enjoys larger profits:

• *Lower acquisition costs.*   A Forrester survey of 24 banks suggests that the cost to a bank of acquiring a checking account varies from $143 to $328, and that for a credit card account from $55 to $115. Importantly, these costs are high relatively to the profitability of a customer, with payback usually only after the second year.

• *More and bigger purchases.*   Many loyal customers eventually grow into more affluent demographics and therefore buy more. And by virtue of their longer tenure with a company, loyal customers also interact more with the company, which then has more opportunities to up-sell or cross-sell to these customers.

• *Lower cost to serve.*   A company and its loyal customers learn more about each other so that their interface can be more efficient. A longtime bank customer would know where the bank's ATMs are, instead of phoning its call center. The bank's financial advisor needs only an update of a customer's finances to know what products suit the latter, instead of spending time reviewing the customer's situation. The added trust developed over a longer tenure makes it easier to persuade a loyal customer.

• *Higher willingness to pay.*   Loyal customers, by selection, are a better fit with the company's products and services and are therefore more willing to pay for these. Conversely, a company can avoid discounts and promotional rates used to entice new customers.

• *Referrals.*   Loyal customers also tend to generate referrals for the company, which are likely to be even better leads than those obtained by spending vast sums of advertising dollars.

As a result of the above, Reichheld reports that—across many industries—customer profitability increases over time (see figure 8.3). The increase for each additional year of tenure increases that year's profitability by 5–10%. What is more surprising is that very small improvements in defection rates can have an enormous impact on the NPV of the entire lifetime profitability of the customer base.

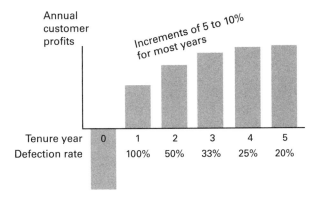

Figure 8.3
Annual customer profitability by tenure.

Reichheld provides a few examples from different industries of how the "impact of a 5-percentage-point" improvement in defection rate can increase the NPV of a company's customers:

- Advertising agency: 95% increase.
- Auto service: 81%.
- Branch bank deposits: 85%.
- Industrial laundry: 45%.
- Life insurance: 90%.

8.3.1   Advanced Topic: Can Reducing Defection Really Double NPV?

Looking at figure 8.3, it may seem unlikely that reducing defection can have a significant impact on the NPV of a customer base. The yearly increment in profitability is on the order of 5 to 10%, so, for example, improving the defection rate from 25% to 20% (a 5 percentage point improvement) does not seem to do much to NPV.

It turns out the intuition is about right. When the defection rate is about middling, improving defection may do the least to increase NPV. But when defection rate is high, the impact can indeed be high.

Suppose, to make things simpler and conservative, the profit bars at present value stay at the same height for all years, as in figure 8.4. If the defection rate is high (toward the left of the figure), the NPV is about zero in year 2, because the bars for years 1 and 2 just about compensate for the year 0 acquisition cost. Then almost any improvement in defection, and hence improvement in profitability, will lead to a spectacular improvement in NPV, from zero to nonzero.

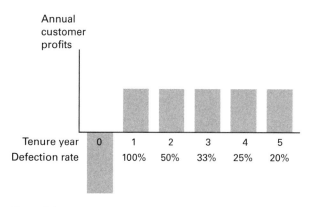

Figure 8.4
Annual customer profitability by tenure (example).

At very low rates of defection (toward the right of the figure), NPV can also increase substantially with a small improvement in defection rate. This is because the small improvement in defection rate, from 10% (average tenure is 10 years) to 5% (20 years) is a dramatic increase in tenure, which affords a dramatic increase in NPV.

A simple mathematical example will show that the claim that a 5 percent reduction in defection rate can double NPV is plausible, but only when defection rates are notably low or high. Say the present value of each bar in figure 8.4 is p and the present value cost of acquisition in year 0 is $A \times p$. When average tenure is n years—or the defection rate is $1/n$ (see the sidebar above on "steady-state analyses")—the NPV is $-A \times p + n \times p$. How does this NPV change with defection rate $1/n$? We just take the derivative:

$$\frac{\partial(NPV)}{\partial(defection\ rate)} = \frac{\partial(-A \times p + n \times p)}{\partial(1/n)} = -p \times n^2.$$

Using this, we can now check the conditions under which a 5 percentage point improvement in defection rate (denoted as $\Delta defection\ rate = -0.05$) would lead to a doubling of the NPV (denoted as $\Delta NPV = NPV = -A \times p + n \times p$):

$$\frac{\Delta NPV}{\Delta defection\ rate} = \frac{-A \times p + n \times p}{-0.05} = -p \times n^2,$$

or

$$A = n - 0.05n^2.$$

The plot is shown in figure 8.5, confirming our intuition. When the tenure n is short, a small increase in tenure significantly improves NPV because, with a short tenure, the average customer is mostly still in payback mode (the bank is still paying back the cost of acquiring the customer).

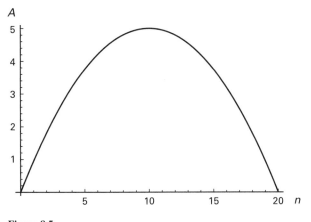

Figure 8.5
Plot of acquisition cost multiple (A) versus tenure (n).

When the tenure is long, a 5 percentage point drop in defection rate translates to a large number of years of added tenure—e.g., going from 10% defection (tenure of 10 years) to 5% (20 years) is a 10-year improvement in tenure.

In between these two cases, acquisition costs have to be staggeringly high to generate a doubling of NPV with a 5 percentage point reduction in defection rate.

To conclude, the Reichheld claim that improving defection significantly increases NPV is sound, but only when defection rates are low or high.

8.4   Impact of Channel Mix on Valuation

Much of the previous discussion—a bank's costs and revenues from a customer over her lifetime—depends on the channel mix a customer uses. For example, the Forrester survey mentioned earlier reports that acquisitions costs are especially low for phone and web channels, compared with branch channels. For checking and savings accounts and credit cards, web channels are about 55% lower than branches and phone channels are 34% lower. For mortgages and home equity loans, web channels are about 38% lower than branches and phone channels are 10% lower. Likewise, costs to serve are also lower for web channels than for phone or branch channels.

Not surprisingly, many studies have documented that heavier users of web channels are also more profitable customers. What is harder to establish is the directionality of the correlation: (1) To what extent do more profitable customers choose to use web channels (e.g., because more profitable customer are generally also more Internet-savvy and value convenience more), and (2) To what extent does getting customers online improve their lifetime profitability?

There is no strong consensus on these questions in the research community, but there is preliminary evidence to suggest that: (1) profitable customers do tend to select into less expensive web channels, whereas (2) while being online enhances sales and reduces the cost to serve for some customers, these effects are not large. For example, Hitt and Frei find that the average retail banking customer who uses the web buys 1.5 times more products (e.g., certificate of deposit, mortgage, credit card) than the customer who does not use the web, but those who use the web buy only 0.17 times more products than they did before web use. Web-using customers also have defection rates than are 3.6 percentage points lower.

Perhaps the most important message from the research literature is not so much a specific number that we can attach to the impact of newer channels such as the Internet, but that we need sophisticated tools to distill the true impact of the newer channels. The following subsection delves into the details of such tools.

8.4.1 Advanced Topic: Does Web Use Really Improve Profitability and Retention?

A simple approach to estimating the impact of web use (as an example of a new type of channel) on profitability is to obtain a sample of customers and run a regression like this:

$$profitability = \alpha \cdot WebUse + \beta X + \varepsilon,$$

where α is the effect of interest, β is the effect of some control variable(s) X such as customer age and address, and ε captures noise.

There are four running themes through modern-day empirics about specification such as the above. Because such empirics are powerful in helping us determine causality in general (e.g., whether the introduction of 5.25-inch disk drives caused a disruption in the disk drive industry, or whether customer dissatisfaction led to defections), it is useful to understand the pitfalls of such empirics.

Specification error. The issue here is whether we are fitting a straight line—as we do above—onto data that really is from a curved relationship (which in the research literature is called a nonlinear relationship). For example, web use might have an inverted-U-shaped relationship with profitability. While increasing web use increases profitability initially, it eventually reduces profitability. This later reduction might be due to customers who increase their volume of interactions with the bank, checking their accounts more often than before, or transfering smaller amounts of funds more regularly than before because of the new convenience. The fix for such specification error is relatively straightforward. Analysts may use a log transformation of the *WebUse* variable, or add terms such as the square of *WebUse* and interactions of *WebUse* with other variables. Generally, a reasonable test is that adding these variables increases the explanatory power of the specification, as captured by measures such as the adjusted R-squared of the estimated regression.

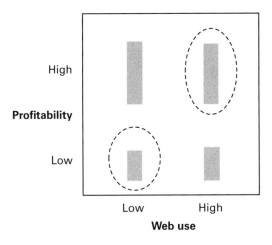

Figure 8.6
Effect of web use and income on profitability. The height of the bars represents income. Dashed circles show where most of the observations are.

Omitted variable bias. The issue here is whether *WebUse* has an observed effect on *Profitability* only because we neglect to control for other variables that correlate with *WebUse*. That is, it is not really *WebUse* but those other missing variables that really have an effect on *Profitability*.

Consider the situation in figure 8.6, where the height of the bars represents the average income of the four groups of bank customers. Suppose that most customers fall into the two groups with circled bars. A regression of *Profitability* on *WebUse* would suggest that higher web use is associated with higher profitability, since the two encircled bars dominate the other two bars in the sample. But once we include *Income* as a variable, we see that web use has little impact on profitability: if we look at just the two high-income groups at the top half, profitability is the same (high) for both low- and high-web-usage customers, and if we look at just the two low-income groups at the bottom half, profitability is again the same regardless of web usage. Conversely, if we control for web usage, we see that it is really higher income that is associated higher profitability: among the two low-web-usage groups on the left, the higher income group is associated with higher profitability, and likewise, among the two high-web-use groups on the right, higher income is again associated with higher profitability.

Despite this guideline, modern empirics have largely moved away from the use of control variables. This is because it is hard to persuade anyone that one has included all necessary controls. Modern empiricists now turn to cleaner tests that involve "exogenous shocks" of the explanatory variable of interest. We discuss this next.

Correlation, causality, and spurious correlations. Correlation is not causality. For example, the presence of doctors and epidemics is correlated, but we would not think that the former causes the latter. In many cases, there could also be bidirectional causality, as in the case of customer profitability and web use described earlier. More profitable customers could choose to go online, and going online could make customers more profitable. What is needed is to carefully disentangle the different impact of these two effects.

Correlation may also be spurious. For example, a high number of swimming pool drownings and high ice cream sales are unlikely to be causally related in either direction. What is more plausible is that a third factor—hot weather—drives up both drownings and ice cream sales.

Empiricists have developed sophisticated techniques to address the issues of causality and spurious correlation. For example, control variables can be used to detect spurious correlations: adding weather temperature as a control, for example, can eliminate the apparent effect of ice cream on drowning.

The issue of causality is much harder to establish and is the holy grail of modern empirical work. The gold standard for estimating causal effects is to run an experiment in which the explanatory variable (such as *WebUse*) is randomly applied to a sample of customers, and see how the dependent variable (such as *Profitability*) changes. In practical settings, of course, it is infeasible and often unethical to run randomness experiments. So sophisticated analysts have turned to ingenious natural experiments. Consider the question of whether retailers manipulate their sales at the end of the fiscal year, when sales bonuses are given based on the attainment of sales targets. A simple regression might be of the form:

$$Sales = \beta \cdot FiscalYearEnd + \varepsilon.$$

The problem is that an estimate of β is likely to be confounded by reverse causality: companies may set their fiscal years to end right after sales are high, at the end of product cycles. For example, if the ski-jacket-selling season ends in February, it is natural for a ski jacket retailer to set its fiscal year to end in February, tallying up the sales for the season. But we would not conclude that high sales near February is due to a February fiscal year end.

To resolve this, we could consider a natural experiment. For example, in Germany a change in tax laws in 2000 incentivized companies to change their fiscal year ends. Such a change is exogenous to changes in sales patterns within the year, so a regression of data around 2000 for firms that change their fiscal year end can more conclusively identify the effect of the fiscal year end on sales.

8.5   Takeaways and Toolkit

In this chapter, we have learned why we have to dig below financial statements to better value a company's customer base. To do that, we need to:

Table 8.1
Toolkit for Reducing Customer Defections

Goal	Key Steps
Loyal customers	Given a company's proposition, some customers are inherently more loyal than others. But this also means that a company can change its proposition to better fit customers. For example, military families might normally be hard to retain for some insurance companies, because the families relocate regularly. However, as Reichheld points out, USAA designs its systems to cater to relocating families, and to USAA, military families are the least likely to defect.
Loyal employees	Reminiscent of the worker-centered spirit of the Toyota production system, the reduction of customer defection goes with the reduction of employee defections. One overriding theme is to ensure that loyal employees are rewarded more than new ones; but to do this without adverse effect requires extremely careful selection of candidates and retrenchment of the inevitable employee who turns out to be an imperfect fit. It is also sensible to tie some forms of compensation to customer retention.
Loyal investors	Many customer service improvements—such as staff training and call center technologies—require immediate investments but show their impact only after a few years. This calls for sacrificing more attractive company valuations for more patient investors—such as some institutional investors—whose horizon and needs are better aligned with the company.
Effective loyalty measures	Reichheld and Sasser advocate measures of defection and referrals across the board, of customers, employees, and investors. In particular, they argue that satisfaction scores do not do the job. These scores are easily manipulated—such as an auto dealer who times his surveys right after customer purchases, when customers are the most receptive—and they do not offer the kind of NPV analyses by customer segment that defection analyses affords.

• Properly measure a customer's profitability, accounting for the customer's lifetime and potential profitability.

• Consider how defection reduction can significantly improve the value of a customer base. In many ways, a program to reduce customer defections is similar to one like the Toyota production system (TPS), to reduce waste. Reichheld and Sasser list some categories for action, which we summarize in table 8.1.

• Consider how the channel mix also affects profitability. Again, the causality of this statement, from channel mix to profitability, needs to be carefully established.

8.6   Survey of Prior Research in One Paragraph

Don Morrison and David Schmittlein are some of the pioneers in valuing and analyzing a customer base. Frances Frei, Patrick Harker, and Lorin Hitt have done some of the most rigorous research on customer profitability analysis in their studies of retail banking. Frederick Reichheld and Earl Sasser are best known for their work on customer retention. In this area, technology plays an important part in designing channels, delivering service, and analyzing and retaining customers. Erik Brynjolfsson, Eric Clemons, Tom Malone,

Carl Shapiro, and Hal Varian are pioneers in developing our understanding in this area. Gary Biddle and Richard Steinberg wrote a seminal paper on the interaction of operations and accounting, on the allocation of costs among activities.

8.7   Further Reading

Biddle, G., and R. Steinberg, R. 1985. "Common Cost Allocation in the Firm." In H. P. Young, ed., *Cost Allocation: Methods, Principles, Applications*, 31–54. Amsterdam: Elsevier Science.

Hitt, L. M., and F. X. Frei. 2002. "Do Better Customers Utilize Electronic Distribution Channels? The Case of PC Banking." *Management Science* 48 (6): 732–748.

Reichheld, F. F., and W. E. Sasser. 1990. "Zero Defections." *Harvard Business Review* 68 (5): 105–111.

Reichheld, F. F., and T. Teal. 1996. *The Loyalty Effect.* Boston: Harvard Business School Press.

Schmittlein, D. C., D. G. Morrison, and R. Colombo. 1987. "Counting Your Customers: Who Are They and What Will They Do Next?" *Management Science* 33 (1): 1–24.

Strothkamp B, and E. Davis. 2008. "Financial Services Firms Open Up about Customer Acquisition Costs." Forrester Research White Paper.

9 Assessing Lean Management

The Toyota production system (TPS) has been so admired that many companies claim that they have implemented it. As Jim Kotek, a vice president of the manufacturing firm ORBIS, said: "At ORBIS' manufacturing plants we have found lean principles to be applicable to not only our on-the-floor production, but also to our warehouse operations, to our purchasing practices and to how we arrange freight for our customers."[1]

Even some service companies claim that they have implemented the TPS. For example, Virginia Mason Medical Center, in Seattle, Washington, is an example of a hospital that has done so. Figure 9.1 shows the process for treating oncology patients before the implementing of the TPS, when 99% of the throughput time—the elapsed time between a patient's entering and exiting the process—is non-value-added, in that the patient is not being attended to. With the TPS, Virginia Mason restructured the process so that the non-value-added throughput time dropped by 70%.

But for an investor doing due diligence on such companies, is looking at outcome improvements sufficient? Indeed, how does one tell whether a company has implemented the TPS?

A note on terminology: many use the phrases "lean management" and "TPS" synonymously, though the two are not identical. We focus on the TPS here, but many of the principles discussed could be applied to lean management.

9.1 How Much of Process Performance Is Revealed in Financial Statements?

Financial statements do show some aspects of process performance. For example, various measures of turns—asset turn (sales/assets), inventory turn (COGS/inventory)—are really measures of technical efficiency. Levels of inventory—especially the level of work-in-progress inventory—capture the level of process imbalance. But by and large, figures in financial statements do not fully reflect process performance in three ways: (1) the figures tend to lag process performance, since the figures are prepared only at the end of every financial period, (2) the figures are aggregated at the firm level, so it is difficult to see

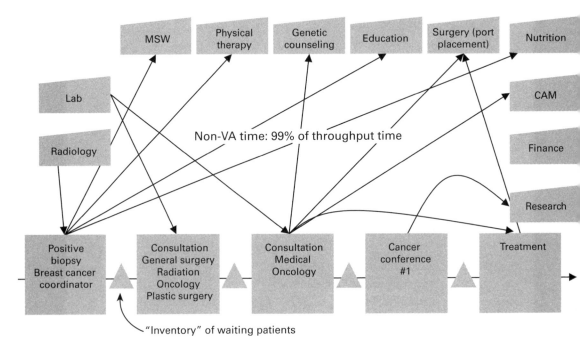

Figure 9.1
The process for treating oncology patients at Virginia Mason, before TPS implementation. Source: Bohmer and Ferlins (2006).

precisely which processes are suboptimal, and (3) the figures do not capture some aspects of processes, such as the quality of service.

For these reasons, we need to dive below financial statements to do operational due diligence of a company, especially of one that purports to have implemented a superior process management system such as the TPS.

9.2 The Toyota Production System (TPS)

This section summarizes the description of the TPS in the text by Gerard Cachon and Christian Terwiesch.

One key point is that the TPS is not just a philosophy that companies can implement only in spirit. It certainly is based on a mindset to reduce waste and variability and to improve quality, and it certainly exhorts managers to tightly couple executing operations with exposing and fixing problems, in real time. But the TPS also comprises a comprehensive set of approaches to problem tracking and solving.

Figure 9.2 shows these specific approaches. The overarching idea is to reduce waste, called 無駄 or *muda*. We operationalize this as four objectives: to achieve zero levels of defects, breakdowns, inventory, and setup.

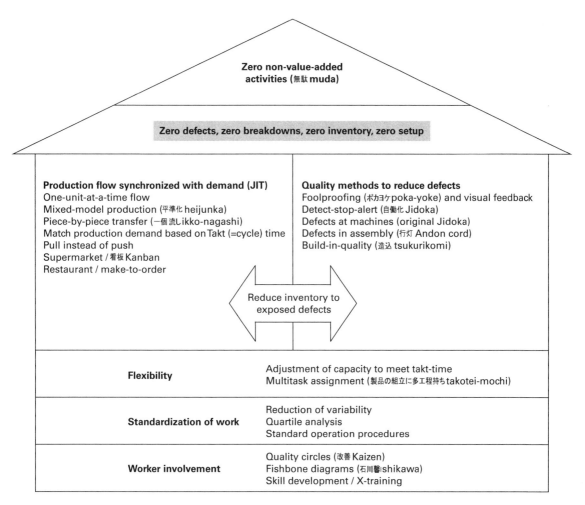

Figure 9.2
The Toyota production system: operational elements. Source: Cachon and Terwiesch (2005).

Table 9.1
Toyota Production System: Organizational Elements

Dimension	More Consistent with TPS	Less Consistent with TPS
Strategy	Differentiation based on cost or quality	Roll-up with mergers and acquisitions, flipping of assets
Structure	Somewhat decentralized	Highly centralized
Systems	Incentives are aligned toward eliminating *muda*; information systems support sharing	Incentives are aligned toward single dimensions, such as sales
Shared values	Common culture fostered over long period	Franchisees who have different agendas and incentives than principals
Skills	Constant training on TPS and problem solving	Professionals, whose skills are more associated with their professions than with the organization
Style	High degree of responsibility at shop floor, emphasis on coaching, strong culture	"Herding cats" as culture, in which autonomy allows staff to go in different directions
Staff	Constant rescheduling to ensure smooth production; part-time employees; roving legions of senior staff to help problem solving	Rigid staffing, perhaps due to difficulty in matching staff's skills with job requirement; or at other extreme, individually incentivized franchisees

Companies can achieve these objectives with two major types of initiatives. One, shown on the left of the figure, is about synchronizing production flow with demand. This involves getting the flow to proceed one unit at a time, so that the process does not produce inventory ahead of demand. The second type of initiatives, shown on the right of the table, reduces defects and breakdowns. This involves exposing and resolving defects as early as possible. These two types of initiatives in turn require flexible capacity and task design, the standardization of work, and the involvement and training of workers.

This description of the TPS suggests two other themes. One is that the system is an internally consistent set of practices and approaches that are interconnected. It would be difficult to synchronize production flow with demand if capacities and tasks are not designed to be flexible. The other related theme is that improvement on one dimension—say removing some steps in a worker's task—often requires improvement on another dimension—such as achieving a smaller probability of machine downtime. Such propagation of improvements is pervasive in any company that implements the TPS.

We can also view the TPS broadly, as an organizational management system, rather than narrowly as an operational management system. In table 9.1, we list the organizational elements consistent with the TPS, grouped along the "7S" dimensions of the McKinsey framework (see Peters and Waterman [1982]).

9.2.1   Limits and Limitations of the TPS

The TPS is surely not the last word on best practices in operations. Indeed, the safety problems associated with Toyota cars around 2010 suggest that not everything is well in the company that defines this system. What are some of the main limits and limitations of the TPS?

The TPS requires that suppliers be located close enough to the TPS plant to ensure quick replenishment. As one Japanese auto maker (Nissan) found out, it could be impractical and overly costly to relocate its geographically diverse plants and their suppliers; the cost advantage of the TPS, calculated at about 20%, did not justify such a move in Nissan's case.

Furthermore, geographic colocation increases the vulnerability of supply chains to natural disasters such as earthquakes. When the 2011 tsunami hit Japan, Toyota's production fell by 62.7%. This was due not to a drop in demand but to a shortage of 150 types of auto parts, because Toyota's suppliers were all hit by the same disaster.

The need to have suppliers in close proximity also limits the ability of a TPS plant to source from the best plants around the world. As connectivity technology and global logistics improve, it has become increasingly possible and competitive to source from the world's best suppliers. A TPS plant may find it difficult to exploit these sourcing opportunities.

There are several other limitations to the TPS, but it is unclear whether some of these are due to poor implementation or to the impossibility of implementing what is in principle a poor design. For example, it is sometimes thought that the low inventory associated with the TPS makes processes rigid. On the other hand, we bear in mind that the TPS is about flexibility and small lots. So does the TPS introduce or reduce rigidity? Paul Zipkin suggests that some firms, prodded by consultants, have put the cart (lower inventory) before the horse (streamline processes). Doing so leads to the possibility that lowering inventory might hamper processes, when it should be smoothing processes that should lead to lower inventory as an outcome.

Finally, there are other perspectives to suggest that the TPS has a dark side in terms of human costs, such as less safe practices with overly fast process lines, excessive social control over employees, and a stifling of genuine creativity. Since we focus on operational issues in this book, we do not delve into these, but bear in mind that the TPS is not just an operational framework.

We conclude this section by noting that both the operational and organizational elements of the TPS have implications for two issues: (1) whether a company should implement the TPS, and (2) how to verify its implementation. We turn to these next.

9.3   Should a Company Implement Lean Management?

While lean management (or the TPS) may appear to be a panacea for many areas of operations, it seems legitimate to ask whether it should really be implemented in some settings. There is the perennial question, for example, of whether lean management works in a service setting, such as that of a hospital or a professional services firm.

Perhaps it might be helpful to divide the question of whether a company should implement lean management into two distinct subquestions: (1) whether the outcomes of lean management are aligned with the company's strategy, and (2) whether lean management would even work in the company's setting.

9.3.1 Are Lean Management Outcomes Aligned with Strategy?

Lean management works to reduce waste, and it seems outlandish that waste should be tolerated in principle. But in practice, the question is whether overenthusiastic staff might set arbitrarily low levels of "waste"—inventory, buffer capacities, some redundancy in staffing—without first implementing the systems needed for such low levels. By putting the cart (low levels of waste) before the horse (a lean management approach to reducing waste), an organization might become vulnerable to variability. For example, if a hurricane hits a city and the hospital is besieged with an unprecedented number of patients, the hospital may not have enough supplies to get through the disaster.

This vulnerability is especially important for low-tolerance industries like healthcare, defense, or aerospace. This is not to say, of course, that such businesses can afford to be bloated, but the practicality of implementation often interferes with the theory that sufficient redundancy can always be arranged.

9.3.2 Does Lean Management Work in the Company's Setting?

Consider first the operational view of lean management. If reducing waste is the primary motivation of lean management, and if waste arises from variability, then it seems important to recognize the source of variability. This also speaks to the question of whether lean management works well in a service setting. One common definition of services is that the primary variability there originates from demand, whereas in manufacturing the primary variability originates from production. For example, in the prototypical services industry of restaurants or airlines, the key is to manage—forecast, properly price, serve— fluctuating demand, without incurring too much perishable capacity. In a prototypical production setting, the key instead is to manage—synchronize, balance, enhance the yield of—the manufacturing process.

This being so, does lean management work better in managing variability from production than managing variability from demand? There is some empirical evidence that lean management is applicable to both types of variability. Taiichi Ohno recalls that many parts of the TPS—such as the 看板 *kanban* system—themselves historically originate from a service setting: US supermarkets. He specifically recognizes the portability of the TPS across many industry boundaries: "Companies make a big mistake in implementing the Toyota production system thinking that it is just a production method. The Toyota production method won't work unless it is used as an overall management system. The Toyota production system is not something that can be used only on the production floors."[2] It is generally recognized that the TPS has been implemented with considerable success not only at Honda and Alcoa but also at service firms such as Vanguard, Southwest Airlines, Jefferson Pilot Financial, the University of Pittsburgh Hospitals, and Virginia Mason

Medical Center. Indeed, Toyota itself is steadily becoming more a service company, it seems, as it evolves from being a mass producer to a mass customizer. If one day it begins to manufacture cars one unique unit at a time on a regular basis, it would truly resemble a service firm, with little inventory and producing on order.

But even for many of these supposed successes, there seem to be implementation issues, suggesting that the last word has certainly not been said about the portability of lean management. At Virginia Mason Medical Center, for instance, the TPS seems to be considerably more successful in the "hoteling" processes—which involve registering patients and managing their way through test scheduling, in-patient check-in, scheduling and administration, and check-out—than in the "clinical" processes—which involves diagnosis, interpretation of tests, treatment, and post-treatment.

One of the critical stumbling blocks is that Virginia Mason physicians are more like free agents than employees, and are more like professionals with allegiance to their professional field than staff with allegiance to the hospital. This suggests that the organizational fit of lean management is also a determinant of implementation success.

9.4   Verifying a Company's Lean Management Implementation

The above discussion provides some guidance for verifying whether a company has the basics of a lean management implementation. Naturally, the answer is unlikely to take a dichotomous yes-no value. We now describe two complementary approaches to verification: one quantitative and the other qualitative.

9.4.1   Data Envelopment Analysis

Consider the hospitals in table 9.2, which use a number of inputs (such as beds available, expenses, productive hours) to produce some outputs (such as the number of discharges, patient survival rates) for acute pediatric divisions. It is difficult to see how lean each hospital is by just eyeballing these data. For example, compared to Pacifica, Rady has $162/24 = 6.75$ times more beds but $10338/644 = 16.05$ times higher expenses. But in terms of output, Rady seems to do well. It has $9.9/0.4 = 24.75$ more discharges and $43/0.7 = 61.4$ times more patient days, and a higher survival rate.

In comparing businesses like these, we can use data envelopment analysis (DEA), a tool that rigorously establishes how lean a business is by looking at multiple inputs, multiple outputs, and multiple peer businesses. Indeed, for the latter, DEA also creates virtual peers out of actual peers, since there may be no actual peers that are directly comparable in terms of size and mix of inputs and outputs. DEA also does not require us to assume how the inputs are transformed into outputs.

To illustrate how DEA works, let us first confine ourselves to a made-up example with just one input—wages—and two outputs—patient days and inpatient survival rate, as in table 9.3.

Table 9.2
Inputs and Outputs for Some California Hospitals

	Pacifica Hospital of the Valley	Rady Children's Hospital San Diego	West Hills Hospital and Medical Center
Beds available	24	162	2
Expenses ($ 000)	**644**	**10,338**	**189**
Wages	514	2,123	131
Depreciation	12	227	1
Employee benefits	116	7,751	51
Purchased services	0.2	119	1
Supplies	0.6	118	4
Outcomes			
Number of discharges (000)	0.4	9.9	0.03
Patient days (000)	0.7	43	0.18
Inpatient survival index (%)*	−29.9	87	−495

Source: Office of Statewide Health Planning and Development, for 2007.
* This is 100 minus the risk-adjusted mortality rate indicator. A 0 means the hospital survival rate is as good as an expected rate. Information is only available for all, not just subacute pediatric, patients. These are risk-adjusted using the All Patient Refined Diagnosis Related Groups (APR-DRGs), a proprietary tool of the 3M Health Information Systems Corporation.

Table 9.3
Example for DEA Analysis

Hospital	A	B	C
Input			
Wages	200	200	200
Outputs			
Patient days (000)	5	4	11
Inpatient survival index (%)	100	60	50

These three hospitals have the same level of input, so we can plot them on an output map, as in figure 9.3. Of course, such a two-dimensional map would not be possible in most real-life cases, where we have not only different input levels but multiple inputs. But for illustration, we could draw two kinds of maps: an output map when businesses happen to have the same input (so points further to the northeast are better, indicating more output for the same input), or an input map when businesses have the same output (so points further to the southwest are better).

Figure 9.3 shows that Hospital B is not as lean as Hospital A, since the former produces fewer patient days and scores lower on the survival index for the same input level. But because B has a different mix of patient days and survival index, it is hard to compare it directly with A. It is even harder to compare B with C, which does better on patient days but not on survival.

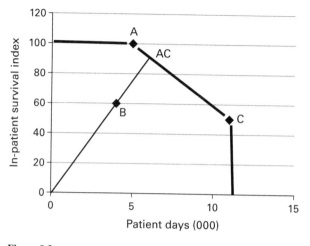

Figure 9.3
A DEA frontier.

What DEA offers is to compare B with the leanest comparable hospital. The leanest ones are on the frontier marked in figure 9.3 by the bold lines through A and C. Implicitly, DEA assumes that it is possible to have a hospital that is some combination of A and C. Which of these leanest hospitals are comparable with B? It is the virtual one marked as AC, which has the same proportion of patient days and survival index. So if the length of the line from (0,0) to AC is indexed as 1.0 in leanness, we can say that B's leanness is some ratio less than 1.0, as determined by the length of the line from (0,0) to B.

Formally, DEA determines the frontier and B's leanness ratio using linear programming.

Since we are comparing different types of outputs and inputs, we first define a hospital's leanness ratio as:

$$\text{leanness ratio} = \frac{Dp_D + Sp_S}{Ww},$$

where D, S, and W are our levels of patient days, survival index, and wages, and p_D, p_S, and w are weights on these levels, respectively. In other words, we need some way to add up D with S, and divide this with W. Another way to think about these weights is that they are prices on outputs and costs on inputs.

Our linear program becomes: what values should p_D, p_S, and w take in order to maximize the leanness ratios of every hospital, given that every leanness ratio must of course be 1.0 or less? Intuitively, think of what the weights p_D, p_S, and w should be so that A, B, and C are all as far northeast as possible, with the furthest points forming a frontier with leanness ratio of 1.0 while the interior points have smaller leanness ratios.

It turns out that the linear program is the same whether we maximize the leanness ratio of A, B, or C,[3] so let us say we maximize the ratio of B:

$$\text{B's leanness ratio} = \frac{4p_D + 60p_S}{200w}.$$

We can constrain the denominator $200w$ to 1 (it does not matter what arbitrary level we set $200w$ to), so this means the linear program is to maximize $4p_D + 60p_S$ subject to $200w = 1$.

Of course, we must add other constraints that say each hospital's leanness ratio is 1 or smaller. For example, the one for A is

$$\frac{5p_D + 100\,p_S}{200w} \leq 1,$$

or

$$5p_D + 100p_S \leq 200w.$$

Put together, the linear program is:

$$\max_{pD, pS, w}\; 4p_D + 60p_S$$

subject to:

$$200w = 1$$

$$5p_D + 100p_S - 200w \leq 0$$

$$4p_D + 60p_S - 200w \leq 0$$

$$11p_D + 50p_S - 200w \leq 0$$

$$p_D \geq 0,\, p_S \geq 0,\, w \geq 0.$$

The solution is $p_D = 0.0588$, $p_S = 0.0070588$, $w = 0.005$, which leads to the following leanness ratios:

$$\text{A's leanness ratio} = \frac{5p_D + 100p_S}{200w} = 1,$$

$$\text{B's leanness ratio} = \frac{4p_D + 60p_S}{200w} = 0.6588,$$

$$\text{C's leanness ratio} = \frac{11p_D + 50p_S}{200w} = 1.$$

As expected, A and C are the leanest, being at the frontier, while B is at 65.88%.

Table 9.4
Leanness Ratios for Ten California Hospitals

Hospital	Leanness Ratio
Valleycare Health System	0.33
West Hills Hospital and Medical	0.48
Arroyo Grande Community Hospital	0.56
Tri-City Medical Center	0.62
Pacifica Hospital of the Valley	1.00
Rady Children's Hospital San Diego	1.00
Children's Hospital and Research Center Oakland	1.00
Mountains Community Hospital	1.00
Coalinga Regional Medical Center	1.00
Madera Community Hospital	1.00

We can use commercial-grade software to calculate the leanness ratios of ten California hospitals, of which a sample of three appear in table 9.2. We use multiple inputs—beds available and the various types of expenses—and outputs—number of discharges, patient days, and the survival index. The resulting leanness ratios are in table 9.4. It turns out that DEA positions both Pacifica and Rady at the frontier, with a ratio of 1.0. Although the position of West Hills may not be obvious from just eyeballing the data in table 9.2, this hospital is substantially penalized in a DEA, with a ratio of 0.48.

To conclude, we list some limitations of DEA analysis. First, the results can be susceptible to noise, in the sense that if the multiple inputs and outputs do not substantively capture the true range of inputs and outputs, the ratios will be suspect. Second, DEA plots a frontier based on the businesses observed. Although it even plots where unobserved virtual businesses might be on a frontier, its frontier is only as good as the number and quality of the businesses we feed into the analysis.

With that in mind, it helps to evaluate how lean a business is qualitatively as well as quantitatively.

9.4.2   Qualitative Verification of Leanness

Theory and empirics suggest that verification is rigorous only if it works well on three dimensions:

• *Comprehensiveness.*   Specifically, the implementation should cover a whole set of the operational elements in figure 9.2 and the organizational elements in table 9.1.

An uneven implementation is often a failed implementation. Consider, for example, a manufacturing line that has a highly sophisticated *kanban* system that constrains inventory buildup, but a still-primitive unbalanced line in which some stations have greater capacity than others. Because of the *kanban* system, the high-capacity stations in the unbalanced line tend to be underutilized, and, as is human nature, tend to introduce work—perhaps unconsciously—to fill the spare time. This in turn makes it hard to see the line's true capacity, making it hard to detect the lack of balance in the line.

• *Sustainability.* Recall that lean management is a highly interlinked management system, so its sustainability requires that all stations can work comfortably at the specified pace without wasted spare capacity. The picture one often has in mind is the *I Love Lucy* episode in which Lucy works in a chocolate factory. The chocolate production line goes at a faster pace than she can manage, and the scene ends with chocolates flying all over.

Since lean management is about continuous improvement, we also want to verify that the implementation has some track record over time.

• *Outcomes.* Ultimately, of course, the proof of the pudding is in the eating, so any rigorous verification of a lean management system must assess the outcome of the system. It would be critical to assess the system not only within-company, but across companies and perhaps even across industries, to see if superior performance is truly being achieved. And of course it is vital to remember that lean management outcomes are represented not just by productivity figures but also by figures on quality, worker satisfaction, line balance, etc.

One of the features of lean management that makes it relatively easy to verify is that lean management specifies that processes and problems are to be visually and aurally explicit. Thus we should find it straightforward to check off the various dimensions of its implementation.

9.5   Takeaways and Toolkit

In this chapter, we have seen that:

• Lean management (or synonymously in this chapter, the TPS) has both operational and organizational elements.

• A company should implement lean management if lean management outcomes are aligned with its strategy, and if lean management works in its operational and organization setting.

• Using data envelopment analysis (DEA), we can verify whether a company has implemented lean management. We should also undertake a qualitative validation, to verify whether the implementation is comprehensive, sustainable, and has produced the expected outcomes.

Table 9.5 summarizes these steps in the form of a checklist.

Table 9.5
Toolkit: Checklist for Assessing Lean Management Implementation

Goal	Key Questions and Analyses
Determine whether the company should implement lean management Verify the company's implementation	• Are lean management outcomes aligned with strategy? • Does lean management work in the company's setting? • Quantitative assessment using data envelope analysis (DEA). Determine the leanness ratio, based on the frontier of all businesses in the industry • Qualitative assessment of: Comprehensiveness Sustainability Outcomes

9.6   Survey of Prior Research in One Paragraph

The defining work on the Toyota production system was by Taiichi Ohno, Shigeo Shingo, and Eiji Toyoda. Some of the most rigorous contemporary research is by Kent Bowen, Marshall Fisher, Takahiro Fujimoto, Chris Ittner, Marvin Lieberman, Masao Nakumura, Roger Schroeder, and Steven Spear. The International Motor Vehicle Program, headed by Charlie Fine and John Paul MacDuffie, has produced some of the most notable reports on the TPS, of which the one by Jim Womack, Dan Jones, and Daniel Roos is the most widely cited. Anita Tucker, Amy Edmondson, and Richard Bohmer are some of the leading scholars of the TPS in healthcare settings. Morris Cohen is a preeminent authority on service management and the application of lean management to the services industry. M. J. Farrell, A. Charnes, W. Cooper, and E. Rhodes are some of the pioneers in data envelopment analysis (DEA).

9.7   Further Reading

Bohmer, R. M. J., and E. M. Ferlins. 2006. "Virginia Mason Medical Center." Harvard Business School Case 9-604-044.

Cachon, G., and C. Terwiesch. 2005. *Matching Supply with Demand: An Introduction to Operations Management*. New York: McGraw-Hill.

Charnes, W. 1978. "Measuring the Efficiency of Decision Making Units* 1." *European Journal of Operational Research* 2 (6): 429–444.

Cusumano, M. A. 1994. "The Limits of 'Lean'." *Sloan Management Review* 35: 27–27.

Farrell, M. J. 1957. "The Measurement of Productive Efficiency." *Journal of the Royal Statistical Society. Series A (General)* 120 (3): 253–290.

Fisher, M. L., and C. D. Ittner. 1999. "The Impact of Product Variety on Automobile Assembly Operations: Empirical Evidence and Simulation Analysis." *Management Science*: 771–786.

Fujimoto, T. 1999. *The Evolution of a Manufacturing System at Toyota*. New York: Oxford University Press.

Hammer, M. 2007. "The Process Audit." *Harvard Business Review* 85 (4): 111–123.

Lieberman, M. B., L. J. Lau, and M. D. Williams. 1990. "Firm-Level Productivity and Management Influence: A Comparison of US and Japanese Automobile Producers." *Management Science*: 1193–1215.

MacDuffie, J. P. 1997. "The Road to 'Root Cause': Shop-Floor Problem-Solving at Three Auto Assembly Plants." *Management Science*: 479–502.

MacDuffie, J. P., K. Sethuraman, and M. L. Fisher. 1996. "Product Variety and Manufacturing Performance: Evidence from the International Automotive Assembly Plant Study." *Management Science*: 350–369.

Mehri, D. 2006. "The Darker Side of Lean: An Insider's Perspective on the Realities of the Toyota Production System." *Academy of Management Perspectives Archive* 20 (2): 21–42.

Nakamura, M., S. Sakakibara, and R. G. Schroeder. 1996. "Japanese Manufacturing Methods at US Manufacturing Plants: Empirical Evidence." *Canadian Journal of Economics/Revue canadienne d'Economique* 29: 468–474.

Ohno, T. 1982. "How the Toyota Production System Was Created." *Japanese Economic Studies* 10 (4): 83–101.

Peters, T. J., and R. H. Waterman. 1982. *In Search of Excellence: Lessons from America's Best-Run Companies*. New York: Harper and Row.

Shinohara, I. 1988. *NPS, New Production System: JIT Crossing Industry Boundaries*. Cambridge, MA: Productivity Press.

Spear, S. J. 2004. "Learning to Lead at Toyota." *Harvard Business Review* 82 (5): 78–91.

Spear, S. J. and H. K. Bowen. 1999. "Decoding the DNA of the Toyota Production System." *Harvard Business Review* 77(5): 96–108.

Womack, J. P., D. T. Jones, and D. Roos. 1990. *The Machine that Changed the World*. New York: Rawson Associates.

Zemell, E. 1992. "Yes, Virginia, There Really Is Total Quality Management." Anheuser-Bush Distinguished Lecture Series, SEI Center for Advanced Studies in Management, Wharton School, Philadelphia.

10 Assessing Risks

Thus far we have looked at risks as something that we want to anticipate—as in the chapters on indicators of disruption and distress—or to manage down—as in the Toyota production system's emphasis on reducing variability. Some investors, such as Berkshire Hathaway, claim, as their risk management strategy, that they only buy into low-risk businesses. Warren Buffett, Berkshire's chairman, said in his 1996 letter to shareholders: "I should emphasize that, as citizens, Charlie [Munger, Berkshire's vice chairman] and I welcome change: Fresh ideas, new products, innovative processes and the like cause our country's standard of living to rise, and that's clearly good. As investors, however, our reaction to a fermenting industry is much like our attitude toward space exploration: We applaud the endeavor but prefer to skip the ride."

But how do we know how much risk a business has? Traditional finance theory has one answer: in a world of efficient markets, a business's risk is captured in its beta. Beta—reflecting *systematic risk*—is the covariance of the business with the market[1] divided by the variance of the market. That part of a business's variance that does not covary with the market—called specific risk—can be diversified away by investors. But there is a growing literature, even in finance, suggesting that specific risk does matter. Therefore, another measure of risk is to consider both systematic risk and specific risk, or *total risk*.

From an operations perspective, there are two types of total risk. The first is process risk, which is recurrent; the second is better viewed as one-off. An example of process risk is the risk of machines breaking down. This can affect the value of a business through higher working capital (inventory) and reduced productivity. An example of one-off risk is the risk that a patent application will not be approved. This affects the value of a business directly.

These definitions raise the question of how we can measure the different types of risks, which we address in this chapter:

• *Systematic risk.* A convenient way to measure this is to return to the definition of beta as the covariance between the expected return from our business and that from the market portfolio. We assess risk mostly in order to value a business. It is vital to directly look to the market for the value of a similar business, rather than try to calculate systematic risk without market validation. Then we expand on our calculation to see how operational leverage increases systematic risk.

• *Total risk.* We describe how you can use a risk map to visualize the severity and probability of changing risks in a business.

   One-off risk. We describe the value-at-risk (VaR) framework to assess this type of risk. The VaR spells out the amount that we might lose (severity), for a given probability and time horizon.

   Process risk. We describe how we can characterize the variability of this type of risk, with coefficients of variation, and how variability reduces productivity and therefore the value of the business.

This typology of risks helps clarify differences that confound even seasoned investors. For example, Warren Buffett declares that "we define risk, using dictionary terms as the 'possibility of loss or injury.' Academics . . . like to define risk differently. . . . In their hunger for a single statistic to measure risk, however, they forget a fundamental principle: it is better to be approximately right than precisely wrong" (Berkshire Hathaway 1993 Annual Report). But it is possible that Buffett is referring to one-off risks, while in finance theory risk is viewed more like process risk, in the ongoing ups and downs of the value of a security.

Furthermore, the typology reveals similarities and differences in the treatment of risks in finance and in this book. For example, finance theory suggests that risks from many sources in a portfolio can be diversified away. In operations, we too model how risk pooling can be helpful—e.g., in reducing inventory needed to serve a given level of demand. But there are also risks, such as process risks, in which the risk sources are in various stations along a process. In this case, the risks cascade and get amplified through the process. We should verify how the amplification could seriously affect our assessment of the risks.

10.1   Why Is Risk Assessment Difficult?

Before we get into some tools for assessing risks, it is helpful to ask why it is difficult to assess risks in the first place.

   Suppose we were to ask the likelihood of facing a shortage in a critical component for production. One way to do this is to simply count the number of past shortages and divide by the time covered (say, 54 shortages in the last 3 years, or 18 shortages per year). This sort of risk assessment has several problems.

   First, it does not account for severity. Some shortages are short, others longer. A histogram of shortages by severity would be useful. Second, even the histogram might convey a false impression of the distribution by severity. The histogram represents data from a sample, but the actual distribution from the population of shortages might be very different—e.g., skewed toward severe shortages. Third, severity also needs to account for our ability to manage the shortage. A production line that can respond effectively to a shortage will find it less severe than another that is crippled by the same shortage. Fourth, a probability measure does not account for seasonality within a year, or a month or week. For example, the component may be more likely to run short at year end than at other times. Fifth, a probability measure also does not account for trends. Suppliers' reliability changes over time. The number of suppliers changes over time. Our responsiveness changes over time. Sixth, the component probability does not consider how failures elsewhere would affect this probability, and how shortage in this component might impact failures elsewhere.

What this discussion suggests is that, given the complexity of the origins and implications of risks, any single measure will have its limitations. A proper risk assessment needs to account for the cost and benefit of undertaking the assessments, and the risk of not doing so.

10.2 Systematic Risk

One way to measure systematic risk of a business is to go back to the definition of beta:

$$beta = \text{Cov}(r_{business}, r_{market}) / \text{Var}(r_{market}),$$

where $r_{business}$ is the expected return from the business in question and r_{market} that from a chosen market portfolio. Although the definition asks for expected returns, a reasonable starting point is to approximate these using historical returns.

Once we have determined beta, we can calculate the discount rate we will use to value the cash flows of our business:

discount rate = risk-free rate + beta × risk premium,

where the risk-free rate might be the treasury note return and the risk premium is the market return less the risk-free rate. Intuitively, the risk-free rate captures the time value of money, and the (beta × risk premium) term captures the riskiness of cash flows.

But in reality, things can get messier. For one, there is "Roll's critique" (named for Richard Roll of the University of Chicago): beta is very sensitive to which market portfolio we have chosen. So it seems wise to construct beta from a number of candidates, such as the Dow, S&P 500, NYSE Composite, Wilshire 5000, or the Morgan Stanley Capital Index.

Second, the discount rate may change over time. In their authoritative textbook, Brealey, Myers, and Allen suggest a way to address this: assume that beta × risk premium is very slow-changing, so that we account for the change in discount rate by tracking the change only in the risk-free rate.

Third, we bear in mind that the market-derived values are usually more accurate than values derived bottom-up using covariances and variances. This is because the former use a more diverse set of information. So before we start calculating covariances and variances to find beta, we should see if there is a peer business with similar risks. "Similar risks" are of course hard to define, and we may only be postponing our problem. One way is to identify companies in the same industry with the same operating characteristics (using factors such as inventory turn or days of accounts receivable, as discussed in section 1.3.1). We can then check our bottom-up derivation against the published beta of our similar companies.

But how does systematic risk, or beta, relate to operations? It turns out that operational leverage—the proportion of assets that is fixed—increases systematic risk. We first give the formulaic explanation for this, then the intuitive sense of it.

The present value (PV) of an asset may be written as follows, since present values are additive (see Brealey and Myers or any standard finance text) and the cash flows from an asset is just revenue minus the two types of costs:

$$PV_{asset} = PV_{revenue} - PV_{fixed\ cost} - PV_{variable\ cost}.$$

Therefore, the beta of an asset can be decomposed into betas of revenue, fixed cost, and variable cost:

$$beta_{asset} = \frac{PV_{revenue}}{PV_{asset}} beta_{revenue} - \frac{PV_{fixed\ cost}}{PV_{asset}} beta_{fixed\ cost}$$

$$- \frac{PV_{variable\ cost}}{PV_{asset}} beta_{variable\ cost}$$

Since fixed costs are fixed (by definition), $beta_{fixed\ cost}$ is zero. Also, $beta_{variable\ cost}$ is about the same as $beta_{revenue}$ since both are covariances with market returns, up to a fixed-cost constant. The above simplifies to:

$$beta_{asset} = \frac{PV_{revenue} - PV_{variable\ cost}}{PV_{asset}} beta_{revenue}$$

Again, using the identity that PV_{asset} is the present value of the revenues minus the costs, we can rewrite the above as:

$$beta_{asset} = \left[1 + \frac{PV_{fixed\ cost}}{PV_{asset}}\right] beta_{revenue}$$

The term $PV_{fixed\ cost}/PV_{asset}$ is a measure of operational leverage, and the above shows that $beta_{asset}$ will increase as leverage increases, given $beta_{revenue}$.

The intuition behind this is that with a higher proportion of assets that are fixed, a business is less able to cope with the vagaries of demand. When market demand is low, the business incurs fixed costs, so its cash flows vary more with the market than they would for a business with a lower proportion of fixed costs.

As mentioned earlier, systematic risks are risks that cannot be diversified away. In the discussion above, even firm-specific factors that change the ratio of fixed costs to assets—perhaps originating from managerial competence or technological advances—would affect $beta_{asset}$. But it may be hard to see other risks—say from information systems that might malfunction or human capital that may defect to the competition—that might also influence operational leverage. In other words, if we stick to just measuring systematic risk, theory does not give us a good indication of which risk is systematic and which is specific. Further, a growing amount of research suggests that even firm-specific diversifiable risks may be important in valuing companies. Finally, if we take the perspective of a manager, and not an investor who can diversify away specific risks, then total risk matters.

Taken together, the above suggests that we would do better to consider both systematic risk and specific risk, or total risk.

10.3 Total Risk

Not surprisingly, there are many ways to characterize the total risk of a business. As before, one useful approach is to appeal to the market. An especially helpful proxy is the divergence among analyst estimates of the business's earnings or sales. Of course, this measure is subject to some limitations—for example, it would not be useful if the business is covered by very few analysts.

At the opposite extreme, we can build a theoretical list of the risks that may arise. One useful framework is to identify risks that may interrupt the smooth addition of value along the value chain—from purchasing and R&D through production to distribution, as well as supporting functions such as human resource and information systems management. Figure 10.1 shows an example, and figure 10.2 shows an even more detailed list of risks in the area of production alone, from Shell's enormous "Comprehensive List of Causes" (ignore the details, which are not visible; the point is that Shell takes risks comprehensively).

We next need a tool to make these lists manageable. One useful tool is the "risk map" that prioritizes the risks for more detailed examination. An important variant is "failure mode and effects analysis" (FMEA), developed by the US military after World War II. In applying this to commercial situations, we focus on two dimensions of risks: the probability of occurrence and the severity of consequences.

10.3.1 Probability

The probability of a risk is often given as a number, but that should be construed as the mean from a more complete characterization of probability, in the form of a probability

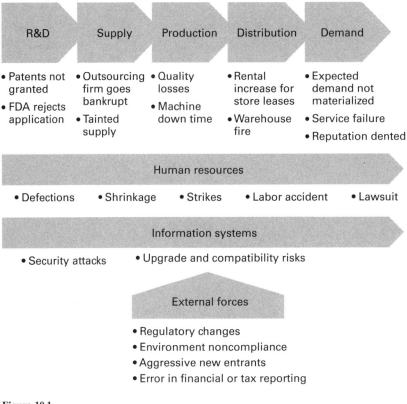

Figure 10.1
Risks in a value chain.

distribution. The confidence of our probability judgment can be measured as the variance of the distribution: the smaller the variance, the more confident we are. This variance depends on how much information we can employ—and the cost of getting that information. For example, Sport Obermeyer, a skiwear maker, uses a six-member committee of purchasers, salespeople, and top managers to make probability judgments about the demand for new skiwear. Empirically, it has been found that this produces a superior demand forecast—in terms of both the bias (the forecast error is on average about zero) and confidence (the forecast error is proportional to the variance of the members' forecast).

In finance, probabilities (or variances) may be reduced through diversification. That is also true in operations—e.g., in risk pooling of workstations. But in operations, probabilities are not only correlated but also amplified. A workstation with a probability of downtime can amplify the probability of downtime at the next workstation. The probability that

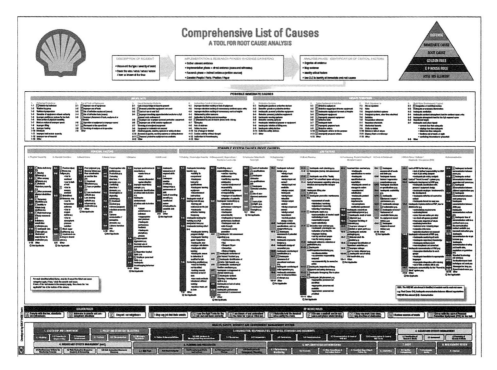

Figure 10.2
Shell's "Comprehensive List of Causes." (Details are not meant to be visible.) © Shell.

a supplier sends tainted supplies and the probability that that supplier goes into bankruptcy may be very high. Indeed, one may cause the other in a vicious amplifying cycle. We address these sorts of relationships between risks below.

10.3.2 Severity

The severity of a risk also depends on three factors. First, of course, there is the raw severity: how bad or what loss amount would be incurred if the risk materializes. Second, this severity depends on the probability and timing of detection; a high probability of early detection could mitigate the raw severity of the risk. Third, the ability of the organization to respond to the risk also mitigates the raw severity. For example, a flexible organization with some redundancy can shift resources to accommodate a temporary shortage. Of course, new investments to better detect risks or to become more flexible and redundant have their own costs. We have to weigh the costs and benefits of "pay now or pay later."

Given the probability and severity of a risk, what can we do about it? As a first step, we need to know in general how we can manage risks. We turn to this next.

10.3.3   A Typology of Risk Management Methods

By definition, the way to manage a systematic risk is to diversify it away, as a financial portfolio manager might do by buying stocks from a variety of companies.

For total risk, there are a number of ways to manage risks:

• **Eliminate.**   It is rare that one can entirely remove a risk, but one example would be to avoid doing something completely. Consider a manufacturer dealing with the risk of shipping delays arising from having a foreign supplier. For this example, we are not referring to the risk that the supplier does not produce on time, but to the risk that on-time productions are delayed by the long-distance shipper. We can eliminate the risk of such delays by relocating our manufacturing plant to the foreign supplier's neighborhood, thus eliminating the need for a long-distance shipper altogether.

• **Avoid.**   More likely, we can avoid a risk by doing something else. For example, we can avoid the risk of delays from a foreign supplier by using a local supplier instead. The difference between "avoid" and "eliminate" is that in the former we change the source of the risk (the fact that the foreign supplier is located far away), while in the latter we do not.

• **Reduce.**   To continue the example of risk of shipping delay from a foreign supplier, we could reduce the risk by using some backup, such as ensuring that the shipping company has spare capacity.

• **Transfer.**   Purchasing insurance is a way to transfer a risk to another party. As another example, if a manufacturer's shipment from a foreign supplier is delayed, the manufacturer might pass that delay to its customer further down the supply chain, protected by a clause in its contract with that downstream customer. The difference between "reduce" and "transfer" in our shipping delay example is that in the former we deal with the risk at source (reducing risk at the foreign supplier), while in the latter we deal with it at destination (transferring the downside of a delay that has already happened to another party).

• **Transform.**   One way to deal with a risk is to transform it into another risk that we can better accept or deal with. For example, one way to handle the risk of shipping delays from a foreign supplier is to have earlier forecasts, so that we can place our orders with the foreign supplier with a longer lead time. This transforms the risk of shipping delay to the risk of having the wrong forecasts.

• **Diversify.**   We have considered diversification as the primary means of dealing with systematic risks. For example, we could diversify by having arrangements with alternate shippers. The distinction between "reduce" and "diversify" is that in the former we stick to the shipper in question, while in the latter we diversify away from that shipper.

• **Monitor.**   Sometimes a risk is small enough that the best way to deal with it is to simply monitor it to ensure that it does not grow to become threatening. For example, suppose in the worst case that a shipment does not even arrive; if we as a manufacturer suffer an amount that is acceptable in such an event, we would do best just to monitor the risk.

• *Accept.* It may be that the cost of managing a risk exceeds the benefit of doing so (e.g., the risk is unlikely to morph into a bigger risk); then we might as well do nothing and accept the risk as is.

With so many ways to deal with risks, what are we to do? This is where probability and severity become useful, as a risk map.

10.3.4 Risk Management with a Risk Map

Figure 10.3 shows a risk map, on which we can plot the probability and severity of each risk. The key point is that the risk map provides different action implications for different types of risks.

Those with high probability and high severity—at the top right of the risk map—require immediate diagnosis. Depending on the diagnosis, we should then neutralize the risk using almost any risk management method except to accept it.

Those with high probability but low severity—at the bottom right—may be monitored. We can also aim to reduce their high probabilities, and to avoid the risk altogether.

For risks with low probability but high severity—at the top left—it would make sense to explicitly prepare a response to their possible occurrence, by transforming the nature of the risks, transferring, or diversifying them away. It also makes sense to insure against such risks.

		Probability	
		Low	High
Severity	High	Transform, transfer, diversify, insure	Immediately diagnose and neutralize
	Low	Accept, insure	Monitor, reduce probability, avoid

Figure 10.3
A risk map, with managerial implications.

Finally, risks that are of low probability and low severity—at the bottom left—should perhaps be accepted, as the cost of managing these risks might not be worth the benefit. At most, perhaps they should be transferred away, via insurance.

In plotting these risks on a risk map, it is useful to differentiate recurrent process risks—such as the risk of machine downtime in a production process—from one-off risks—such as the risk of a drug application being rejected by the FDA.

Importantly, these two types of risks have different value implications. As we show below, process risks usually affect value by reducing productivity. One-off risks usually affect value by directly reducing the value of a business. The two types also have different state-of-the-art tools to assess their riskiness. Therefore, we discuss them separately.

10.3.5 Advanced Topic: Process Risks

These risks are recurrent and routine. They involve processes in our business, such as purchasing, production, or forecasting.

Consider a prototypical production process with multiple stations. First, we analyze the probability and severity of risk—or downtime—at each station. These may be characterized by the mean time to failure (MTTF) and mean time to repair (MTTR). For example, if the MTTF of a station is 100 hours and the failure probability is constant over time, then the probability of failure is 1/100 over an hour. A long MTTF represents a low probability of failure, and a long MTTR represents a high severity of failure.

We now describe how MTTF and MTTR affect the value of the business in question, at the station and process level.

One Station

Consider first a station in the process. Suppose this station has a capacity of r units per hour if there were no risk of it being down. Now, with the MTTF and MTTR, its reduced capacity is:

$$r\frac{\text{MTTF}}{\text{MTTF}+\text{MTTR}}. \tag{4}$$

That is, r is now scaled down by the station's availability, represented by the quotient. This, then, is the first performance effect of process risk: high probability (small MTTF) or high severity (big MTTR) leads to large reductions in capacity.

Process risk also has a second performance effect: it increases working capital in the form of inventory.

Consider figure 10.4. In panel (a), we have a station with no process risk—i.e., no breakdowns. Recall that it can produce units at a rate of r if there are no breakdowns. Suppose its inputs arrive at a rate of r_a. For simplicity, we consider the case when r_a is unvarying and is lower than r, so that the outflow rate—which is the minimum of r_a and r—is just r_a. In this case, the average inventory at the station is r_a/r.

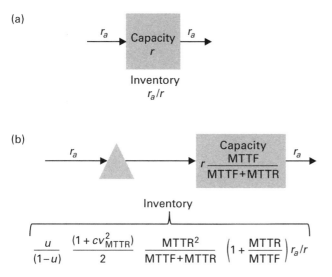

Figure 10.4
Process risk (variability) and working capital (inventory) at a station. No process risk (no downtime) (a); with process risk (MTTR, MTTR, cv^2_{MTTR}) (b).

Now consider what happens when we have process risk, as in panel (b). As explained earlier, the first performance degradation is that the station has a reduced capacity, which is now $r \times \text{MTTF}/(\text{MTTF} + \text{MTTR})$.

Inventory at the station is now higher, at

$$r_a \left/ \left(r \frac{\text{MTTF}}{\text{MTTF} + \text{MTTR}} \right), \right.$$

or

$$\left(1 + \frac{\text{MTTR}}{\text{MTTF}} \right) r_a \left/ r. \right.$$

Intuitively, a station with reduced capacity needs more time to process an input, so on the average the station now holds more inventory.

Worse, the MTTR itself is just a point estimate of process risk (it is the mean) from a probability distribution. Its variability may be measured by its *squared coefficient of variation* (denoted cv^2), which is the variance divided by the square of the mean. Let us denote the cv^2 of the MTTR by cv^2_{MTTR}. This variability cv^2_{MTTR} increases inventory even more.

To see this, note that a variable MTTR means that the processing time at the station is now variable, instead of being a constant. In queueing theory, the formula for the cv^2 of a station's processing time is given by:

$$r\left(1+cv_{\text{MTTR}}^2\right)\frac{\text{MTTF}}{\left(\dfrac{\text{MTTF}}{\text{MTTR}}+1\right)^2}. \tag{5}$$

From queueing theory, we know that a variable processing time means that queues (i.e., inventory) will form when incoming units cannot be processed because they arrive when the station happens to be busy. Assuming that the incoming units themselves arrive with certainty, the average queue length is given by:

Station queue inventory =

$$\frac{u}{(1-u)}\times\text{station processing time}$$

$$\times\frac{\left[cv^2 \text{ of station input arrivals}\right]+\left[cv^2 \text{ of station processing time}\right]}{2}, \tag{6}$$

where u is the utilization of the station. The utilization is also the average inventory in the station

$$\left(1+\frac{\text{MTTR}}{\text{MTTF}}\right)r_a / r \ ;$$

a high utilization is equivalent to high average inventory, since the unit stays in the station to be processed for much of the time. Returning to the queue inventory in equation (6), we can now substitute into it the station processing time, which is the reciprocal of equation (4). The cv^2 of the input arrivals is 0, since by assumption, input arrivals do not vary. The cv^2 of the station processing time is given in equation (5). Taken together, we get:

Station queue inventory =

$$\frac{u}{(1-u)}\frac{\left(1+cv_{\text{MTTR}}^2\right)}{2}\frac{\text{MTTR}^2}{\text{MTTF}+\text{MTTR}}.$$

Therefore, as shown in figure 10.4, panel (b), not only do we have higher inventory at the station, we also have new inventory in a queue into the station. Both types of inventory—in the station as well as in the queue—increase with MTTR/MTTF. This makes intuitive sense, since a longer time for repairs compared to time to failure degrades performance. The inventory in the queue also increases with cv_{MTTR}^2, which again makes intuitive sense.

Sequential Stations in a Process

Next we move from one station to a process with multiple stations. To keep the discussion manageable, suppose we have just two stations. We consider how performance is affected when the two stations are in sequence and when they are pooled in parallel.

Consider first a sequence of two stations, as in figure 10.5. As before, process risk has these effects:

- it reduces each station's capacity from r to

$$r\frac{\text{MTTF}}{\text{MTTF}+\text{MTTR}},$$

- it increases inventory at each station, from r_a/r to

$$\left(1+\frac{\text{MTTR}}{\text{MTTF}}\right)r_a/r, \text{ and}$$

- it introduces inventory, in the form of queues, in front of each station.

What is different now is that Station 1's output is used as the input to Station 2, and because of that the input to Station 2 is varying—unlike that into Station 1, which is unvarying by assumption. Buzacott and Shanthikumar give a formula for the cv^2 of the input into Station 2 as the product of u^2 and the cv^2 of Station 1's processing time from equation (5); that is:

cv^2 of Station 2 input arrivals $=$

$$u^2 r\left(1+cv^2_{\text{MTTR}}\right)\frac{\text{MTTF}}{\left(\dfrac{\text{MTTF}}{\text{MTTR}}+1\right)^2}. \qquad (7)$$

This will in turn escalate the inventory in the queue in front of Station 2 further, to:

$$\frac{u}{(1-u)}\times\text{Station 2 processing time}$$

$$\times\frac{\left[cv^2 \text{ of Station 2 input arrivals}\right]+\left[cv^2 \text{ of Station 2 processing time}\right]}{2}. \qquad (8)$$

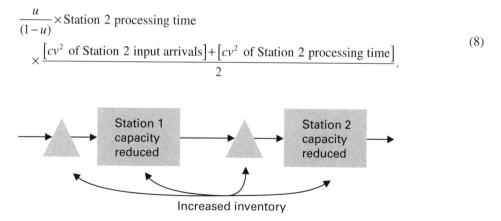

Increased inventory

Figure 10.5
Process risk for two stations in sequence.

The cv^2 of Station 2's input arrivals is in equation (7), and the cv^2 of Station 2's processing time is the same as that for Station 1, as given in equation (5).

Therefore, the Station 2 queue inventory is:

$$\frac{u}{(1-u)}\frac{\text{MTTF}+\text{MTTR}}{r\text{MTTF}}\frac{\left[u^2 r\left(1+cv^2_{\text{MTTR}}\right)\dfrac{\text{MTTF}}{\left(\dfrac{\text{MTTF}}{\text{MTTR}}+1\right)^2}\right]+\left[r\left(1+cv^2_{\text{MTTR}}\right)\dfrac{\text{MTTF}}{\left(\dfrac{\text{MTTF}}{\text{MTTR}}+1\right)^2}\right]}{2}.$$

$$=\frac{u(u^2+1)}{(1-u)}\frac{\left(1+cv^2_{\text{MTTR}}\right)}{2}\frac{\text{MTTR}^2}{\text{MTTF}+\text{MTTR}}.$$

In other words, the queue inventory for Station 2 is amplified by $(u^2 + 1)$ over that for Station 1. The higher Station 1's utilization u, the greater the amplification. At the extreme when Station 1's utilization is 1, Station 2's queue inventory is double that of Station 1.

Pooled Stations in a Process

Finally, we consider stations pooled together, as in figure 10.6.

How does process risk affect performance in this case? In some ways, the impact is similar to the previous case of sequential stations: (1) station capacities are reduced, (2) station inventories are increased, and (3) inventory appears in a queue before the stations. The difference here is the last. The formula for inventory in the queue when there are m pooled stations is:

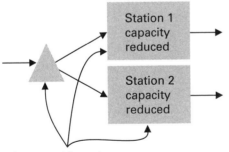

Figure 10.6
Process risk for two stations pooled together.

$$\frac{u^{\sqrt{2(m+1)}-1}}{(1-u)} \times \frac{\text{MTTF} + \text{MTTR}}{mr\text{MTTF}} \times \frac{[cv^2 \text{ of station processing time}]}{2} =$$

$$\frac{u^{\sqrt{6}-1}}{(1-u)} \frac{\left(1 + cv_{\text{MTTR}}^2\right)}{4} \frac{\text{MTTR}^2}{\text{MTTF} + \text{MTTR}}.$$

(9)

While this is larger than the queue inventory for a single station as in equation (6), it is smaller than just the queue inventory for Station 2 in equation (8).

Taken together, this shows that process risk affects capacities and inventories. Unlike in finance, where risks are often thought of as pooled in a portfolio,[2] operational processes may amplify risks as they cascade through many stations in the processes.

Risk of Inadequate Warranty Reserves

In December 2006, Clay Sumner, an FBR Equity Research analyst, claimed that Dell Computers reported artificially high earnings by not setting aside adequate reserves to cover the warranty of computers sold. For many products from electronics to cars, the inadequate provision of warranty reserves is a major source of risk. How do we know how big the reserve ought to be? Intuitively, that should depend on:

- S = the sales rate, or how many units we sell per year,
- MTTF = mean time between failures, as above,
- w = length of the warranty period (we assume this is exogenously given here; in section 15.4.3, we show how it is determined),
- p = the unit price to the customer,
- c = the unit cost to us,
- t = time to when the unit fails, following its purchase at $t = 0$,
- b = our rebate to the customer when the unit fails during warranty.

There are two major types of warranties: (1) free replacement, in which $b = c$; and (2) pro rata rebate, in which we give the customer a rebate of the price p she paid proportionate to the remaining life of the warranty; see figure 10.7.

The warranty reserve is then the expected cost of failures, or the sum (or integral, since we are dealing with continuous variables) of the failure probability and failure cost. The failure probability—assuming that failures are random—is given by the probability density function:

$$P_{(\text{unit fails at time } t)} = e^{-t/\text{MTTF}}/\text{MTTF},$$

and the failure cost is $\$b$ per unit, which depends on the warranty type: free replacement or pro rata. So for free replacement, the warranty reserve ought to be:

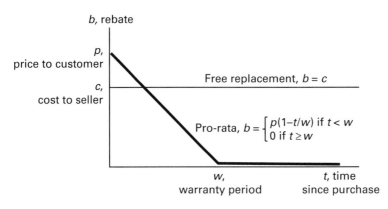

Figure 10.7
Two types of warranties: free replacement and pro rata.

$$\int_0^w \left(\frac{e^{-\frac{t}{\text{MTTF}}}}{\text{MTTF}} \right) Sc\, dt = Sc\left(1 - e^{-\frac{w}{\text{MTTF}}} \right)$$

and that for pro rata warranty ought to be:

$$\int_0^w \left(\frac{e^{-\frac{t}{\text{MTTF}}}}{\text{MTTF}} \right) \left[Sp\left(1 - \frac{t}{w}\right) \right] dt = Sp\left[1 - \frac{\text{MTTF}}{w}\left(1 - e^{-\frac{w}{\text{MTTF}}}\right) \right].$$

In both cases, we see that as MTTF becomes larger—as failure becomes rarer—the appropriate warranty reserve goes down, as shown in figure 10.8 for an example in which $S = 100$ units per year, c is \$1 per unit, p is \$1.2 per unit, and w is 5 years.

Finally, bear in mind that the reserves we just calculated are for one year. We should get the cumulative NPV of the reserves; for example, if the yearly reserves grow at g every year and should be discounted at r, the cumulative NPV is the yearly reserve divided by $(r - g)$.

10.3.6   One-off Risks and Value at Risk (VaR)

Like process risks, one-off risks can be evaluated on the basis of their probability and severity. But while the consequences of process risks tend to be gradual (e.g., lower capacity, higher inventory), the consequences of one-off risks tend to be categorical (e.g., patent application rejected, supply is tainted). In other words, one-off risks are less forgiving, and they require a different tool to evaluate their impact on valuation.

The most common tool comes under the value-at-risk (VaR) framework, in which we assess how much we would lose, given a probability and a time horizon. VaR is defined

Warranty reserve

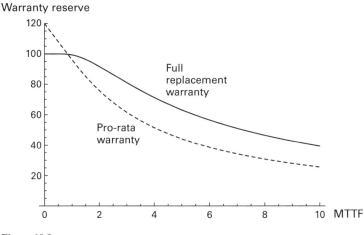

Figure 10.8
Warranty reserves decrease with MTTF.

as the loss that would be incurred with some prespecified probability (say 1%) for a pre-specified portfolio (say $100 million of real estate holdings). VaR was popularized by Banker's Trust and J. P. Morgan, the latter of which spun off a group called RiskMetrics to further develop the VaR tool.

Even though VaR was originally developed for assessing the risks of securities and credit portfolios, with some tweaking it offers a useful and simple method for assessing real assets. For example, in March 2000 thunderstorms hit Philips's semiconductor plant in Albuquerque, New Mexico. The plant furnace was hit by lightning, and the resulting fire destroyed the plant's clean room. The risk involved in this sort of one-off event could be quantifiable using the VaR methodology.

We describe two common methods for calculating VaR, then compare them.

Parametric Method

The original RiskMetrics description of VaR uses historical data to estimate the parameters of an assumed normal probability distribution of financial assets. We can use it for real assets, although there are some necessary departures. First, the horizon for financial VaRs is usually in days, while that for real assets can reasonably be a lot longer. Suppose we want to find the 1%-probability-over-three-months VaR for a $100 million portfolio of real risks: 40% of the value is in rentals for a clutch of retail stores and 60% in a three-month demand for our collection of skiwear products. We first assemble the historical three-month percentage changes for rentals and demand. The further back we go into the historical returns, the more confidence we have with our estimation of the probability distribution, *provided* the underlying distribution has not changed much. Using these

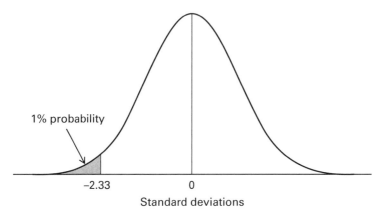

Figure 10.9
Standard normal distribution.

historical percentage changes, we estimate the mean percentage change of the portion as $40\% \times E(r_g) + 60\% \times E(r_m)$, where $E(.)$ is the expectation operator to represent the mean, and r_g and r_m are the variables that represent the three-month percentage change of rental and demand. In some variants of this method, the percentage changes are the lowest within the three months. We calculate the variance of the portfolio acknowledging the covariance between the two stocks. The portfolio variance is $40\%^2 \times \text{Var}(r_g) + 60\%^2 \times \text{Var}(r_m) + 2 \times 40\% \times 60\% \times \text{Cov}(r_g, r_m)$, where $\text{Var}(.)$ is the variance operator and $\text{Cov}(.)$ the covariance operator.

Importantly, the parametric method assumes that the portfolio return is normally distributed with the estimated mean and variance. The 1% probability mark is 2.33 standard deviations lower than the zero mean in the standard normal distribution (see figure 10.9).

Let us suppose that the mean portfolio percentage change is 10% and the standard deviation (the square root of the variance) is 20%. Therefore, there is a 1% probability that the three-month percentage change is as much as $10\% - 2.33 \times 20\% = -36.6\%$. The $100 million portfolio of risks will therefore have a VaR of $100 million $\times 36.6\% = \$36.6$ million.

How realistic is this VaR? As we suggested, this depends on how representative the past is of the future. The more comprehensively we can model the risks, the more accurate can be our VaR. For example, we could account for changes in the mix of store locations, or changes in their retail formats. (As the clutch of rental locations expand from urban to rural areas, we should account for this change in mix.)

What about categorical risks like whether a patent application is approved? These VaRs tend to be volatile. For example, a patent valued at $10 million may have a VaR of $0 if the probability is 1%, but all $10 million if the probability is (as an example) 0.1%. The

VaR amount is either $0 or $10 million, depending on what probability threshold we pick. In these cases, it makes sense to think through these risks differently. For example, we might focus on correlations—that is, if this patent application is rejected, will almost all related patent applications likewise be rejected? We might also think about divesting or hedging this sort of risk, perhaps through real options (see chapter 11).

Historical Method

A major criticism of the parametric method is that it assumes a normal distribution. Simulation methods construct empirically based distributions instead. In this method, we use three-month changes in rentals and demands—going as far back as we might in the parametric method—to calculate the change in our portfolio. For example, for the three-month period of January-March 1983, rentals might have gone down 2% and demand 3%, and if this had been the case today, our portfolio would have gone down 40% × 2% + 60% × 3% = 2.6%.

This 2.6% downturn would constitute one of very many historical three-month changes, and we next put these changes into a histogram—rather than using them to estimate a normal distribution. Then the rest of the steps are as before: find the percent change corresponding to the 1% percentile in the probability distribution, and translate that percent change to a dollar change to get the VaR.

This simple historical method assumes that all historical changes are of equal weight. One modification is to place greater weight on more recent changes.

Monte Carlo Method

A more sophisticated way is to explicitly model how values change over time, rather than using historical percentage changes.

Let us stay with our example of determining the 1%-probability-over-three-months VaR for a $100 million portfolio of real risks: 40% of the value is in rentals for a clutch of retail stores and 60% in three months' demand for our collection of skiwear products.

We first build models of how rentals and demand might change. To do this, we postulate factors that drive these two risks. For example, we might have:

$$\text{rental}_{t+1} = \beta_1 + \beta_2 \times \text{rental}_t + \beta_3 \times t + \beta_4 \times \text{demand}_t + \varepsilon, \tag{10}$$

$$\text{demand}_{t+1} = \alpha_1 + \alpha_2 \times \text{demand}_t + \alpha_3 \times \text{SKU}_t + \alpha_4 \times \text{rental}_t + \eta. \tag{11}$$

The t subscripts indicate three-month periods. In other words, rental in the next three months depends on rental in this three-month period, a trend term (the t term), demand in this period, and a random noise term with zero mean and a normal distribution. Demand in the next three-month period depends on demand in the current period, the number of stock-keeping units (SKUs) in this period, the rental in this period (which also provides a proxy for the total retail square footage), and another random noise term, also with zero mean and a normal distribution. Notice how we connect rental and demand in the two equations, so as capture the correlation between the two.

Using historical data containing observations of rental, inflation, demand, stores, and number of SKUs for three-month periods, we can run regressions to get the β and α terms. The regression results also produce the variance for ε and η.

Now we create a distribution of the value of the portfolio consisting of 40% of its value in rentals for a clutch of retail stores and 60% in skiwear demand. To do this, we plug in what we now know for all the values on the right-hand side of equations (10) and (11), as well as randomly generate values of ε and η based on normal distributions with their variances estimated from the regressions. Then we put these generated portfolio values in a histogram to find the value corresponding to the 1% percentile in the probability distribution. The difference between this value and the current value is the VaR.

Of course, we can add more realism—and complexity—to the procedure just described. Importantly, we have assumed that the connection between rental and demand is static, and that the stochastic components ε and η are independent. We could add more realism by explicitly correlating ε and η with, say, a bivariate normal distribution. Also, we actually make only one forecast, so all the histogram is showing is the randomness in ε and η. We could use short historical periods—say one month rather than three months—and use a sequence of one-month predictions to get our three-month VaR. We could also add more explanatory factors other than just a trend term or the number of SKUs. And we could assume that ε and η do not follow the normal distributions.

Comparison and Critique

We can compare the methods along several dimensions, and suggest situations in which one method might be superior to another:

• *Distributional assumptions.* The parametric method assumes that the probability distribution is normal, and can be completely parameterized by the mean and variance. The historical and Monte Carlo methods escape this criticism. But like the parametric method, the historical method still assumes that the past distribution is representative of the future. If we are dealing with very liquid risks—such as those in the pricing of financial assets— the normality assumption under the parametric method seems reasonable. At the opposite extreme, if we are dealing with rare risks, then the Monte Carlo method seems to be appropriate, since in principle it simulates as many different scenarios as are needed. Nevertheless, the Monte Carlo method is still susceptible to "model risk"—that is, the model used deviates too much from the actual distribution. It also assumes that we know the probability distributions of the risk factors.

• *Computational requirements.* Not surprisingly, the parametric method—which requires only two parameters—is computationally the easiest. At the opposite extreme is the Monte Carlo method, which is known to take several orders of magnitude more of computational power and time.

Apart from the problems just indicated, the VaR methodology in general is subject to many other criticisms. For one, it provides only a threshold loss amount. A VaR amount of $1 million with 1% probability could also represent a risk of losing $100 million with 0.9% probability. For another, by providing just a single statistic, it could offer a false sense of security in a black box. The Monte Carlo regressions in which we can explicitly model what is driving changes in value are very helpful, but they are only as helpful as the models themselves. Using VaR does not make us less susceptible to risks we do not know about. And finally, the provision of a single statistic also subjects it to manipulation, as when managers decide to provide "the number that the CEO likes to see." But many of these criticisms can also be leveled against most other measures of risk, and the VaR has withstood several decades of practical use in industry.

10.4 Takeaways and Toolkit

In this chapter, we learn why we have to dig below financial statements to better value a company's risks. To do that, we need to:

• Differentiate between systematic and total risk. If our risks can be diversified away, then it is useful to think only about systematic risk, which is the undiversifiable part of total risk.

• To find systematic risk, we calculate beta. Operations affect beta through operational leverage: the higher the proportion of costs that are fixed, the higher the beta.

• To find total risk, we first have to specify the myriad of risks that might occur. A risk map of probabilities and severity can help. In finance, probabilities (or variances) may be reduced through diversification. That is true in operations; but in operations, probabilities could also be amplified.

• It is also helpful to analyze two types of total risk: process and one-off risks. They affect firm value differently, and are amenable to different tools for assessment.

• Process risk reduces capacity and increases working capital (inventory). One-off risks can be assessed using a value-at-risk framework.

In table 10.1, we summarize the formulae for systematic and total risk.

10.5 Survey of Prior Research in One Paragraph

The leading researchers who have developed the idea of beta include Harry Markowitz, Bill Sharpe, John Lintner, and Jack Treynor. Recent research argues that specific risks are

Table 10.1
Toolkit: Formulae for Systematic and Total Risk

Type of Risk	Formula
Systematic risk	$beta = \mathrm{Cov}(r_{business}, r_{market}) \,/\, \mathrm{Var}(r_{market})$ $= \left[1 + \dfrac{PV(\textit{fixed cost})}{PV(\textit{asset})}\right] beta_{revenue}$
Total process risk	Inventory needed to buffer process risks (captured by MTTF and MTTR): • One station: $\dfrac{u}{(1-u)} \dfrac{\left(1+cv_{\mathrm{MTTR}}^2\right)}{2} \dfrac{\mathrm{MTTR}^2}{\mathrm{MTTF}+\mathrm{MTTR}} + \left(1+\dfrac{\mathrm{MTTR}}{\mathrm{MTTF}}\right) r_a \,/\, r$ • Two stations in a sequence: as above for first station plus below for second station: $\dfrac{u(u^2+1)}{(1-u)} \dfrac{\left(1+cv_{\mathrm{MTTR}}^2\right)}{2} \dfrac{\mathrm{MTTR}^2}{\mathrm{MTTF}+\mathrm{MTTR}} + \left(1+\dfrac{\mathrm{MTTR}}{\mathrm{MTTF}}\right) r_a \,/\, r$ • Two stations in a pool: $\dfrac{u^{\sqrt{6}-1}}{(1-u)} \dfrac{\left(1+cv_{\mathrm{MTTR}}^2\right)}{4} \dfrac{\mathrm{MTTR}^2}{\mathrm{MTTF}+\mathrm{MTTR}} + 2\left(1+\dfrac{\mathrm{MTTR}}{\mathrm{MTTF}}\right) r_a \,/\, r$
Total one-off risk	Calculate the value at risk (VaR) using one of these methods: 1. Parametric 2. Historical 3. Monte Carlo

not completely diversifiable. Two leading finance scholars are Andrei Shleifer and Robert Vishny. Richard Bettis makes a similar point, from the strategy angle, and John Birge and Paul Glasserman are leading scholars in applying operations research techniques to risk assessment. The treatment of warranty reserves here is by Warren Menke. Kevin Hendricks and Vinod Singhal pioneer the quantification of operational disruptions on firms' financial performance. Marshall Fisher, Jan Hammond, and Ananth Raman have done rigorous analyses on collective forecasting and the staging of production capacities to increase flexibility, so as to mitigate the risk of demand-supply mismatches. Yossi Sheffi has written a useful reference called *The Resilient Enterprise*. Value at risk has long been known in statistics, but its current form is popularized by J. P. Morgan under the name RiskMetrics™.

10.6 Further Reading

Bettis, R. A. 1983. "Modern Financial Theory, Corporate Strategy and Public Policy: Three Conundrums." *Academy of Management Review* 8 (3): 406–415.

Brealey, R. A., S. C. Myers, and F. Allen. 2006. *Principles of Corporate Finance*. Boston: McGraw-Hill/Irwin.

Buzacott, J. A., and J. G. Shanthikumar. 1993. *Stochastic Models of Manufacturing Systems*. Englewood Cliffs, NJ: Prentice-Hall.

Foster, D. P., and R. A. Stine. 2006. "Being Warren Buffett: A Classroom Simulation of Risk and Wealth When Investing in the Stock Market." *American Statistician* 60: 53–60.

Lintner, J. 1965. "The Valuation of Risk Assets and the Selection of Risky Investments in Stock Portfolios and Capital Budgets." *Review of Economics and Statistics*: 13–37.

Markowitz, H. 1952. "Portfolio Selection." *Journal of Finance*: 77–91.

Menke, W. W. 1969. "Determination of Warranty Reserves." *Management Science* 15 (10): 542–549.

Morgan, J. 1995. *Riskmetrics Technical Manual*. New York: J. P. Morgan.

Sharpe, W. F. 1963. "A Simplified Model for Portfolio Analysis." *Management Science* 9 (2): 277–293.

Sheffi, Yossi. 2007. *The Resilient Enterprise*. Cambridge, MA: MIT Press.

Treynor, J. 1961. "Toward a Theory of Market Value of Risky Assets." Unpublished manuscript.

11 Assessing Options

On September 15, 2006, Freescale Semiconductor agreed to a buyout by the Blackstone Group for $17.6 billion. Freescale's profits were just $584 million in 2005. If these profits were considered cash flows into the future, with a discount rate of say 10%, the net present value of Freescale would have been just $5.8 billion. What could account for Blackstone's bold valuation?

One possibility is that Blackstone was buying the option that Freescale would grow tremendously. Freescale had been making static random access memory (SRAMs), which was at the tail end of its product lifecycle. However, more importantly, SRAM manufacturing positioned Freescale well for the anticipated next technology, magnetoresistive random access memory (MRAMs), which has enduring memory facilitated by electron spins that create "nonvolatility." In 2006, the MRAM market was in its infancy: it might have become huge or it might have become nothing. So Blackstone was also in essence paying for the option to enter the MRAM market. Indeed, in June 2008, the MRAM market was looking bright enough that Freescale spun off Everspin to make MRAMs.

Table 11.1 shows the value of growth options, estimated as the difference between the value of market equity and the discounted cash flow (DCF) value of earnings discounted at a conservative 15%. The value of growth options as a percent of the market equity value is substantial, with this rough but conservative estimate; when the DCF value is discounted using higher rates, the importance of growth options is even higher.

Options include more than just growth opportunities. We can frame research and development investment as the price of an option; we invest in a major way only if the R&D produces promising results. We can also frame the opportunity to terminate a business as an option.

All these suggest that we need to better assess the value of options, which in turn raises these important questions:

• *How do we calculate the value of options on operational assets*—often called "real assets"—such as factories and patents? Is there any difference from the valuation of options on financial assets?

Table 11.1
Value of Growth Options

	Market Value ($ mil)	DCF Value ($ mil)	Growth Value ($ mil)	Option % of Market Value
Electronics				
Motorola	5,250	1,400	3850	73%
Genrad	550	113	437	79%
RCA	2,200	1,600	600	27%
Computers				
Apple	2,000	660	1340	67%
Digital Equipment	5,690	1,900	3790	67%
IBM	72,890	36,433	36457	50%
Chemicals				
Celanese	1,010	520	490	49%
Monsanto	4,260	2,733	1527	36%
Union Carbide	4,350	1,867	2483	57%
Tires and rubber				
Firestone	1,090	587	503	46%
Goodyear	2,520	2,000	520	21%
Uniroyal	400	313	87	22%
Food				
Carnation	1,790	1,367	423	24%
Consolidated Foods	1,190	1,140	50	4%
General Foods	2,280	2,113	167	7%

Source: Kester (1984). "Market value" is the value of equity. "DCF value" is the discounted cash flow value, calculated by discounting earnings at 15%.

• *Where do options come from and what are the main types?*   In many cases, they originate from operational decisions, in terms of changing the investment timing (i.e., to start or expand later, or end or shrink earlier) and flexibility (i.e., the mix of what to produce).

The rest of this chapter addresses these two questions, and shows how we can value different types of options.

11.1   Refresher on Valuing Financial Options

From most finance texts, you will recall that a call option gives you the right, but not the obligation, to purchase an underlying asset—say an equity share—at a specified exercise price, and at a future exercise date (for a "European option") or by a future exercise date (for an "American option"). A put option gives you the right, but not the obligation, to sell rather than buy.

The popular methods for valuing options are the Black-Scholes formula and the binomial method (which we will describe later). These use five inputs, and table 11.2 shows how these inputs affect option values.

Table 11.2
How Call and Put Option Values Change with Input Parameters

If the following increases. . .	. . . then the value of the following changes as below	
	Call	Put
Value of underlying asset (S)	↑ Higher chance that the value at expiration will exceed the exercise price ("upside").	↓
Uncertainty of value of underlying asset (σ)	↑ Higher chance of an upside; size of downside is irrelevant since the option will be valueless in any case.	↑ Same as for calls.
Time to expiration (t)	↑ Option has a credit element: pay option price now to defer paying (usually larger) exercise price later. This extends the credit term. For American options, longer time also provides more opportunities for upside.	↑ Same as for calls.
Risk-free interest rate (r_f)	↑ The credit nature of an option also means that when interest is high, paying a small amount upfront is valuable.	↓
Exercise price (X)	↓ A higher exercise price means a higher hurdle to get some upside.	↑

11.2 Real versus Financial Options

Financial options are well known, so before we proceed it is helpful to define the difference between real and financial options.

Real options use much of the machinery used to value financial options, but there are some differences. The main ones are that: (1) real assets are usually not traded, nor do they have much history; therefore, it is difficult to assess the value of the real option; (2) real options often do not incur direct costs as in the purchase of financial options; (3) the distribution of volatilities is unlikely to be lognormal, as is assumed in financial options models; for example, the probability distribution of costs is likely to be skewed toward cost overruns rather than underruns; and (4) real options are often exposed to more than one uncertainty; while a financial option is typically exposed to the uncertainty of the market price of its underlying assets, a real option on, say, a patent related to a new product might be exposed to uncertainty in the product's demand quantity and price.

There are also similarities. For example, real options are often multistaged; while more complex than one-shot financial options, they are similar to complex financial options called compound options (options on options). Also, the value of the underlying asset in real options might erode over time, say because the competition may preempt our exercising our option. This is similar to the erosion of the underlying asset in financial options because of, say, dividend payouts. In any case, the issue really is not whether real and financial options are substantively different, but whether we can get a reasonable enough assessment of options so as to make the best business decisions.

11.3   Options to Start or Expand Later

In many business processes, we can time our investment. In section 7.4, we described how the due diligence process can be organized in stages. In this way, we invest a little up front, so that we invest more only if a potential deal looks promising, creating an option. Similarly, Dell employs options by using a make-to-order instead of a make-to-stock process. In the latter, a business would assemble computers as soon as stock (say in its warehouse) runs out. In Dell's case, it assembles computers only when it gets a customer order. This has the advantage of deferring the expense as much as possible, to capture the time value of money. But the more important advantage is that it assembles a computer only when the demand for it is certain.

More generally, the option to delay investing can also be analyzed as an option to expand later. The point is that, in assessing a business, we should ask whether budgeted investments can be delayed. If so, what is the option value of delay?

Suppose the assembly of a computer incurs a cash outflow of $1,200; we have to buy the parts, put in the labor, stock the computer. The computer stays as inventory for one "period"—you will remember this as "days of inventory" from section 2.1.2. Then it is sold either at the full price of $1,978 or, if there is weak demand, at a discounted price of $728. This is depicted in figure 11.1, panel (a).

What if we can delay the assembly, so that we assemble the computer only if we can sell at the full price of $1,978? In that case, we either get $1,978 less $1,200 (the cost of assembling the computer), which is $778, or we get $0 because we do not even bother assembling the computer. How much is the value of this delay, which we can denote as c? This situation is depicted in figure 11.1, panel (b).

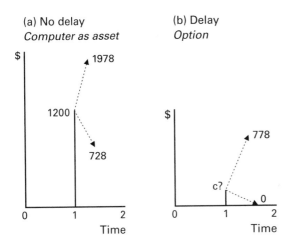

Figure 11.1
The value of delaying assembly of a computer.

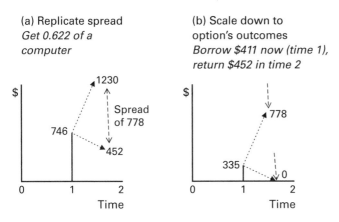

Figure 11.2
Option to start later: replicating an option.

11.3.1 Binomial Method Using Replication

We can find c by replicating the cash flows at the end of the period. First, we scale the outcome spreads—that is, we find what has been called "delta":

$$\text{delta} = \frac{778 - 0}{1978 - 728} = 0.622.$$

This means that if we assemble "0.622 of a computer" without delay and then sell it, we get the same spread of $778 between the good and bad outcomes as with the delay: see figure 11.2, panel (a). Specifically, the 0.622 of a computer gives us $1,978 \times 0.622 = \$1,230$ upside and $728 \times 0.622 = \$452$ downside, a spread of $778.

But to completely replicate the option, we need to scale the $1,230 down to $778 and the $452 down to $0—i.e., reduce both by $452. To do this, we can borrow some money now so that we need to pay $452 at the end of the period, thus neutralizing the $452 from selling the 0.622 of the computer. Since this borrowing is risk-free, we can use the risk-free interest rate. Say this rate is 10%. So we borrow

$$\frac{452}{1+10\%} = \$411.$$

To summarize, the method involves two steps in replicating a call option:

1. *Create the same spread as the option:*   purchase delta $\times$ one unit of the underlying asset. This is $0.622 \times \$1,200 = \$746$.

2. *Scale the outcomes to the option's levels:*   borrow an amount now at the risk-free rate to scale both the outcomes later. This is borrowing $411.

The method determines that delaying has value, at $c = 746 - 411 = \$335$.

Should we delay? That depends on whether not delaying has a higher value than \$335. For example, if "not delaying" is fairly priced with a zero net present value, then delaying is better.

11.3.2   Advanced Topic: Binomial Method Using Risk-Neutral Probabilities

One interesting discovery about the binomial method just described is that replication is independent of investors' risk preferences. This provides another and often easier method to value an option: find the probabilities associated with the outcomes of the underlying asset, and use these to value the option.

Here's how, using the previous example:

1. *Find the probabilities associated with the outcomes of the underlying asset*—see figure 11.1, panel (a). The probabilities should be commensurate with the appropriate discount rate. Since we have the risk-free discount rate (assumed to be 10% above), let's use risk-neutral probabilities p for the upside of \$1,978 and $(1 - p)$ for the downside of \$728 and discount with the risk-free rate to \$1,200:

$$\frac{p \times 1978 + (1-p) \times 728}{1.1} = 1200 . \tag{12}$$

This gives $p = 0.4736$.

2. *Use these probabilities to value the option*—see figure 11.1, panel (b). So we have, using the just-obtained $p = 0.4736$:

$$\frac{p \times 778 + (1-p) \times 0}{1.1} = 335 .$$

This, of course, is the same figure we obtained earlier, with less fuss.

11.3.3   Binomial Method in Continuous Time

In figure 11.1, we are given the upside and downside values. Another way to specify these values is to obtain σ, the standard deviation of how these values spread out. In the previous example, we actually used $\sigma = 0.5$.

In continuous time, the period Δt can be any fraction of t, the time to expiration. The formulas to get the upside and downside are:

upside $= e^{\sigma\sqrt{\Delta t}} = e^{0.5\sqrt{1}} = 1.65$.

The base value is \$1,200; the upside value is $1.65 \times 1,200 = \$1,978$;

downside $= 1/$upside.

This is $(1/0.65) \times 1,200 = \$728$.

In continuous time, we discount values by $e^{r_f \Delta t}$ rather than by $(1 + r_f)^{\Delta t}$ as we had before. For example, equation (12) would look like:

$$\frac{p \times 1978 + (1-p) \times 728}{e^{0.1 \times 1}} = 1200.$$

11.3.4 Black-Scholes Method

The binomial method just described has only one period. It would be more accurate to divide that period into subperiods. At the extreme, we arrive at the Black-Scholes method.

Let us denote the five inputs to option valuations in table 11.2:

S = value of underlying asset

σ = standard deviation of S, capturing the uncertainty of the value of the underlying asset

t = time to expiration

r_f = risk-free interest rate

X = exercise price

The structure of the Black-Scholes method is similar to that from the binomial method:

1. *Create the same spread as the option:* purchase delta × one unit of the underlying asset. In this case, the delta is $N(d_1)$. N is the probability that a variable with normal distribution is less than d_1; d_1 is $\dfrac{\log\left(\dfrac{S}{PV(X)}\right)}{\sigma\sqrt{t}} + \dfrac{\sigma\sqrt{t}}{2}$, where $PV(X)$ is the present value of X discounted using r_f.

2. *Scale the outcomes to the option's levels:* borrow an amount at the risk-free rate to scale both the outcomes. In this case, we get an amount $N(d_2) \times PV(X)$, where d_2 is $d_1 - \sigma\sqrt{t}$.

In other words, the value of an American call option is:

$N(d_1) \times S - N(d_2) \times PV(X)$.

Returning to our example, we have:

S = value of underlying asset = \$1,200

σ = standard deviation of S = 0.223[1]

t = time to expiration = 1 period

r_f = risk-free interest rate = 10%

X = exercise price = \$1,200.

This gives a call value of $165.3, which is about the same order of magnitude as the $211.4 we obtained with the binomial method. As the binomial method uses more subperiods, it will approach the Black-Scholes number.

The Black-Scholes method makes a number of assumptions. Some—such as no restriction on short selling, no arbitrage opportunity, and exercise possible only at expiration—seem less reasonable in the context of real options. But the method does not suffer the disadvantages of the binomial method—such as the tradeoff between a small number of periods and computational complexity—so it provides a reasonable check.

11.3.5   Black-Scholes with Deteriorating Assets

The Black-Scholes formula can be enhanced to accommodate underlying assets that deteriorate in value. This deterioration may come in many forms. For example, inventory may become obsolete. The possibility of new entrants may intensify competition. There might also be an explicit cost of keeping the option alive. For example, some governments require oil tracts, while fallow, to pay a "flame tax," so as to induce tract owners to drill the tracts. And keeping a factory unused but ready to start has its obvious costs: some minimal labor force, maintenance.

If d is the deterioration rate (e.g., 20% per period), then we need to modify d_1:

$$d_1 \text{ for deteriorating assets} = \frac{\log\left(\frac{S}{PV(X)}\right) - dt}{\sigma\sqrt{t}} + \frac{\sigma\sqrt{t}}{2}.$$

The rest of the formula is as before.

11.3.6   Example: Accurate Response at Sport Obermeyer

Sport Obermeyer, a ski apparel maker, postpones its production as much as possible, learning better information as time goes by. Figure 11.3 shows how much better forecasts get with new information. In the left panel, we see that the initial forecasts for demand have an error rate of 55%. But in the right panel, when we include orders from the first two weeks of sales in our forecasts, the error rate drops significantly to just 8%.

This delay and other initiatives at Sport Obermeyer (see sections 12.3 and 13.2) resulted in the business's reducing its mismatch costs—the cost of over- and understocking—by half.

11.3.7   Detecting an Option to Start or Expand Later

How do we know we have such an option on our hands? The following situations would be indicative:

Much Learning over Time

For example, over time we might be able to size up demand much more accurately. This happens at Sport Obermeyer, in which forecast accuracy improves dramatically over time.

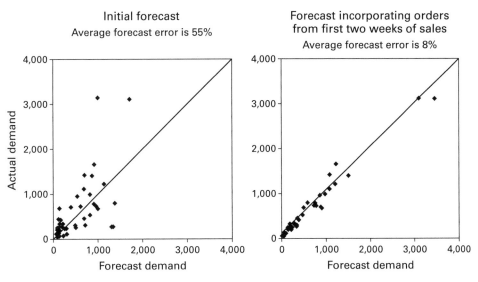

Figure 11.3
Demand forecasts improve over time. Source: Fisher (2009).

Learning can be significant over time because we have:

• *New fashion products.* This is the situation faced by Sport Obermeyer. There is little about old products that can inform the demand for new products.

• *Asset intangibility and specificity.* In the investing context, this could also be significant because an investee company's assets are mostly intangible (e.g., human capital) and are specific to that company (e.g., proprietary technologies not used elsewhere).

The "Ticket to Play" Is Needed Early

Since an option, by definition, offers the right to something, it goes without saying that without the option, we should not have that right. Think of this as an extreme form of first-mover advantage, without degrees of advantages. A firm is either in the game (e.g., has a patent) or not. But this "right" is not always obvious. For example, how much is a "toehold" in China really an option for expansion? And while a license may be needed to produce a drug, do we really need the license early if no one else is interested in procuring it just yet? In short, the "ticket to play" is not only needed to obtain the right, it must be needed early, because it would not be available later.

11.4 Option to End or Shrink Earlier

The option to start later is about making cash outflows (investing) *later*: we decide to invest only when we learn that the outlook is *good*. The mirror image is an option to end *earlier*: we decide to abandon and receive salvage value only when we learn that the outlook is *bad*.

More generally, the option to end early is an extreme version of the option to shrink a business.

Suppose we are considering buying a machine line with a four-year lifespan. The expected cash flow every year is $1 million, so if we calculate the net present value of these cash flows, it would be:

$$\text{NPV} = 1 + = 1 + \frac{1}{1.1} + \frac{1}{1.1^2} + \frac{1}{1.1^3} = \$3.49 \text{ million.}$$

But depending on demand, this line generates cash flows indicated in gray in figure 11.4. That is, the subsequent cash flows change over time, with ups and downs.[2] Importantly,

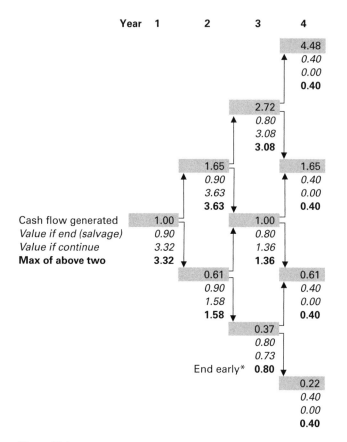

Figure 11.4
The value of abandoning a machine line. (All figures are in $ million.) At "End early," the salvage value in year 3 is higher than the value of continuing.

in any year we can give up the line for a salvage value. For example, in year 1 the salvage value is $0.9 million but then it deteriorates over time.

The crux here is that the cash flow for some years might be so low that we should end the machine line and get a good salvage value, before the four years are up. This issue is operationalized in a comparison between these two values:

· *The value if we end.*   This is the salvage value, indicated by the italicized figures just below the gray boxes in figure 11.4. We take as given the numbers shown there.

· *The value if we continue.*   This is the second italicized figure below the gray boxes. To determine the latter, we work backward, as usual. In year 4, the value if we continue is naturally zero, since that is the end of our machine line's life. Therefore, the decision would be to get the salvage value. This value is indicated by the bold figures, third down from each gray box.

Consider now the topmost situation in year 3. In the following year (year 4), the good outcome has value 4.48 (from cash flow) + 0.4 (from salvage) = $4.88 million. The bad outcome has value 1.65 + 0.4 = $2.05 million. This is actually an option because in year 4, we decide whether to end or continue.

To value this option, we use the usual replication technique (see section 11.3.1). Figure 11.5 shows, on the left, the values for the underlying asset. In other words, this is the equivalent of our "No Delay" option in figure 11.1. We pick the values from years 1 and 2, but it would make no difference if we had picked other years, since what matters is the amount by which the value goes up and down. The figure shows, on the right, the option in year 4 whose value—denoted by the "?"—we are trying to determine.

As before, we have the following:

$$\text{delta} = \frac{4.88 - 2.05}{1.65 - 0.61} = 2.72.$$

Again, assuming that the risk free interest rate is 10%,

$$\text{borrow now} = \frac{2.72 \cdot 0.61 - 2.05}{1 + 10\%} = -\$0.36 \text{ million.}$$

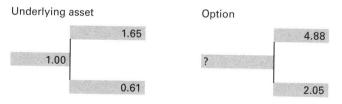

Figure 11.5
Option to end earlier: replicating an option.

The negative sign on borrowing means we actually lend. The value of this option is $2.72 + 0.36 = $3.08 million. This is the italicicized number two boxes below the topmost gray box for year 3.

Now the critical decision is clear: we should continue and get $3.08 million rather than end early in year 3 and get the salvage value of $0.8 million. This is shown in bold as the third box below the topmost gray box for year 3; that is, we should continue, for $3.08.

We repeat the above procedure for all gray boxes.

In year 3, when the worst outcome occurs, the salvage value is higher than the value of continuing (see the "End early" mark in figure 11.4).

When we complete the calculations, the value of the business would include the $1 million cash flow in year 1 and the value of continuing from then, which is $3.32 million, making a total of $4.32 million. Compare this with the net present value of $4 million, which is the sum of the present value of $1 million from each of the four years, obtained by discounting the *expected* cash flows from each year at the risk-free rate of 10%. The option of ending early has value.

11.4.1   Example: Staging in Due Diligence and Investing

Among venture capital (VC) firms, the issue of learning more about a portfolio company over time is especially pertinent. Therefore, it is not surprising that many VC firms undertake their core activities in a staged manner. We have already seen how they use staging in due diligence (section 7.4; see in particular figure 7.1). If a deal does not look promising, it is dropped, and not much due diligence time would have been invested in it.

VC firms also use staging in their disbursements to their portfolio companies. The idea is that these companies need to show they can reach preset milestones, or the VC firm discontinues further funding.

11.4.2   Detecting an Option to End or Shrink Earlier

As with an option to start later, an option to end earlier works only if there is learning over time. Other situations also indicate the presence or absence of such an option.

Some Branches Produce Negative NPV

The option has value only if ending/shrinking earlier has some benefits, such as reaping the salvage value or forestalling substantial upcoming costs. In contrast, there is no urgency to shutting or shrinking a business that has nonnegative net present value going forward. When determining the net present value, we also have to consider the costs of ending or shrinking the business, such as severance pay, cleaning up environmental pollution, or non-compete clauses.

Viable Release Clause

In order to end a business, the option must allow for a viable exit. The terms should not be overly onerous, and the timing should be definite.

An interesting note is that many options to end are not executed because of inertia. For example, research has shown that consumers tend not to cancel their purchases even when cancellation makes economic sense, possibly because of behavioral biases.

11.5   Option in Being Flexible

So far, we have considered the option of changing our timing: can we start or expand later? Can we end or shrink earlier? Here we consider the option of flexibly switching between, say, products or production facilities.

Suppose you are considering buying a chain of run-down movie theaters.[3] These theaters sit on prime land, so there are two options: refurbish the theaters or convert the land to hotels. We have some idea of how theater and hotel cash flows look in the future. Question: what is this option to switch to hotels worth?

The complication is that now we have two underlying assets: theaters and hotels. Suppose their characteristics are as in table 11.3. With a smaller σ, theaters have less uncertain cash flows. This translates to smaller upsides and downsides, and smaller probability of upside. The exercise price X is also smaller for theaters; this is the cost of refurbishing the theaters before they can generate cash flow. The cost of converting theaters to hotels is represented by the higher X for hotels.

In this example, the correlation between theater and hotel cash flows is represented by ρ. At 0.2, there is some correlation, but not a lot. We will see how this affects the flexibility option.

If we have the option to stay with just theaters or hotels, we are back to options to delay paying X to get the respective cash flows. To value these options, we once again start from the last year (year 2) and work back to the present time (year 1). In figure 11.6, panel (a), we consider theaters, whose cash flows are given in the gray boxes; for example, $1.22 is the upside from $1, as in table 11.3 (let us say that all units are in billions of dollars).

The value of investing in year 2 is shown just below the gray box. Each value is the cash flow less X, the $0.8 exercise price (recall table 11.3). There is no value of deferring

Table 11.3
Characteristics of Theater and Hotel Cash Flows

	Refurbish Theaters	Switch to Hotels
σ	0.2	0.9
Upside = e^{σ}	1.22	2.46
Downside = 1/upside	0.82	0.41
$p = (e^{r_f} - \text{downside})/(\text{upside} - \text{downside})$	0.71	0.34
X	0.8	1.0
r_f	10%	
ρ	0.2	

Note: The derivation of the formulas is described in section 11.3.3.

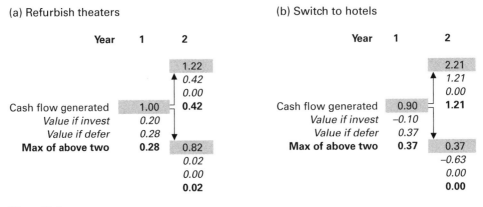

Figure 11.6
Option for theaters and hotels, individually.

in year 2, so these are the zeroes two rows below each gray box. And the decision, represented by the maximum of investing versus deferring, is obvious: these are the bold figures, representing investing in year 2.

In year 1, the value of investing is $1 less X (= $0.8), which is $0.20, shown just below the gray box. Below this is the value of deferring, obtained by the binomial method:

$$\frac{p \times 0.42 + (1-p) \times 0.02}{e^{0.1 \times 1}} = 0.28,$$

where p is 0.71, from table 11.3.

So between investing now to get $0.20 and deferring the investment to get $0.28, we defer.

Panel (b) of figure 11.6 shows the same for hotels. Notice that hotels start with a smaller cash flow of $0.90, but, with their enormous variance, the upside and downside here are a lot higher. So if we have an option to defer, and therefore avoid the downside, we have the chance of capturing the high upside. Correspondingly, the value of deferring is $0.37, higher than the value of investing (−$0.10), and higher than even the option for theaters.

Now consider what happens when we have the option of either refurbishing theaters or converting to hotels. In figure 11.7, we see that there are now four possible outcomes in year 2, representing the cross of the theater's and hotel's up and down outcomes. As before, the italicized figures just below the gray boxes represent the cash flows net of respective X. We take the maximum of these figures, representing our decision about whether theaters or hotels are the better investment.

Below these are the values of deferring, which are all zeroes since year 2 is the last year of the option. And as before, the bold figures represent the higher of the two figures above.

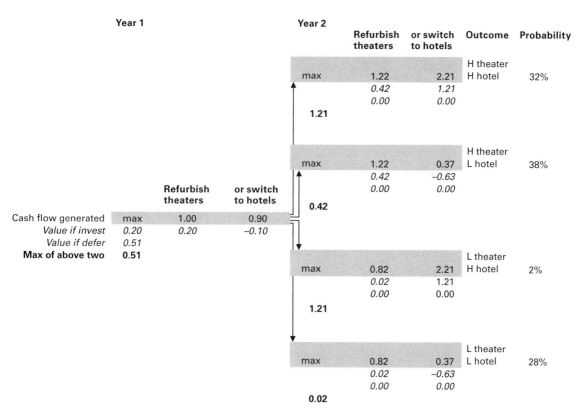

Figure 11.7
Option in being flexible between refurbishing theaters and switching to hotels.

In year 1, the value of investing is again shown in the italicized figures just below the gray boxes, representing the cash flows less the respective X. As before, the maximum of this is $0.20, for theaters. To calculate the value of deferring, we need probabilities p for each of the four outcomes. The usual binomial (two outcomes) as in equation (12) does not apply. Instead, following Boyle (1988), the probabilities for each outcome are as follows, with subscripts t for theaters and h for hotels:

$$p_{\text{up}_t\text{up}_h} = \frac{1}{4}\left[1 + \rho + \sqrt{\Delta t}\left(\frac{r_f - \frac{1}{2}\sigma_t^2}{\sigma_t} + \frac{r_f - \frac{1}{2}\sigma_h^2}{\sigma_h}\right)\right],$$

$$p_{\text{up}_t\text{down}_h} = \frac{1}{4}\left[1 - \rho + \sqrt{\Delta t}\left(\frac{r_f - \frac{1}{2}\sigma_t^2}{\sigma_t} - \frac{r_f - \frac{1}{2}\sigma_h^2}{\sigma_h}\right)\right],$$

$$p_{\text{down}_t \text{up}_h} = \frac{1}{4}\left[1 - \rho + \sqrt{\Delta t}\left(-\frac{r_f - \frac{1}{2}\sigma_t^2}{\sigma_t} + \frac{r_f - \frac{1}{2}\sigma_h^2}{\sigma_h}\right)\right],$$

$$p_{\text{down}_t \text{down}_h} = \frac{1}{4}\left[1 + \rho + \sqrt{\Delta t}\left(-\frac{r_f - \frac{1}{2}\sigma_t^2}{\sigma_t} - \frac{r_f - \frac{1}{2}\sigma_h^2}{\sigma_h}\right)\right].$$

Notice that ρ, the correlation of theater and hotel cash flows, increases the probabilities of the extreme outcomes and reduces the probabilities of the two middle outcomes. But it is the two middle outcomes that provide value, since we now have the flexibility of choosing the theater upside if we encounter a hotel downside and vice versa. Therefore, a low—indeed negative—correlation increases the value of our option, as in figure 11.8. The $\rho = 0.2$ point is the case in our example.

Using these probabilities, we value the flexibility option at $0.51. Importantly, this is higher than any of the options to defer when we have only theaters or hotels.

In our example, this flexibility option is more valuable than investing immediately, so we should defer and then, depending on theater and hotel outcomes, decide whether to go with theaters or hotels in year 2.

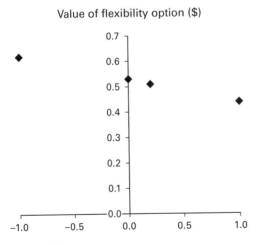

Figure 11.8
The value of the flexibility option depends on correlation of cash flows from the two underlying assets.

11.5.1 Example: Delayed Differentiation

The idea of delayed differentiation (also called postponement) is that products are not customized—such as colored (for apparel) or accessorized (for cars)—until we have information about what colors or accessories customers want.

Delayed differentiation has reportedly been successful in Benetton, Sun Microsystems, General Motors, and Compaq. For example, Hewlett Packard's printers are made in the Vancouver, Washington, plant and then shipped to distribution centers around the world. But printers for many markets in Asia and Europe require voltage, plug convention, and manuals that are different from those for the US market. By making printers without power supplies, plugs, or manuals, the Vancouver plant can ship undifferentiated printers anywhere. Only in Asia or Europe are the localized power supplies, plugs, and manuals installed.

An extreme form of differentiation is reported for IBM computers, which are manufactured using the same chips. Computers to be sold to the lower-end, slower market have their chips switched to a lower clock speed only just before they are shipped.

Delayed differentiation incorporates two options. One is the option to invest later. This has the benefit of the time value of money since the investment is postponed. More important, the investment—such as the customization of a printer with a 220V rather than 110V power supply—is not wasted in that we accurately produce the right type of printer.

The other option in delayed differentiation is the flexibility option. Here it is important to bear in mind that delayed differentiation works best only if the undifferentiated product can be used for multiple product lines that have uncorrelated demand. In this way, delayed differentiation is related to the idea of risk pooling (see section 10.3.1).

11.5.2 Detecting an Option for Being Flexible

As before, there is always the prerequisite that we learn about outcomes over time. In addition, an option for being flexible is usually present when the following conditions appear.

Multiple Types of Outcomes

Unlike other options in which there are simply alternative outcomes, an option for being flexible is, by definition, an option on different *types* of outcomes, such as hotel and theater outcomes.

Imperfectly Correlated Outcomes

As we have seen, these outcomes should also be imperfectly correlated for the option to be valuable. The imperfect correlation is the source for the risk-pooling effect, so that when the outcome for one type (say hotels) is down, the outcome for another (say theaters) is up. Since the option allows us the right to pick the best outcomes, we can avoid the downs and capture the ups.

Similarly Sized Outcomes

The two types of outcomes should also be similarly sized. If one type (say hotels) has much better outcomes than another (say theaters) under most circumstances, then there is little value in the flexibility: we would always pick the type with better outcomes.

11.6   Takeaways and Toolkit

In this chapter, we discussed why we have to dig below financial statements to better value a company's options.

• There are three main types of real options: options to start or expand later, options to end or shrink earlier, and options for being flexible in choosing between multiple *types* of outcomes.

• There are two main approaches to valuing options: the binomial and the Black-Scholes methods. The second is a continuous version of the former, which is discrete.

• An option to start or expand later is usually present when we can learn much about outcomes over time and there is a "ticket to play" that is needed early.

• An option to end or shrink earlier is usually present when there is negative net present value going forward and there is a viable release clause.

• An option for being flexible is usually present when we have different types of outcomes which are imperfectly correlated and are not similarly sized.

Table 11.4 summarizes the formulae for pricing the key options in the chapter.

11.7   Survey of Prior Research in One Paragraph

Real options have been an active topic for many years. Some experts include Avinash Dixit, Ian C. MacMillan, and Robert Pindyck, who have an authoritative text on the

Table 11.4
Toolkit: Pricing Formulae for Real Options

Option Type	Pricing Formula
Option to start or expand later	Binomial method: 1. Find the no-delay cash flows and their price today. 2. Compute the delta. 3. Replicate the option cash flows with borrowing/lending.
Option to end or shrink earlier	1. Construct a cash flow tree using up and down probabilities at each branch. 2. Assign abandonment values at the tree leaves. 3. Working back to the tree root, use the binomial method to price options at each branch.
Option in being flexible	1. Price the various options, as above. 2. Construct an option tree with these options at its leaves. 3. Now work backwards to the tree root to obtain the value of the flexibility option.

subject. From an operational angle, Marshall Fisher, Jan Hammond, and Ananth Raman have shown how firms like Sport Obermeyer, a skiwear maker, delay the production of less certain product lines, effectively incorporating an option to expand or shrink production according to later and better information. John Birge wrote an influential paper to show how we can use options in capacity planning. Awi Federgruen, Leroy Schwarz, Chris Tang, Paul Zipkin, and Hau Lee with Corey Billington are some of the pioneering researchers on the option embedded in delayed differentiation. Morris Cohen and Arnd Huchzermeier develop the early results on how multinationals can value the option of having production facilities in many countries. Some leading scholars who study operational flexibility include Rene Caldentey, Jiri Chod, Paul Enders, Vishal Gaur, Roman Kapuscinski, Sunder Kekre, David Simchi-Levi, Jan van Mieghem, Nils Rudi, Alan Scheller-Wolf, Nicola Secomandi, Sridhar Seshadri, and Beril Toktay.

11.8 Further Reading

Bettis, R. A. 1983. "Modern Financial Theory, Corporate Strategy and Public Policy: Three Conundrums." *Academy of Management Review* 8 (3): 406–415.

Birge, J. R. 2000. "Option Methods for Incorporating Risk into Linear Capacity Planning Models." *Manufacturing and Service Operations Management* 2 (1): 19.

Boyle, P. P. 1988. "A Lattice Framework for Option Pricing with Two State Variables." *Journal of Financial and Quantitative Analysis* 23 (1): 1–12.

Brealey, R. A., S. C. Myers, and F. Allen. 2006. *Principles of Corporate Finance*. Boston: McGraw-Hill/Irwin.

Buzacott, J. A., and J. G. Shanthikumar. 1993. *Stochastic Models of Manufacturing Systems*. Englewood Cliffs, NJ: Prentice-Hall.

Dixit, A. K., and R. S. Pindyck. 1994. *Investment under Uncertainty*. Princeton: Princeton University Press.

Enders, P., A. Scheller-Wolf, and N. Secomandi. 2008. "Interaction between Technology and Extraction Scaling Real Options in Natural Gas Production." Tepper School Working Paper 2008-E04.

Fisher, M. L., J. H. Hammond, W. R. Obermeyer, and A. Raman. 1994. "Making Supply Meet Demand in an Uncertain World." *Harvard Business Review* 72: 83–83.

Foster, D. P., and R. A. Stine. 2006. "Being Warren Buffett: A Classroom Simulation of Risk and Wealth When Investing in the Stock Market." *American Statistician* 60: 53–60.

Huchzermeier, A., and M. A. Cohen. 1996. "Valuing Operational Flexibility Under Exchange Rate Risk." *Operations Research* 44 (1): 100–113.

Kester, W. C. 1984 "Today's Options for Tomorrow's Growth." *Harvard Business Review* 62 (2): 153–160.

Lintner, J. 1965. "The Valuation of Risk Assets and the Selection of Risky Investments in Stock Portfolios and Capital Budgets." *Review of Economics and Statistics*: 13–37.

Markowitz, H. 1952. "Portfolio Selection." *Journal of Finance*: 77–91.

Morgan, J. 1995. *Riskmetrics Technical Manual*. New York: J. P. Morgan.

Sharpe, W. F. 1963. "A Simplified Model for Portfolio Analysis." *Management Science* 9 (2): 277–293.

Treynor, J. 1961. "Toward a Theory of Market Value of Risky Assets." Unpublished manuscript.

IV OPERATIONAL TURNAROUNDS

So we've invested. We now have to turn around the situation. The first three chapters of this part address the turnaround of three vital parts of the value chain: purchasing, production, and distribution. In the final chapter, we consider operational initiatives that are ongoing, to sustain a turnaround.

12 Turning Around Purchasing

For the average US manufacturer, purchases from suppliers constitute as much as 50% of its sales revenues. This percentage has been trending up, with increasing reliance on outsourcing even of services. Not surprisingly, the purchasing function has become strategic.

Yet there appear to be many challenges with the function. Many businesses cannot buy products at the right time and place. As a result, suppliers find themselves writing off and marking down enormous amounts of inventory, to the tune of about $30 billion for the food industry. These problems arise despite enormous efforts by businesses. To enhance feedback for purchasing, they have sunk substantial amounts in all manner of technologies, from point-of-sale scanners to electronic data interchange (EDI) and efficient consumer response (ECR). To follow customers' changing demands and to obtain better pricing and mitigate supplier stockouts, many businesses also now face "supplier creep," from the proliferation of suppliers over the years.

In many turnaround situations, rationalizing the supplier base can deliver significant benefits. We document some steps to reap these benefits.

12.1 Caveats about Rationalization

There is no denying that rationalization can be simultaneously rewarding and painful. A successful rationalization is likely to take heed of some caveats.

12.1.1 Balancing Short- and Long-Term Impact

We bear in mind that rationalizing operations can not only provide much needed degrees of freedom in a turnaround situation but, if properly thought out, may also offer the same for longer-term strategy—for example, smart capacity withdrawals and investments can reconfigure the competitive space. At the same time, we must be cautious about how less thoughtful rationalization can harm long-term prospects. For example, overly aggressive cost reduction may hamper flexibility and innovation. Therefore, these operational initiatives need to be considered in a broader picture that involves issues in marketing, finance, organization, and strategy.

12.1.2 Prioritizing Opportunities

Another caveat is about prioritization. In any turnaround situation, there are vast opportunities for improvement, but limited capacity for change. Not surprisingly, there is tremendous value in prioritizing these opportunities by: (1) the size of the potential improvement, and (2) the ease of accomplishing that improvement.

12.1.3 Accounting for Human Considerations

Issues of equity, social compacts, and other human considerations often arise in turnaround situations. While we do not elaborate on these in this book on operations, we should bear in mind that these issues are real and often interact with operational decisions.

12.2 Rationalize Supplier Base

Buying more from fewer suppliers increases the buyer's leverage in a number of ways. We should also not discount the value of *threatening* to rationalize the supplier base; sometimes that alone might be enough to deliver some of the benefits of increased leverage. It is important to emphasize that we have to be cautious about damaging long-standing relationships, and about the risks of having too few suppliers without backup capacity.

In many turnaround situations, the rationalization of the supplier base can deliver one of the quickest and most significant benefits, described below.

• *Better pricing.*   This might include compromising on buying in greater volume. It might also include better and more frequent promotional terms, especially passing on trade promotions given by the supplier's supplier to the supplier.

• *Better credit terms.*   As we know from section 2.1.3, standard business credit terms in the US range from 30 to 90 days. In a turnaround situation when cash is critical, the extension of credit terms can be a life-and-death issue. Furthermore, a buyer with more leverage can also negotiate for better discounts for payment on time, lower interest on late payment, or even consignment arrangements, in which the buyer does not take inventory until the stock is sold by the buyer.

• *Higher quality of service.*   This includes services such as responsiveness to changes in orders, queries about orders being shipped, shipping speed, etc. It can also include terms for returns and other quality problems.

• *Faster learning.*   With greater scale in the business with a buyer, a supplier can more rapidly learn what the buyer wants. There is some evidence that this learning is proportional to the volume of business between supplier and buyer, an effect called the "experience curve" (see section 3.2.2).

• *Greater investment by the supplier.* A major issue faced by suppliers is whether to invest in buyer-specific improvements. A rationalized supplier base, particularly when it is rationalized into a single-source purchasing strategy, can be a credible signal that the buyer wishes to enter into a long-term relationship with the supplier, alleviating the supplier's concern about "holdup" problems (concern that the buyer, after the supplier has invested in buyer-specific improvements, might turn around and press for lower prices by threatening to switch to another supplier).

• *Lower cost and higher quality of monitoring.* Not surprisingly, fewer suppliers can mean lower cost of monitoring. An important side effect is that the quality of monitoring can also improve if the buyer spends more time on the fewer suppliers. Another quality effect is that the reduction in monitoring effort is likely to be disproportionate to the number of suppliers, since fewer suppliers also means less heterogeneity among them. A final quality effect is that problems can surface earlier, leading to quicker and less costly resolution.

So how do we rationalize the supplier base? The number of suppliers may depend on the following factors, and an important way to think about them is whether these factors fit the business's overall strategy.

12.2.1 Competition versus Commitment

For example, Intel uses dual sourcing in which two competing suppliers keep each other on their toes. Toyota, on the other hand, emphasizes commitment in its overall strategy (see section 9.2), so it tends to use single sourcing.

12.2.2 Homogeneity versus Diversity

There is an argument for a small, homogeneous set of suppliers who can serve as backups for each other; for example, they may use similar production standards. However, some purchasing strategies also call for innovative suppliers, who tend to be nonstandard.

12.2.3 Hungry Newbies versus Strong Incumbents

New entrants—whether new to the supplier's industry or simply new to us—may offer better terms for their products, but they might also be financially less stable. Strong incumbents may be financially very solid, but could carry with them the baggage of bureaucracy. Some buyers insist on a threshold level of financial viability—for example Wal-mart insists that its suppliers not rely too much on just Wal-mart's business—but otherwise aim for "hungry newbies."

12.3 Design for Supply

We first need to address the issue of what strategy our supply chain should have. Then we consider the role our suppliers should play in the chosen strategy. Then we address two more specific issues: what types of products should be outsourced or offshored to suppliers, and whether we can even design products to make it easier for purchasing. In short, these are issues of strategic rather than tactical importance.

12.3.1 Architect the Right Supply Chain

A suitable starting point is to consider the nature of the demand for our product. At the extreme, we may classify the demand into functional and innovative products (see table 12.1). An example of a functional product is soup. It is a staple and its demand is fairly predictable. In contrast, fashion products are innovative, and their demand is hard to forecast accurately. There are, of course, products between these two extremes, but this spectrum serves to highlight the different implications for an appropriate supply chain (see table 12.2).

Research suggests that businesses with matching product and supply chain types do the best operationally and financially (see figure 12.1). But why would businesses have mismatched supply chains? For one, the type of product is only obvious after it is stated. Many personal computers may be functional, but some (e.g., iMacs) may be innovative. Conversely, many fashion items may seem innovative, but some (e.g., Gap T-shirts) may be functional. Another reason for mismatches is that businesses often start with a clean setup—selling functional products with an efficient supply chain—as reflected in the top left corner of figure 12.1. Over time, as they strive to match the competition, they introduce more innovative products, creeping to the top right cell.

This theory, backed up by empirical observations, also implies that most turnaround opportunities are in the top right rather than the bottom left cell. Fisher (2003) tells a

Table 12.1
Functional versus Innovative Products

	Functional	Innovative
Predictability (forecast accuracy at production)	High (90%)	Low (0% to 60%)
Product life cycle	More than 2 years	3 months to 1 year
Gross margin (price less variable cost, as a percent of price)	Up to 20%	More than 20%
Product variety (SKUs per category)	Up to 20	More, often millions
Stockout rate	1% to 2%	10% to 40%
Forced markdowns at season end (percent of full price)	0%	10% to 25%
Lead time for made-to-order products	6 months to 1 year	1 day to 2 weeks

Adapted from Fisher (1997). Figures are typical averages and ranges.

Table 12.2
Physically Efficient versus Market-Responsive Supply Chains

	Physically Efficient	Market Response
	→For functional products	→For innovative products
Primary purpose	Supply predictable demand at low cost	Respond quickly to unpredictable demand, to minimize over- and understocking
Inventory strategy	Generate high turns and minimize inventory throughout the supply chain	Deploy significant buffer stocks of parts or finished goods
Lead-time focus	Shorten lead time as long as it does not increase cost	Invest aggressively in ways to reduce lead time
Product design strategy	Maximize performance and minimize cost	Use modular design to postpone product differentiation
Approach to choosing suppliers	Select primarily for cost and quality	Select primarily for speed, flexibility, and quality

Source: Fisher (1997).

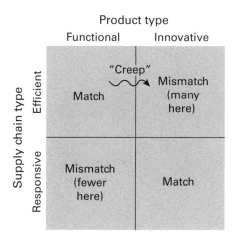

Figure 12.1
Match between type of product and supply chain.

typical story of how this happens. For years until the 1980s, IBM had an efficient but unresponsive supply chain, so that it had to tell its customers to wait for up to 14 months for a 360 mainframe. As the market pulled IBM toward more innovative products—minis and personal computers—its lag in restructuring its supply chain led it to the top right corner of mismatch in figure 12.1.

The type of supply chain in turn implies different roles for suppliers, which we discuss next.

12.3.2   Consider a Full Range of Possible Supplier Roles

There is really a wide range of supplier roles, and the chosen role should fit with the buyer's (and supplier's) purchasing strategy. This is summarized in table 12.3.

The table suggests that these roles are sufficiently distinct. For example, it is difficult to maintain a coherent operational stance while taking on both transactional and equity ownership roles. It makes more sense to adopt one primary role, even if this may be supplemented by other roles.

12.3.3   Outsource or Offshore with Differentiated Capacities

The opportunity to outsource or offshore is often tied to the strategic questions of "what is core" and what is not, and whether the tasks to be outsourced or offshored have agency problems (e.g., are difficult to monitor, difficult to evaluate, give the supplier no incentive to invest in improvements). Here, we focus on operational aspects of outsourcing and offshoring, assuming that the decision has been taken to do so.

An important example is the accurate response technique. In section 11.3.6, we described how Sport Obermeyer, a skiwear maker, is able to accurately forecast demand by delaying

Table 12.3
Range of Supplier Roles

Supplier's Role	Buyer's Purchasing Strategy
Consignment	"Buyer" does not take ownership of supplies. Can be viewed as supplier leasing distribution space from a distributor.
Transactional	Cost-based. Information technology and price discovery mechanisms (e.g., an auction market) are prevalent.
Value-added	Vendor-managed inventories (VMI); third- and fourth-party logistics (3PL, 4PL). Other value-added could include joint efforts in design, production, marketing, information sharing (such as forecast sharing), and certification programs (e.g., ISO 9000).
Relationship-based	"Toyota production system" relationships. Supply is mission-critical to buyer. This is a long-term version of the value-added role of suppliers.
Licensing and franchising	The supplier is a licensee of the buyer, or the buyer is a franchisee of the supplier. Each is legally liable to use the other's services for the bulk of its business; a captive relationship.
Equity ownership or long-term credit arrangement	The buyer may take an equity stake in the supplier, or provide long-term credit to the supplier in the form of a bond.

production. But Sport Obermeyer does something even smarter: it divides its products into low-certainty and high-certainty categories (this is described in section 13.2). The high-certainty category is the one with the option to start later. This category of products is produced in US factories, where the lead time is short.

However, the company makes its low-certainty products in Chinese factories. While the lead time needs to be longer, the cost is much lower. This allows Sport Obermeyer to intelligently allocate the products to be outsourced or offshored, with a reasonable lead time and cost.

12.3.4   Standardize and Modularize Product Requirements

This is sometimes known as design to cost. The idea is that, without compromising product design or quality, we can often specify product requirements at higher, more abstract levels. This allows the purchasing function greater leeway to find standard parts, explore substitutes, and importantly to buy modules rather than components. Failure rates tend to increase with the number of suppliers; procuring modules from one supplier can increase reliability.

12.4   Reconfigure Sourcing Contracts

The demand for most products is uncertain. Suppose we are John Lewis, a department store in London, and one of the products we sell is the Apple iPod. We purchase iPods at the wholesale price of £172 a unit from Apple and resell them at £189. But the tricky thing about iPods—and many other products—is that they can be dated quickly. If we cannot sell the iPod this season, we have to mark it down to just £70. So our question is how many iPods we should carry to balance over- versus understocking costs.

One approach is to use a formulation called *newsvendor analysis*. Let us use these symbols:

C_o = unit cost of overstock,

C_u = unit cost of understock,

$\Phi(I)$ = cumulative probability that demand is lower than inventory stock I. That is, $\Phi(I)$ is the probability of overstocking if we hold I units of inventory, and $1 - \Phi(I)$ is the probability of understocking.

To maximize profit, we want to balance these two costs:

$$C_o \times \Phi(I) = C_u \times [1 - \Phi(I)], \tag{13}$$

or

$\Phi(I) = C_u/(C_u + C_o)$, which we can call the service probability.

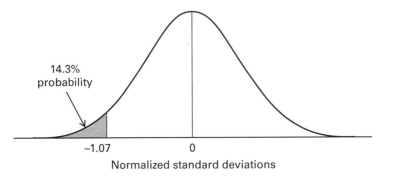

14.3%
probability

−1.07   0

Normalized standard deviations

Figure 12.2
The probability of overstocking when demand is below stocking level.

In our John Lewis-and-iPod example, we have:

$C_o = £172 − 70 = £102,$

$C_u = = £189 − 172 = £17,$

$\Phi(I) = 17/(17 + 102) = 0.143.$

Now how do we translate this to I, the stocking quantity we wish to determine? This depends on the probability distribution of demand, and for large values we can assume a normal distribution.

So first we find the standard normal Z statistic corresponding to the probability of 0.143. Using a standard normal table or the Excel function normsinv(0.143), we see that the Z is −1.07. This is shown in figure 12.2.

Next we estimate the mean and standard deviation of the demand distribution, say from historical numbers. Say we have these:

μ = mean of demand = 1,000 copies, and

σ = standard deviation of demand = 500 copies.

Then the optimal inventory is given by this formula:

$I = \mu + Z \times \sigma = 1,000 − 1.07 \times 500 = 467$ units.   (14)

We can interpret the μ as that part of inventory catering to our mean demand, and $Z \times \sigma$ as the additional safety stock we need in case demand is more than mean demand.

The above is an analytical result. Do retailers stock this optimal level? One intriguing observation is that stockouts are pervasive. A typical blogger comment is: "Today I went shopping for an 8GB iPod Touch in [sic] John Lewis . . . but . . . they didn't have any 8GB iPod Touches, or the 16 GB model, or even the 32 GB . . ."[1]

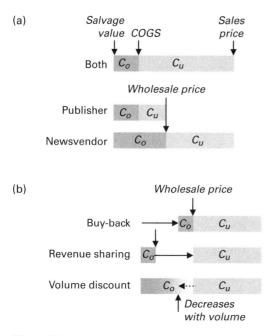

(b)

Figure 12.3
Double marginalization and its fix. Double marginalization (a); reconfiguring the newsvendor's situation (b).

Is this just a consumer perception despite John Lewis's optimal stocking level, or do retailers indeed stock less than optimally? It turns out that newsvendor analysis does provide the optimal stocking level for the retailer, but this optimal is small than the optimal for the supply chain as a whole—that is, if manufacturer and retailer were the same company. In other words, in a supply chain where the manufacturer and retailer are separate, the retailer—looking at its own situation—would stock less than if the manufacturer and retailer were the same company.

Figure 12.3 illustrates what C_u and C_o might be in the two setups. First consider the case in which Apple is both manufacturer and retailer ("both"), as in panel (a). We can picture that the service probability $C_u/(C_u + C_o)$—the light gray bar divided by both dark and light gray bars—is fairly high. To explain with numbers, suppose Apple's manufacturing cost is £108 (see table 12.4). If Apple were both manufacturer and retailer, we would have:

$C_o = £108 - 70 = £38,$

$C_u = = £189 - 108 = £81,$

$\Phi(I) = 81/(81 + 38) = 0.681.$

Table 12.4
Apple's Cost of Manufacturing an iPod

Supplier(s)	Component Type	£
Toshiba Semiconductor, Samsung, Hynix, Micron	Flash memory: NAND, 32Gbit x 2 (8GB total)*	25.30
EPSON, Toshiba, Matsushita, Sharp	Display: 3.5-inch diagonal, 16M color TFT, 320 × 480 pixels	13.91
Balda/TPK, Wintek, Optrex, HonHai	Touchscreen assembly and integration	13.73
Samsung Semiconductor	Video/applications processor, ARM core	8.34
Samsung Semiconductor	K4X1GA53PE-XGC3, SDRAM, mobile DDR, 1Gb(bit), package-on-package	7.59
Murata	WLAN module value line item, IEEE 802.11b/g	4.11
WUS Printed Circuit Co. Ltd.	Main PCB, 8-layer rigid/flex FR4/Kapton, 2+4+2, lead	2.71
Broadcom	BCM5974 touchscreen controller	1.87
NXP	Power management IC	1.65
	Battery: lithium ion, 3.7V, 800mAh	1.49
STMicroelectronics	LIS302DL motion sensor/accelerometer	1.42
Texas Instruments	THS7318YZFT video driver	0.70
National Semiconductor	LM2512ASN 24-bit RGB interface serializer	0.68
Wolfson Microelectronics	WM8758BG audio codec	0.66
	Other material costs	10.21
	Currency conversion from manufacturer's costs	3.70
	Delivery to London	9.80
	Total delivered to John Lewis	108

Source: iSuppl, October 2007.

Now the optimal stocking level aims to overly low demand 68.1% of time; see figure 12.4. Put another way, we can stock higher, because the optimal Z is a higher normsinv(0.681) = 0.469.

With the same mean (1,000 units) and standard deviations (500 units), our optimal stocking level is now 1,000 + 0.469 × 500 = 1,235 iPods, almost three times that when John Lewis was optimizing its own stocking level.

We can see this in figure 12.3, panel (a), where the bottom part shows Apple selling iPods to John Lewis at a wholesale price. Notice that their *individual* service probabilities—the light gray bar divided by both dark and light gray bars—are now a lot smaller than that for both as a whole. This means that each will stock a lot less than is maximally profitable for both of them as a whole. This suboptimal situation is called *double marginalization*.

There are opportunities to enlarge the pie by reconfiguring how Apple sells to John Lewis. In panel (b) of figure 12.3, we see that one solution is to reconfigure the contract so that Apple has to buy back John Lewis's unsold copies at some price. Now, from the latter's perspective, we have reduced C_o, so that its service probability $C_u/(C_u + C_o)$ is closer to the size we have for both as a whole. The disadvantage of buy-back contracts is

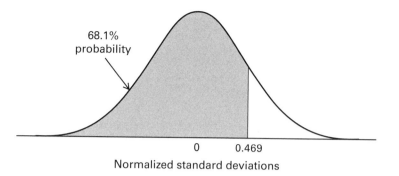

Figure 12.4
The probability of overstocking when demand is below stocking level (combined manufacturer and retailer).

that there are now additional costs incurred with the returns, and indeed such contracts may dampen the newsvendor effort to sell more.

Another way to reduce C_o is to reduce the wholesale price. This might leave too much for John Lewis. Partly to counter that and to incentivize the retailer to put in the maximum effort and set the best retail price, the contract could also specify that the revenue (or margin) be shared with Apple. Looking at panel (b), we see that the service probability is again closer to that for the manufacturer-and-retailer as a whole. A key issue with revenue-sharing contracts is that the manufacturer has to find a cost-effective way to ensure that the revenues are truthfully reported.

Yet another way to increase the pie is to use volume discount contracts. As panel (b) indicates, the reduction of the wholesale price when John Lewis buys more both incentivizes it to put in more effort and moves toward a service probability that once again goes closer to the probability when manufacturer-and-retailer are as treated as a whole. One issue with volume discount contracts is for durable goods is that it encourages the retailer to place lumpy volume orders and sell the goods at the regular pace. The retailer loses information on actual demand, and the lumpy orders increase its variability.

A final important approach is to let the retailer get more information before placing orders. This way, the retailer may have a suboptimal service probability as in panel (a), but, with more information and therefore a smaller standard deviation, the deviation in safety stock—which is the Z from the service probability times the standard deviation in equation (14)—will also be proportionately smaller.

In short, there are many ways to reconfigure sourcing contracts so that we enlarge the pie between manufacturer and retailer. How much each gets depends on each party's bargaining strength, but enlarging the pie is often the best first step.

12.5   Reengineer Purchasing Process

In the 1980s, Ford was surprised to find that its accounts payable department had 400 people while Mazda's had just 5, even though the two companies had similar sales volumes. What followed at Ford, a reengineering of its purchasing process, led to a 75% headcount reduction and a revolution in the operational processes of many departments across many corporations.

Some specific examples of process reengineering are given below.

12.5.1   Design End-to-End Processes, Eliminate Handoffs

Many processes are fossilized with multiple handoffs from one party to another. In rationalizing processes, it makes sense to start afresh, taking the viewpoint of the "customer"— whether a supplier or an internal client.

Figure 12.5 shows a simple example of designing from the supplier's point of view. The supplier takes the buyer as one entity, not three, in which documents are handed off from purchasing to receiving, and receiving to accounts payable.

By eliminating these handoffs, we can substantially reduce the elapsed time and cost of the process. Actual cost savings can be much larger, since this example does not show complications arising from associated processes such as returns, payment to and from the buyer's and supplier's banks, or linkages to logistics partners.

12.5.2   Balance the Load

Purchasing work almost always get bunched up, say, at month end, because many suppliers issue invoices at that time to fit with their fiscal calendars. To the extent possible, it makes sense to find ways to level out the load over time. An important contributor to load requirements is variability (see also section 7.2.3, and note 2 in that chapter). This might involve standardizing purchase orders and invoicing forms and timing, and reducing errors and returns.

12.5.3   Differentiate versus Standardize

Not all purchases and suppliers are of the same importance, so it would make sense to provide stronger support for more critical purchases. For instance, we might involve critical purchases and suppliers in much tighter roles—even assuming equity ownership of suppliers as in table 12.3—but adopt a transactional pose with other suppliers. On the other hand, there are situations—such as in processing—where standardization helps. Examples include standardized order forms and payment procedures.

12.5.4   Automate

Automation could reduce errors and labor cost; more importantly, it could reduce inventory. A key idea is that information and inventory could be substitutes for one another.

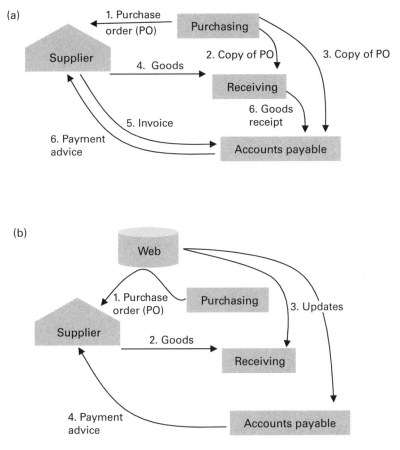

Figure 12.5
Process redesign. Before (a); after (b). Adapted from Hammer (1990).

When we have more information (properly used), we can reduce the amount of inventory we carry. A particularly important type of information is that on inventory up the supply chain, on suppliers and their suppliers. This is because information distortion becomes greater as the supply chain becomes longer.

12.5.5 Centralize versus Decentralize

How much to centralize? One answer to this perennial question is to centralize when the benefits of centralization—such as scale and risk control—outweigh the benefits of decentralization—such as greater latitude to experiment and the opportunity to leverage information available at the front line. The purchasing strategy (as in table 12.3) plays an important role in this decision. For example, if most purchasing decisions are transactional, it makes sense to centralize. If most decisions are relationship-based, it makes sense to rely on those managing the relationships.

12.6   Takeaways

Turning around a business is complicated, but it can be made less so by going through it systematically. In this chapter, we start with purchasing. This involves a few strategic initiatives:

• Rationalize the supplier base: should your suppliers compete for your business or commit to it? Should they be homogeneous or diverse, new or old?

• Design for supply: design for efficiency if your product is function, for responsiveness if it is innovative.

• Reconfigure supply contracts. Address double marginalization using buy-backs, revenue sharing, or other devices.

• Reengineer the purchasing process: load-balance, automate, eliminate handoffs, and consider how much differentiation and centralization the process should handle.

12.7   Survey of Prior Research in One Paragraph

Marshall Fisher and Saibal Ray are some of the leading scholars on the design of supply chains. Double marginalization dates back to the prolific economist Abba Lerner. Sourcing contracts became a major field of study in operations management led by, among others, Gerard Cachon, Fangruo Chen, Awi Federgruen, Martin Lariviere, Sergei Netessine, V. Padmanabhan, Erica Plambeck, S. J. Whang, Terry Taylor, and Yusheng Zheng. In particular, Justin Ren and Y. P. Zhou consider contracts for outsourcing call centers, and Gad Allon and Jan van Mieghem study global dual sourcing. John Birge looks at trade credit and its impact on operations, for which we provide a reference below. The reengineering revolution was popularized by Michael Hammer.

12.8   Further Reading

Allon, G., and J. A. van Mieghem. 2010. "Global Dual Sourcing: Tailored Base-Surge Allocation to Near-and Offshore Production." *Management Science* 56 (1): 110.

Cachon, G. P. 2003. "Supply Chain Coordination with Contracts." In S. Graves and T. de Kok, eds., *Handbooks in Operations Research and Management Science*, 229–340. New York: North-Holland.

Cachon, G. P., and M. A. Lariviere. 2005. "Supply Chain Coordination with Revenue-Sharing Contracts: Strengths and Limitations." *Management Science* 51 (1): 30–44.

Chen, F., A. Federgruen, and Y. S. Zheng. 2001. "Coordination Mechanisms for a Distribution System with One Supplier and Multiple Retailers." *Management Science* 47 (5): 693–708.

Fisher, M. L. 2003. "What Is the Right Supply Chain for Your Product?" *Operations Management* 105: 73.

Hammer, M. 1990. "Reengineering Work: Don't Automate, Obliterate." *Harvard Business Review* 68 (4): 104–112.

Lerner, A. P. 1934. "The Concept of Monopoly and the Measurement of Monopoly Power." *Review of Economic Studies* 1 (3): 157–175.

Ray, S., S. Li, and Y. Song. 2005. "Tailored Supply Chain Decision Making under Price-Sensitive Stochastic Demand and Delivery Uncertainty." *Management Science* 51 (12): 1873.

Taylor, T. A., and E. L. Plambeck. 2007. "Supply Chain Relationships and Contracts: The Impact of Repeated Interaction on Capacity Investment and Procurement." *Management Science* 53 (10): 1577–1593.

Ren, J., and Y. P. Zhou. 2008. "Call Center Outsourcing: Coordinating Staffing Level and Service Quality." *Management Science* 54 (2): 369.

13 Turning Around Production

In production, the core turnaround opportunities are in installing the appropriate process, building forecasting capabilities, addressing capacity investments, and driving down costs. Another opportunity arises from rationalizing production processes; this is similar to the reengineering described in the previous chapter.

13.1 Ensuring Process-Product Fit

Many high-performing businesses—or at least companies that stay in business—match their process structure with their product type. In figure 13.1, we see examples at the industry level. There tends to be a migration of product and process type to the lower right over time, as products and processes mature. This provides a way to anticipate future process changes and perhaps necessary investments.

Should we find ourselves off the diagonal, we should ask whether our processes have been misconfigured. That may not always be the case. Hayes and Wheelwright (1979) give an example of a circuit board maker who uses an assembly line to create low-volume products. On the surface, this looks like misconfiguration. But on closer inspection, the circuit board maker is really selling design capability—there are many designs on a board—so its configuration is really in line with the matrix.

13.2 Building Forecasting Capability with a Consensus Approach

Broadly speaking, there are two ways to match supply with uncertain demand: put in place a responsive supply process, or better forecast demand.

Sport Obermeyer provides an interesting example of a company that is able to achieve better demand forecasting ("early detection" of demand conditions) and more responsive production by reconfiguring its processes, rather than just by investments in capabilities and capacities.

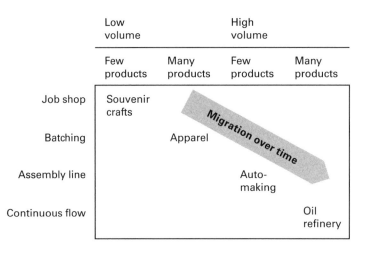

Figure 13.1
Matching process to product. Adapted from Hayes and Wheelwright (1979).

To better forecast demand, Obermeyer uses a forecasting committee of six staff with different functions such as purchasing and sales. This exploits the diversity of information the staff have among them, and allows the company to get a sense of not just the mean forecast, but the probable forecast error. Empirically, they find that low agreement among the committee members is highly suggestive of high forecast error (see figure 13.2). This provides more accurate early detection of demand. As time goes on, the committee updates its forecasts, further improving them.

13.3   Rationalizing Production Assets with Newsvendor Analysis

In turnaround situations, it is not surprising to find that many types of assets—inventory, cash holdings, and capacities—are bloated. But determining the right level is critical for many businesses. We focus here on inventory as an important example: the average US retailer holds as much as 53% of its current assets as inventory. For retailers as well as many other industries, inventory is also a key determinant of profitability.

Although this section studies the question of how much inventory our business should hold, the technique is applicable to working capital in general—such as cash held and plant capacities. The crux is to balance the cost of overinvesting versus underinvesting. The newsvendor analysis of section 12.4 is the right tool for this.

The newsvendor situation is distinctive in that understocking leads to lost sales, and each analysis is for just one period. But we can extend it to situations in which sales are not lost but are backlogged (we would modify the understocking cost to exclude lost margins), or in which orders placed get delivered only after a lead time (we would modify

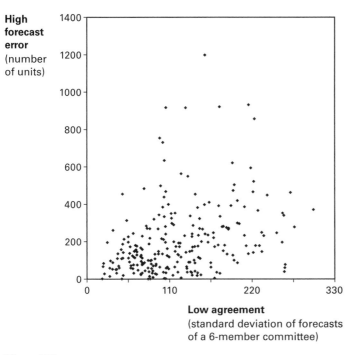

High forecast error (number of units)

Low agreement
(standard deviation of forecasts
of a 6-member committee)

Figure 13.2
Low agreement among committee members suggests high forecast errors. Source: Fisher (2009).

the probability distribution of demand so that its mean and standard deviation are over the duration of the lead time, rather than over just one period).

13.3.1 Additional Rationalization with Pooling

Another extension is to reduce inventory by risk pooling. It might seem obvious that pooling is a good idea, but many warehouse managers "actively horde inventory for 'their own' customers. This often happens with regional customer service departments that are linked to specific warehouses. . . . Some managers say, 'we don't want to fill orders from other warehouses because the sales figures get into our demand history and cause us to carry more inventory."[1] Therefore, pooling needs to be accompanied by a restructuring of incentives and some education.

We described one type of pooling with delayed differentiation (section 11.5.1) in which we can delay differentiating our work in progress into finished products as long as possible. We now go into the analytics of pooling two products. Suppose we have:

μ = mean of each product's demand,

σ = standard deviation of each product's demand, and

ρ = correlation coefficient of the products' demands.

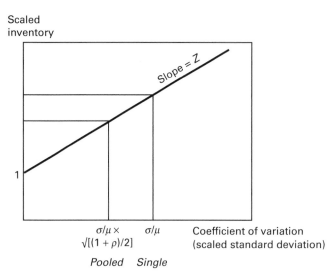

Figure 13.3
Lower inventory with product pooling.

If demand for the differentiated finished products is imperfectly correlated, then we can reduce the undifferentiated work-in-progress inventory, because the standard deviation of the pool of products increases less than the mean of the pool:

μ' = mean of the two products' demand = 2μ, and

σ' = standard deviation of the two = $\sigma\sqrt{(2 + 2\rho)}$.

To see how this reduces inventory proportionately, we scale equation (14) by dividing both sides by μ:

$$I/\mu = 1 + Z\,(\sigma/\mu).$$

In other words, scaled inventory increases with scaled standard deviation σ/μ, which is called the *coefficient of variation*; see figure 13.3.

When we pool two products, the coefficient of variation is $\sigma\sqrt{(2 + 2\rho)}/2\mu = \sigma/\mu\sqrt{[(1 + \rho)/2]}$. Since ρ is between 0 and 1, the factor $\sqrt{[(1 + \rho)/2]}$ is at most 1, so the pooled coefficient of variation is at most σ/μ. At its best when the products are perfectly negatively correlated ($\rho = -1$), the scaled inventory is 1, or I is just the mean demand, and we do not need any safety stock.

13.3.2   Even Smarter Rationalization with Chaining

It turns out that we do not really need completely flexible assets—such as inventory or capacities—to achieve pooling. Consider figure 13.4, panel (a), in which each asset can

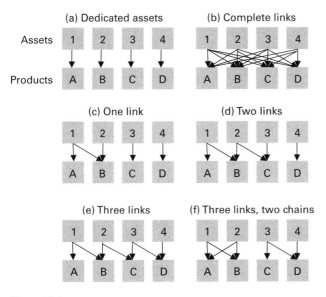

Figure 13.4
Chaining achieves flexibility. Adapted from Jordan and Graves (1995).

only produce one type of product. The kind of pooling described in the previous section is shown in panel (b), in which any asset can be used for any product. But what if, as in panel (c), only asset 1 is flexible enough to produce products A or B? This is a one-link configuration. Panels (d) and (e) show two- and three-link configurations.

Suppose demand not immediately served is lost. In figure 13.5, we compare these configurations on two dimensions, expected sales and lost sales, and it turns out that just a few links go a long way in reaching almost the best results we expect from the complete linkage configuration.

In figure 13.4, panel (f), we show a different configuration, in which we also have three links but configuration is broken into two chains. Another finding is that such fragmentation greatly degrades performance.

Finally, research also shows that in deciding for which product types an asset should be flexible, it does not matter too much that we connect the most negatively correlated products. As long as a chain is linked, the performance is almost as good no matter how we configure the flexibility.

More generally, this is about where the best places to be flexible are. Analytical solutions are still being developed, and current efforts have mostly used algorithms and simulations.

13.4 Rationalizing Service Assets with Queueing Analysis

Production assets handle the uncertainty of demand by having inventory. Of course, there are variants of what happens when there is insufficient stock: lost sales (when customers

Figure 13.5
Illustrative performance of chain configurations.

take their business elsewhere) or backlogged sales (when they wait until new inventory arrives).

In the service industry, there is no inventory. In these cases, the uncertainty of demand is also reflected directly in lost sales (when customers can't wait) or waiting time (when they can wait). But instead of using inventory to manage the demand uncertainty, we have to directly use the capacity of service assets such as hotel rooms, hospital operating rooms, and bank tellers.

13.4.1   When Customers Cannot Wait

Consider the case of hospital operating rooms. We have two ways to go: increasing the capacity of these rooms (e.g., more support staff for surgeons so as to turn these rooms around more frequently) or having more rooms.

Consider the first approach: sizing the capacity with just one operating room. Customers (i.e., patients who need surgery) cannot wait and are diverted to other hospitals, so the diversion constitutes lost profits to the hospital in question. Our hospital has to balance the cost of higher capacity against the cost of losing customers. These are reflected in its profit function:

$$\pi(C) = margin\,with\,no\,loss - server\,cost - lost\,margin$$
$$= D \times m - C \times c_c - D \times P_1 \times m$$

where:

D = demand rate, in units per year,

m = margin per unit, in \$,

C = capacity, in units per year,

c_c = cost of capital, in \$ per year for every unit of capacity,

P_1 = fraction of customers lost with one server[2] = $D/(C + D)$.

Using some calculus,[3] we see that profit is maximized at that value of C when

$$c_c = \frac{mD^2}{(C+D)^2},$$

or $C = D\left(\sqrt{\frac{m}{c_c}} - 1\right).$

This value of C is defined only when m is at least c_c, which is what we would expect since otherwise this is not a viable business. And as we would also expect, the more important lost margins—captured by m—are relative to capacity cost—captured by c_c—the more we invest in capacity C over some level of demand D.

Taking the second approach, we can see whether adding a second operating room might provide higher profits. To do this, we simply compare the profit function above (now assuming that C is given and fixed) and the function with two operating rooms:

$$\pi(C) = margin\, with\, no\, loss - servers\, cost - lost\, margin$$
$$= D \times m - 2C \times c_c - D \times P_2 \times m,$$

where P_2 is fraction of demand lost when we have two operating rooms (see note 2 of this chapter). Naturally, if two rooms are better, we would check whether three might be even better, and so on.

Not surprisingly, this gets more complicated as we investigate both approaches simultaneously: having higher capacity and having more rooms.

13.4.2 When Customers Wait

Again, there are two approaches: increasing the capacity of the operating room or having more rooms. But now our cost is not in lost customers but in customer waits. This cost could manifest itself, for example, in lost goodwill or future sales.

In the case where we have one server, the tradeoff is reflected in the profit function:

$$\pi(C) = margin\, with\, no\, wait - server\, cost - waiting\, cost,$$
$$= D \times m - C \times c_c - D \times \frac{1}{C} \frac{D}{C-D} \frac{cv_D^2 + cv_C^2}{2} \times c_w,$$

where D, m, C, and c_c are defined as in the previous section, $\frac{1}{C} \frac{D}{C-D} \frac{cv_D^2 + cv_C^2}{2}$ = hours of waiting time per unit, in a standard formula, cv_D^2 and cv_C^2 are the squared coefficients of variation related to D and C,[4] and c_w = cost of waiting, in \$ per hour of waiting time per unit.

Again, using some calculus and using the reasonable assumption that

$$\frac{cv_D^2 + cv_C^2}{2}$$

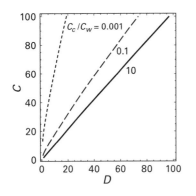

Figure 13.6
Capacity response to demand when customers wait, for different values of c_c/c_w.

is 1,[5] we see that profit is maximized at that C when:

$$\frac{c_c}{c_w} = \frac{(2C-D)D^2}{\left(C^2 - CD\right)^2}.$$

Although we cannot solve for C, we can see how it responds to D for different values of c_c/c_w (that is, the ratio of capacity to waiting cost).

In figure 13.6, we see that when the c_c/c_w ratio is small—capacity is a lot less costly than waiting—the optimal capacity C is high for every level of demand D. When the ratio is high, waiting is relatively costless and we need much lower C for every level of D.

As in the previous section, we should also investigate other ways of sizing capacity, by increasing the number of rooms or increasing both the capacity and the number of rooms.

13.5   Rationalizing Capacities with Competitive Capacity Analysis

In the early 1970s, Du Pont significantly expanded its capacity to manufacture titanium dioxide, a whitener used in materials such as paint. As a consequence, it was able to preempt capacity expansion by key competitors such as Kerr McGee, contributing to Du Pont's leadership in the industry. Indeed, research by McKinsey and academics suggests that businesses can sometimes even shrink their capacities preemptively to gain leadership. We now turn to this issue of rationalizing capacity.

So far, our analysis has been internally focused on our own business. We take as given that unit cost of the assets (for example, a unit of inventory stock) is going to be about the same no matter how much inventory we hold. While this may be true in many cases, it is not always so and most likely not for assets that involve large, fixed-cost investments. Recall from section 3.2 that the unit cost of plant capacity tends to go down by the cube of the square root of capacity size.

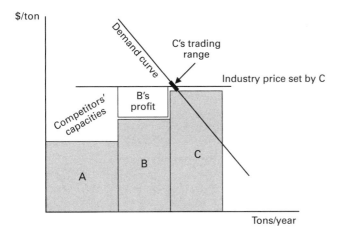

Figure 13.7
Competitive capacity analysis.

This connection between how much capacity we should invest in and our unit cost also affects pricing, and in particular how we and our competitors set prices. So we have to start accounting for competitive dynamics. In particular, because the capacity investments are large, they can greatly affect the dynamics.

Such scenarios are most common for commodity- and asset-intensive industries. In these scenarios, a useful tool for assessing how much capacity a business should have is competitive capacity analysis, based on the microeconomic supply curve.

Consider three plants A, B, and C with capacities and per-unit costs as shown in figure 13.7. The capacities effectively form the supply curve. Suppose that the demand curve is as shown. In this scenario, the price and quantity traded are decided by plant C, and indicated by the thick-line trading range. At the left end of the trading range, C has some margin but sells nothing. At the right end, C sells something but at zero margin. So C sets its price somewhere within the range to maximize its profit. At this price, both A and B are comfortably profitable; B's profit is as shown in the black empty box. We say that C offers a *price umbrella* for A and B.

Competitive capacity analysis provides a mechanism for exploring the dynamics of capacity expansion and shrinkage. Suppose we expand plant B, as in figure 13.8. Crucially, plant B expands by an increment so that C is pushed off to the right beyond its old trading range. Now C is no longer profitable and has to withdraw from the market; it could be mothballed or dismantled altogether, depending on the option value of these decisions (see section 11.4).

The new trading range is set by B. Indeed, B's profit increases (compare the size of the old dashed rectangle to the size of the new full-line rectangle). Of course, we have made a few assumptions. For example, new entrants do not have a lower cost structure than C,

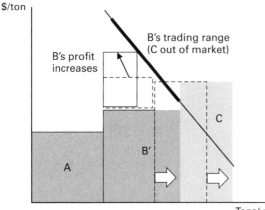

Figure 13.8
Competitive capacity analysis with expansion by plant B to B′.

so that they can enter the market and therefore decide the price. We also assume that the demand curve is steep enough so that when B shrinks its production, price increases more than demand shrinks. We also assume that B does not own C, for if it did, B would not even need to expand capacity to improve its profit. It could just shrink the amount produced.

But what if B is not allowed to push out a competitor C only to increase prices? What if B shrinks its production so that it affords C a wider trading range? Figure 13.9 shows that it is possible that B's profit will again increase. As before, this increase, if any, depends on a steep demand curve. This time, it also depends on how C responds to the opportunity of a wider trading range.

The framework of competitive capacity analysis provides a mechanism for us to explore all sorts of other capacity scenarios. For example, there might be new capacities, perhaps added by incumbents and perhaps by new entrants, at different unit cost levels. The framework provides a way for us to think through what happens to the price umbrella and what happens to each competitor's profits.

Another consideration: what if the optimal capacity as determined from the competitive capacity analysis deviates from the optimal capacity suggested by the newsvendor analysis? Suppose we want to hold more inventory I' rather than the optimal inventory. Then the cost of deviation comes into play because the expected cost of overstocking exceeds the expected cost of understocking. Following equation (13), and recalling that C_o and C_u are the costs of overstocking and understocking and $\Phi(.)$ is the cumulative probability function, this is:

$$\text{cost of deviation} = C_o \times \Phi(I') - C_u \times [1 - \Phi(I')].$$

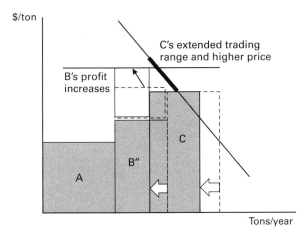

Figure 13.9
Competitive capacity analysis with reduced production by plant B to B″.

We can find $\Phi(I')$ by looking up the standard normal table using $Z' = (I' - \mu)/\sigma$, where, as before, we first determine μ and σ, the mean and standard deviation of the distribution of I'. We should then make our final capacity decision by weighing the benefit of the capacity decision from the competitive capacity analysis against the cost of deviating from the newsvendor analysis.

13.6 Driving Down Unit Costs with Experience Curves

In section 3.2.2 we saw how unit costs may go down with cumulative units. Instead of passively waiting for cumulative units, we can actively push down the experience curve in a turnaround situation.

Consider the situation in figure 13.10. We could reduce prices to point X, which could increase our units produced and sold. The increased cumulative units leads to lower unit cost—shown by the first downward arrow—which allows us to further reduce prices, gain cumulative volume, and further reduce unit costs. With diverging price and experience curves as shown, we enter a virtuous cycle. But we might also (and eventually) face a situation as in figure 13.11, in which the price and experience curves converge. Then we face a limit to how much cost reduction we can drive.

When do we face diverging and converging curves, and more pertinently, how can we get diverging curves? To answer these questions, we need to understand not only the slope of the experience curve but also the slope of the price curve. And pricing is importantly driven by the interaction of consumer demand and competitive pressure.

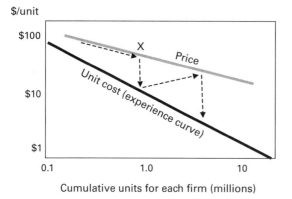

Figure 13.10
Driving down unit cost with an experience curve.

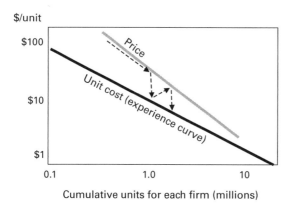

Figure 13.11
Limits to driving down unit cost with an experience curve.

13.6.1 Competitive Dynamics

Figure 13.12 shows the typical dynamics of an industry. Consider first the "aggressive pricing" curve indicated by the curving solid gray line. In the early stages, to the left of point A, there is little consumer demand, and prices are below cost. But once past A when unit costs have dropped, incumbents might be aggressive in keeping prices high. They enjoy superior margins until point B, when the margins attract new entrants, which quickly squeeze margins until C, when the industry stabilizes. At each point, of course, there may be some turbulence, with some competitors dropping out. But the overall pattern has been observed for an enormous number of industries, from handheld calculators and electronic

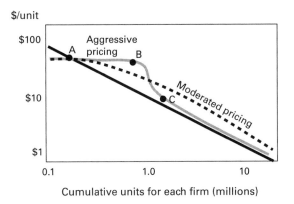

Figure 13.12
The dynamics of experience and price curves.

watches to steel and polyvinyl chloride. The price and experience curves diverge between A and B, resembling the situation we see in figure 13.10. The curves converge between B and C, resembling figure 13.11.

An alternative pricing strategy is to be more moderate, as indicated by the dotted line in figure 13.12. We need to carefully analyze each situation so as to determine whether the overall value of our business is better off with aggressive or moderated needs. But these dynamics suggest that, in seeking to turn around the fortunes of a business, we need to be cognizant of how short-term gains—represented by the fat margins between A and B—might be gained at the expense of long-term value.

The dynamics also suggest that it might be possible to leapfrog the competition by preempting investments in capturing market share and therefore cumulative units, especially when the curves diverge. Bausch & Lomb aggressively expanded its Soflens manufacturing capacity, keeping prices down and gaining market share from 55% in 1980 to 65% in 1983. It achieved competitively lower unit costs so that, despite its aggressive pricing, it earned margins 20 to 30 percentage points greater than its competitors.

13.6.2   Advanced Topic: How Long Does It Take to Catch Up on the Experience Curve?

To see how difficult it is to catch up, consider how fast a second-mover firm has to grow to catch up with the first mover's cumulative units. Suppose the first mover's volume (not cumulative volume) grows at a compounded rate of g percent a year, and the second mover starts later at time L. If it wants to catch up with the first mover by time T, how fast does it need to grow?

Denote the second mover's continuously compounded growth rate as h. The units sold by each firm at time t are as follows, since they are continuously compounded:

Units

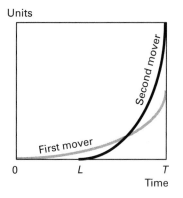

Figure 13.13
Units sold over time, for first and second movers.

First mover: $e^{gt} - 1$ units, and

Second mover: $e^{h(t-L)} - 1$ units.

Figure 13.13 depicts these growth rates. Note that we draw them as increasing, but they could well be straight lines when the growth rates are zero.[6] The cumulative units are represented by the area under the curves, which can be obtained by integration. For these areas to be equal (for the second mover to catch up with the first mover in cumulative units sold), we set:

$$\int_0^T \left(e^{gt} - 1\right) dt = \int_L^T \left(e^{h(t-L)} - 1\right) dt$$

$$\left[\frac{e^{gt}}{g} - t\right]_0^T = \left[\frac{e^{h(t-L)}}{h} - t\right]_L^T$$

$$\frac{e^{gT}}{g} - T - \frac{1}{g} = \frac{e^{h(T-L)}}{h} - T - \frac{1}{h} + L$$

$$\frac{e^{gT}}{g} - \frac{1}{g} = \frac{e^{h(T-L)}}{h} - \frac{1}{h} + L$$

Suppose the first mover grows at $g = 10\%$. Figure 13.14 shows when the second mover is able to catch up (time T) versus how fast it has to grow (growth rate h) if it enters the market late at L = year 1 or even later at L = year 2. For example, when $L = 1$, it has to grow about 20% a year to catch up with the first mover's cumulative volume by year 3. If $L = 2$, it has to grow by more than 70% a year to do that.

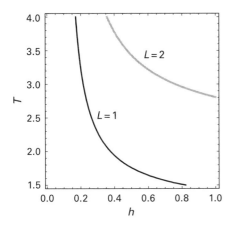

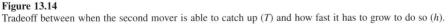

Figure 13.14
Tradeoff between when the second mover is able to catch up (T) and how fast it has to grow to do so (h).

13.6.3 Caveats

So much controversy has stirred over the misuse of the experience curve that it is useful to remind ourselves of where the tool might not work, or has to be used carefully. For example, Bausch & Lomb's success mentioned earlier did not last. It priced so aggressively low that it drove out its competitors, only to have them be acquired by well-capitalized and stronger competitors: Revlon, Johnson & Johnson, and Schering-Plough.

Another set of challenges surrounds the issue of determining what cumulative units count. For example, NEC garnered enormous cumulative experience over its vast array of businesses—from telecommunications to computers—in a way that single businesses like AT&T and IBM could not catch up with. Conversely, we must bear in mind how one component in our product may eventually have only a limited impact on the product as a whole. For example, our electronic calculator may have a memory chip whose cost we can drive down with the experience curve. This has two effects on the cost of the calculator: (1) it reduces the calculator's cost, and (2) the chip's share of the calculator's cost drops. Over time, the latter effect might overwhelm the former, so that further drops in the chip's cost have only minimal effect on the calculator's cost.

13.7 Takeaways

In this chapter, we turn from purchasing to production. This involves a few strategic initiatives:

• Ensuring that the process fits the product type.

• Building forecasting capability with a consensus approach. Sport Obermeyer uses a six-member team, and the team's consensus gives a good indication of the accuracy of its forecasts.

• Rationalizing production assets with newsvendor analysis. These assets—inventory, cash holdings, capacities—are often held in anticipation of uncertain demand, and newsvendor analysis provides a rigorous approach to determining the profit-maximizing holding levels.

• Rationalizing service assets with queueing analysis. Service assets such as teller counters and restaurant tables do not have inventory, but their equivalent is waiting customers. Queueing analysis provides the equivalent rigorous approach to finding the profit-maximizing investment in service assets.

• Rationalizing capacities with competitive capacity analysis. For large capacities—such as manufacturing plants—investments have a competitive and often preemptive element. This tool provides an approach to figuring out capacity investment in these situations.

• Driving down unit costs with experience curves.

13.8   Survey of Prior Research in One Paragraph

Rob Hayes and Steve Wheelwright introduced the process-product matrix analysis. The work on Sport Obermeyer was done by Marshall Fisher, Jan Hammond, Walter Obermeyer, and Ananth Raman. The newsvendor and queueing analyses are classics in the literature. Some of the leading scholars on risk pooling include Morris Cohen and Leroy Schwarz. Steve Graves, William Jordan, and Brian Tomlin pioneered the analysis of chaining. Jan van Mieghem is an authority on capacity investments. Pankaj Ghemawat is a pioneer in the analysis of preemptive capacity addition, from the angles of industrial organization and game theory; the Du Pont case is from his seminal doctoral dissertation. Don Watters and others at McKinsey popularized competitive capacity analysis. Louis E. Yelle did the early analysis of experience (or learning) curves.

13.9   Further Reading

Fisher, M. L. 2009. "Rocket Science Retailing: The 2006 Philip McCord Morse Lecture." *Operations Research* 57 (3): 527–540.

Fisher, M. L., and A. Raman. 1996. "Reducing the Cost of Demand Uncertainty through Accurate Response to Early Sales." *Operations Research* 44 (1): 87–99.

Fisher, M. L., A. Raman, and A. S. McClelland. 2000. "Rocket Science Retailing Is Almost Here—Are You Ready?" *Harvard Business Review* 78 (4): 115–124.

Ghemawat, P. 1984. "Capacity Expansion in the Titanium Dioxide Industry." *Journal of Industrial Economics*: 145–163.

Graves, S. C., and S. P. Willems. 2000. "Optimizing Strategic Safety Stock Placement in Supply Chains." *Manufacturing and Service Operations Management* 2 (1): 68–83.

Hayes, R. H., and S. C. Wheelwright. 1979. "The Dynamics of Process-Product Life Cycles." *Harvard Business Review* 57 (2): 127–136.

Jordan, W. C., and S. C. Graves. 1995. "Principles on the Benefits of Manufacturing Process Flexibility." *Management Science* 41 (4): 577–594.

Van Mieghem, J. A. 2008. *Operations Strategy: Principles and Practice*. Belmont, MA: Dynamic Ideas.

Van Mieghem, J. A. 2003. "Commissioned Paper: Capacity Management, Investment, and Hedging: Review and Recent Developments." *Manufacturing and Service Operation Management* 5 (4): 269–302.

Van Mieghem, J. A. 1999. "Coordinating Investment, Production, and Subcontracting." *Management Science* 45 (7): 954–971.

Van Mieghem, J. A. 1998. "Investment Strategies for Flexible Resources." *Management Science* 44 (8): 1071–1078.

Yelle, L. E. 1976. "Estimating Learning Curves for Potential Products." *Industrial Marketing Management* 5 (2–3): 147–154.

14 Turning Around Distribution

We have already discussed a strategic aspect of designing distribution, which is to match the type of supply chain—physically efficient or market-responsive—to the product type (see section 12.3). Here we dive into tactical issues, focusing on what distribution strategy we should have.

It often pays to start from customer needs and profitability. Customers have different needs, buying different products and incurring different costs to serve. For example, a very profitable bank customer might be one who purchases a range of products—deposits, credit cards, loans, investment products, financial advice—and prefers a light touch with easy accessibility, using mainly the Internet channel.

Customers are also unquestionably different in terms of their profitability. It is not unusual for a retail bank to have 80% of the customer base contributing more than 100% of the profits, as in figure 14.1, which we have first seen as figure 8.2.

Having recognized that there are different customer segments by needs and profitability, we consider the implications for three issues:

• **_Determining the right set of channels._**   Which channels meet which needs and maximize customer profitability? For example, in retail banking, the bank and its customers have needs that might be best met by sets of channels that differ by customer segment (see table 14.1).

• **_Matching customers with channels._**   For example, this involves migrating customers with low profit potential toward lower-cost channels, and encouraging customers with high profit potential toward channels that are particularly suited for cross-selling and up-selling.

• **_Rationalizing the delivery architecture_**   to ensure that its parts are individually efficient and collectively integrated. For example, once a bank migrates a large number of customers away from branches to the web, it makes sense to rationalize the branch network.

We consider each of these in turn.

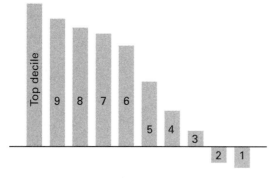

Figure 14.1
Customer base by profitability deciles (illustrative).

Table 14.1
Needs and How Channels Fulfill Them

Need	High-End Banking Customers	Mass-Market Banking Customers
Acquisition	• Expert advisors, relationship managers, selected high-touch branches	• Call centers, targeted e-mailing, online ads, supplementary accounts of high-value customers
Up-selling, cross-selling	• Call centers, paid referrals from third parties and internal staff	• Call centers, targeted mailing, online ads
Transactions	• Dedicated lines in select branches, web, ATM, voice recognition units (VRU)	• Web, ATM, VRU, charges imposed beyond threshold use in higher-cost channels such as tellers
Retention, recovery	• Relationship managers, call centers	• Computerized monitoring, VRU

Note: We take "need" to mean both needs of the customer and needs of the bank, say to acquire customers.

14.1   Determining the Right Set of Channels with the Rangan-Zoltners-Becker Model

Suppose we want to find which C candidate channels—distributors, franchisees, company-owned storefronts, sales agents, websites, and such—should serve our N customer needs (e.g., 24-hour service, advisory). A customer segment might be represented by several needs. Since we focus on the operational issue of matching, we take as given that the customer needs are well defined.

Kasturi Rangan of Harvard, Andris Zoltners of Kellogg, and Robert Becker of Digital Equipment constructed a useful integer program to solve this problem. Figure 14.2 depicts the basic setup.

Specifically, we want to maximize the net present value of our choice:

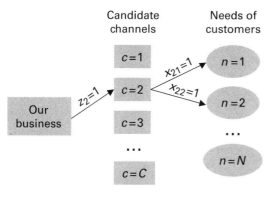

→ Solution link (illustrative)

Figure 14.2
The Rangan-Zoltners-Becker model. Source: Adapted from Rangan, Zoltners, and Becker (1986).

$$\max \sum_{c=1}^{C}\sum_{n=1}^{N}\sum_{t=1}^{T} d_t \left(p_{cnt} - v_{cnt}\right) u_{cnt} x_{cn} - \sum_{c=1}^{C} s_c z_c,$$

where the first term captures the gross margin—margin times units less variable costs—and the second captures fixed costs. The symbols are defined as follows (see figure 14.2 for clarification):

$c = 1$ to C indexes the channels,

$n = 1$ to N indexes the customer needs,

$t = 1$ to T indexes the year so T is our planning horizon,

x_{cn} is our decision variable that is 1 if we have c sell to n,

z_c is also our decision variable that is 1 if we link with channel c,

d_t is the discount rate for year t,

p_{cnt} is the our price of selling one unit through channel c to need n in year t; the model does not need to assume who sets the price,

v_{cnt} is our variable cost of using c for selling to n in year t,

u_{cnt} is the units we expect to sell through c to n in year t,

s_c is the setup cost of linking with channel c.

We impose a number of constraints:

Capacity. We need three constraints, one each for our capacity, the channels' capacities, and the consumers' expected demand rate:

$$\sum_{c=1}^{C}\sum_{n=1}^{N}u_{cnt}x_{cn} \leq k_t, \forall t = 1,2..,T$$

$$\sum_{n=1}^{N}u_{cnt}x_{cn} \leq k_{ct}, \forall c = 1,2..,C; t = 1,2..,T$$

$$\sum_{c=1}^{C}u_{cnt}x_{cs} \leq k_{nt}, \forall n = 1,2..,N; t = 1,2..,T$$

where:

k_t is our capacity in year t,

k_{ct} is the capacity of channel c in year t,

k_{nt} is the expected demand rate of need n in year t.

Budget. We also need to bind our variable cost and the setup cost with our budgets:

$$\sum_{c=1}^{C}\sum_{n=1}^{N}v_{cnt}x_{cn} \leq b_t, \forall t = 1,2..,T$$

$$\sum_{c=1}^{C}s_c z_c \leq b$$

where:

b_t is our budget for variable costs to all channels in year t,

b is our budget for setup cost to link to all channels.

Channel performance. We also require the expected units sold to be a function of a number of parameters:

$$u_{cnt} = inventory_{cnt} \times turn_{cnt} \times resources_{cnt} \times interest_{cnt} \times \left(\sum_{h=1}^{C}h \cdot num_{hn}\right)^{-2} \qquad (15)$$

where:

$inventory_{cnt}$ is the estimated inventory that channel c will hold for need n. This might be obtained from discussions with channels or formally from supply contracts. For service reps who carry no inventory, this is the expected number of sales calls made;

$turn_{cnt}$ is the expected inventory turn, and could be estimated from historical data or industry data. For service reps, this is the expected sales per call made;

resources$_{cnt}$ is a fraction representing c's ability. This is obtained by qualitative assessment;

interest$_{cnt}$ is a multiplier representing c's interest. For Rangan et al. this ranges from 0.75 to 1.75. For proprietary channels, this might be pegged at 1. For third-party channels, small channels have lower effort, intermediate-sized ones have the highest, and large channels also have lower effort because we might be only a small portion of their business;

$\sum_{h=1}^{C} h \cdot num_{hn}$ is the number of channels assigned to serve need n; and

$\left(\sum_{h=1}^{C} h \cdot num_{hn} \right)^{-2}$ captures channel conflict in a power law: if there is one channel, this is 1; if there are 2 channels, this becomes a factor of $2^{-2} = 1/4$; and so on.

To construct

$$\sum_{h=1}^{C} h \cdot num_{hn},$$

we define *num$_{hn}$* as a 0–1 indicator variable which is 0 when the number of channels for need n is h, and impose the following constraints:

$$\sum_{c=1}^{C} x_{cn} = \sum_{h=1}^{C} h \cdot num_{hn}, \forall n = 1, 2.., N,$$

$$\sum_{h=1}^{C} num_{hn} \leq 1, \forall n = 1, 2.., N.$$

So if there are 3 channels, we see that $\sum_{h=1}^{C} h \cdot num_{hn}$ is $1(0) + 2(0) + 3(1) + \ldots + C(0) = 3$; that is, all the indicators *num$_{hm}$* are zero except for the one for 3.

Decision variables. Finally, we have constraints on the decision variables:

$$\sum_{n=1}^{N} x_{cn} \leq N z_c, \forall c = 1, 2.., C,$$

$$\sum_{c=1}^{C} x_{cn} \geq 1, \forall n = 1, 2.., N,$$

$$x_{cn} = 0 \, or \, 1, \forall c = 1, 2.., C, n = 1, 2.., N,$$

$$z_c = 0 \, or \, 1, \forall c = 1, 2.., C,$$

$$num_{hn} = 0 \, or \, 1, \forall h = 1, 2.., C, n = 1, 2.., N.$$

14.1.1 Embellishments

There are many embellishments to make the model more realistic. An important one is to set up expected units sold not as mostly given but as functions of prices. Modifying equation (15), we can add the last term:

$$u_{cnt} = inventory_{cnt} \times turn_{cnt} \times resources_{cnt} \times interest_{cnt} \times$$

$$\left(\sum_{h=1}^{C} h \cdot num_{hn} \right)^{-2} \times \left(p_{cnt}^{\alpha_{cn}} \prod_{\substack{q \in (1,2,..,C) \\ q \neq c}} p_{qnt}^{\beta_{qcn}} \right), \tag{16}$$

where:

α_{cn} is the direct price elasticity of c selling to n with respect to price p_{cnt},

β_{qcn} is the cross price elasticity of c selling to n when competing channels q sell to n at price $p_{qnt.}$.

The prices are now decision variables, and we would impose nonnegative constraints on them. If the channels are primarily cost centers (like automatic teller machines) rather than profit centers (like sales reps), we might include a term for elasticity not with respect to price but with respect to costs.

And while we are on embellishments, we can also take various components to the next level. For example, we could model $inventory_{cnt}$ using the newsvendor formulation described in section 13.3.

All these significantly complicate our model. The most serious implication is that we would have a nonlinear objective function, and would have to use more sophisticated optimization techniques.[1]

14.2 Matching Customers with Channels

Even though we might have set up an appropriate set of channels, in a turnaround situation our customer base is unlikely to match up with these channels right away.

Consider the retail bank example in figure 14.3. The bank uses a premium channel—like a premium banking network—as the primary platform for serving high-profitability customers, and a mass-market channel—a regular branch network—to serve low-profitability customers. But observe that, for the premium channel, most high-profit customers are underserved, and decile 5 seems grossly overserved. For the mass-market channel, all but decile 4 is overserved. This situation is typical. The difference between the two channel types is too narrow. And with just two channel types, there might not be enough differentiation among the ten deciles. Finally, very low-cost channels—like web and ATM networks—tend to be underutilized, resulting in many unprofitable deciles.

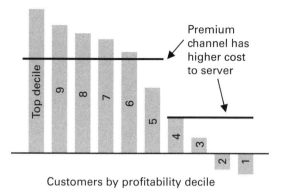

Figure 14.3
Mismatch between customer profitability and cost to serve.

Much harder is finding ways to migrate lower-potential customers to lower-cost channels. Some examples of these initiatives in banking are below. Many include carrot-and-stick incentives:

• Install enough low-cost channels such as ATMs to reduce waiting time, and shift staff from costly channels such as manual teller counters to other customer service functions;

• Station greeters at bank branches who guide customers toward web kiosks;

• Introduce an online deposit product with better rates but with fees for using branches;

• Introduce fees for excessive use of high-cost channels;

• Rebalance the load at high-cost channels. For example, it may be difficult to migrate elderly customers to web channels, but they might be encouraged to go to branches at nonpeak times.

We should mention two accompanying initiatives that, from experience, seem to be necessary conditions for a successful transition: (1) appropriate training and incentives for employees, and (2) a safety net for customers during the transition. The latter implies that it is often necessary to maintain both old and new infrastructure simultaneously, so that costs will go up before they come down.

14.3   Rationalizing the Delivery Architecture

Many channels are suboptimal. They will be even more suboptimal after we migrate customers from one channel to another. Therefore, the clearest initiative is to invest in the capacity of channels to which customers are migrating and (often forgotten) to cull the capacity of channels from which customers are migrating.

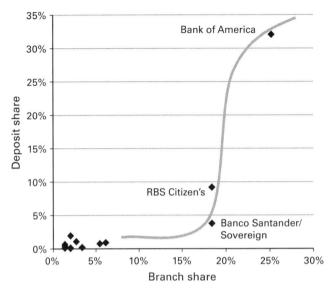

Figure 14.4
Banks' share of branches and deposits in Boston, on June 30, 2008. Source: Capital IQ.

A second category of initiative concerns process and capacity reengineering—such as balancing loads. Many of these apply (see sections 12.5 and 13.3).

A third type of initiative is to be smart about the nature of channel investments. For example, a bank's share of branches in a local market tends to determine its share of deposits in that market in an S-curve.

Figure 14.4 shows this effect in Boston. Clearly, it makes sense to invest in branch networks to just above the critical branch share, which seems to be slightly above 20% in Boston and is generally 20–30% in other markets. This effect is important enough that it seems to empirically hold for many types of store-based retail businesses in which convenience is important, such as gasoline stations, convenience stores, fast-food restaurants, or coffee joints.

14.4   Takeaways

We focus on only the operational aspects of turning around distribution. This comprises three steps:

• Determining the right set of channels with the Rangan-Zoltners-Becker model. Using an integer program, this model determines which channels we should use to serve which needs, while maximizing the net present value of the sales from the channel-needs assignments.

• Matching customers with channels. Having decided on the set of channels to use in principle, we need to migrate customers to the intended channels.

• Rationalizing the delivery architecture. Not only do we need to get customers into the new channels, we also need to restructure the old channels into the new ones.

14.5 Survey of Prior Research in One Paragraph

Robert Becker, Kasturi Rangan, and Andris Zoltners developed the model described in this chapter. Marcel Corstjens and Peter Doyle also pioneered work with these models. Marshall Fisher and Monique Guignard-Spielberg are leading authorities on integer programming. Dennis Campbell and Frances Frei studied the migration of retail bank customers between online and offline channels.

14.6 Further Reading

Ansari, A., C. F. Mela, and S. A. Neslin. 2008. "Customer Channel Migration." *Journal of Marketing Research* 45 (1): 60–76.

Boyd, S., S. J. Kim, L. Vandenberghe, and A. Hassibi, A. 2007. "A Tutorial on Geometric Programming." *Optimization and Engineering* 8 (1): 67–127. Available at http://stanford.edu/~boyd/papers/gp_tutorial.html.

Campbell, D., and F. Frei. 2010. "The Cost Structure, Customer Profitability, and Retention Implications of Self-Service Distribution Channels: Evidence from Customer Behavior in an Online Banking Channel." *Management Science* 56 (1): 4–24.

Corstjens, M., and P. Doyle. 1981. "A Model for Optimizing Retail Space Allocations." *Management Science* 27 (7): 822–833.

Fisher, M. L. 1981. "The Lagrangian Relaxation Method for Solving Integer Programming Problems." *Management Science* 27 (1): 1–18.

Guignard, M., and K. Spielberg. 1979. "A Direct Dual Method for the Mixed Plant Location Problem with Some Side Constraints." *Mathematical Programming* 17 (1): 198–228.

Neslin, S. A., D. Grewal, R. Leghorn, V. Shankar, M. L. Teerling, J. S. Thomas, and P. C. Verhoef. 2006. "Challenges and Opportunities in Multichannel Customer Management." *Journal of Service Research* 9 (2): 95.

Rangan, V. K., A. A. Zoltners, and R. J. Becker. 1986. "The Channel Intermediary Selection Decision: A Model and an Application." *Management Science* 32 (9): 1114–1122.

15 Sustaining the Turnaround

We have seen in the previous chapters how we can reconfigure our various functions: purchasing, production, distribution. We end this book by assuming that we have optimized our configurations—supplier base, sourcing contracts, production capacities, distribution channels, and so on. Now we consider how we need to run some core areas day to day so as to sustain an operational turnaround. We focus on five vital areas:

1. *Quality management.* How do we maintain or improve quality—a particularly tall order during turnaround situations. We will see that a key is to drive down variability.

2. *Innovation management.* Like quality, innovation is often relegated to a backseat in turnaround situations.

3. *Revenue management.* How do we maximize value from customers while minimizing our asset investments?

4. *Performance management.* How do we measure and track operational improvements?

5. *Investor management.* How do we tell an operational narrative to an audience that might be skeptical, uninterested, or not ready?

As we emphasized before, this description is not meant to be complete; there are many other issues—strategy, marketing, organization, law, finance, and accounting—that we do not seek to cover. Nevertheless, the subject of managing between two extreme forms of turnarounds is so vital to setting the tone and pace of even operational transformations that we begin with a short discussion of that.

15.1 Operational and Organizational Turnarounds

Table 15.1 illustrates the key differences between operational and organizational turnarounds.[1] Of course we do not expect that all turnarounds will be of only one type or the other, but the dichotomy usefully highlights the differences and, importantly, that the

Table 15.1
Characteristics of Operational and Organizational Turnarounds

	Operational Turnarounds	Organizational Turnarounds
Goals	Maximize shareholder value	Develop organizational capability
Leadership	Manage top-down	Encourage bottom-up
Focus	Structure and systems	Style and shared values
Process	Plan, execute, debug	Experiment, evolve
Reward	Financial	Mutual commitment

Adapted from Beer and Nohria (2000).

differences seem irreconcilable—that is, it is difficult (perhaps not impossible) to simultaneously have characteristics of both operational and organizational turnarounds.

Not surprisingly, we see actual examples falling into one or the other type. Al Dunlap's stint at Scott Paper in 1994 is illustrative of an operational turnaround. He increased market value from $3 billion in 1994 to $9 billion in 1995, was directive, focused on restructuring and paring down of assets, with a plan that had almost military precision. The rewards are richly financial; Dunlap himself was paid over $100 million.

In contrast, Andrew Sigler at another paper company, Champion International, led an organizational turnaround in 1981. Sigler launched "Champion Way," whose goal was to develop employee competence. He delegated detailed change, focused on developing a culture of trust, and encouraged employees to problem-solve. The reward was both skill-based with some profit sharing with the company.

The surprising result: neither company had a sustainable turnaround. Scott Paper became embroiled in alleged accounting scandals[2] and Champion "had not seen a significant increase in the economic value of the company in more than a decade" (Beer and Nohria, 2002).

If a company undertakes both types of turnaround, it seems that a specific sequence works best: first operational and then organizational. GE's Jack Welch undertook an operational turnaround in the early 1980s, earning the moniker "Neutron Jack," but by 1985 he switched to an organizational strategy and started cultivating top managers. GE's stock saw a continuous climb.

Simultaneous operational and organizational turnarounds are hard, but British grocer ASDA may have pulled it off. In 1991, its new CEO Archie Norman adopted an operational strategy but hired COO Allan Leighton to simultaneous undertake an organizational turnaround. The company multiplied its shareholder value eightfold by 1999.

In short, it seems that successful turnarounds require some combination—perhaps in a sequence—of operational and organizational changes. In the rest of this chapter, we focus on fairly neutral operational matters, but we would do well to bear the ideas of operational and organizational change in mind.

15.2 Quality Management

In a turnaround situation, it is tempting to put quality on the back burner. But it is often in this period that we need to better control quality to ensure that it does not compromise long-term sustainability.

Say we have put in place a quality management program of the sort described in chapter 9. Here we describe how we control quality on a day-to-day basis: how to control the quality of a process—such as a production process—and of the outputs of a process.

15.2.1 Value-Maximizing Output Control

Suppose we produce batches of precision bolts, which must be of a certain length. For simplicity, suppose we produce only two types of batches: good and bad, with defect rates of 4% per batch versus 15%. In the trade, these percentages are called:

a = acceptable quality level (AQL) = 4% here,

b = lot tolerance percent defective (LTPD) = 15% here.

It is rare that we can check every bolt in every batch to find the defect rate, so we have to sample each batch. Let us denote the parameters of our sampling:

N = batch size,

n = sample size,

c = cost of sampling each bolt,

d = number of defects in a sampling of a batch,

t = threshold number of defects: if a batch has more than t defects, we reject it; otherwise, we send it to the customer.

In particular, we compare d against t and arrive at one of the outcomes in table 15.2 (where we also indicate some illustrative values in each cell). For example, selling a bolt gets us $10, in the top left cell. A wrong reject incurs the cost of losing the margin that we could otherwise have made. A wrong accept is when we accept the batch and send it to our

Table 15.2
Four Possible Outcomes of Output Control, with Illustrative Values per Bolt Shown in Each Cell

	Good batch (defect probability is a)	Bad batch (defect probability is b)
$d \leq t$ = we accept	Correct accept $10	Wrong accept −$15
$d > t$ = we reject	Wrong reject −$3	Correct reject −$1

customer, who (we assume) will find that it is defective because she has to use the bolt. The cost of handling that wrongly accepted bolt is \$15. If we reject a bolt correctly, that would cost us \$1, in the bottom right cell.

This raises the questions of how we can determine n and t. We should select n and t to maximize our NPV. If the profitability of each batch is constant and is discounted by a constant rate, then maximizing NPV is the same as maximizing the profit from each batch.

The profit of each batch includes these components:

Profit per batch $= N[\$10 \times P(\text{correct accept}) - \$15 \times P(\text{wrong accept})$

$- \$1 \times P(\text{wrong reject}) - \$3 \times P(\text{correct reject})] - n \times c.$

We can determine the probabilities thus:

$P(\text{correct accept}) = P(d \le t \mid \text{defect probability is } a)$

$$= P\left(Z \le \frac{t - n \cdot a}{\sqrt{n \cdot a \cdot (1-a)}} \right) = \Phi\left(\frac{t - n \cdot a}{\sqrt{n \cdot a \cdot (1-a)}} \right),$$

$P(\text{wrong accept}) = P(d < t \mid \text{defect probability is } b)$

$$= P\left(Z < \frac{t - n \cdot b}{\sqrt{n \cdot b \cdot (1-b)}} \right) = \Phi\left(\frac{t - n \cdot b}{\sqrt{n \cdot b \cdot (1-b)}} \right),$$

$P(\text{wrong reject}) = P(d > t \mid \text{defect probability is } a)$

$$= P\left(Z > \frac{t - n \cdot a}{\sqrt{n \cdot a \cdot (1-a)}} \right) = 1 - \Phi\left(\frac{t - n \cdot a}{\sqrt{n \cdot a \cdot (1-a)}} \right),$$

$P(\text{correct reject}) = P(d > t \mid \text{defect probability is } b)$

$$= P\left(Z > \frac{t - n \cdot b}{\sqrt{n \cdot b \cdot (1-b)}} \right) = 1 - \Phi\left(\frac{t - n \cdot b}{\sqrt{n \cdot b \cdot (1-b)}} \right).$$

The resulting expression may be difficult to analyze in closed form, but it is easy to find its maximum via simulation or even a simple contour plot. For example, if $N = 1,000$ and $c = \$9$, the batch profit is shown in figure 15.1, where the highest point is about \$7,530, at integer values of $n = 111$ and $t = 9$.

15.2.2   Advanced Topic: Value-Maximizing Process Control

We have just described the control of the quality of output. Suppose we go back into the production process and control quality there. Specifically, we want to know when the process deviates "enough" from some desired bolt length. Let us use these symbols:

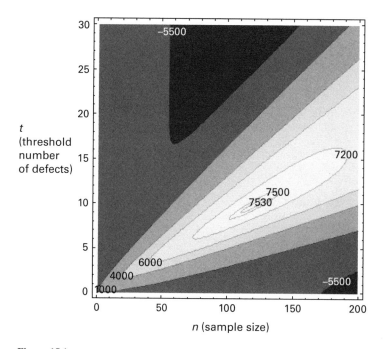

Figure 15.1
Batch profit of output control.

μ = a prespecified desired mean bolt length of process,

σ = a known standard deviation of process,

$\theta \times \sigma$ = a prespecified acceptable tolerance, in θ number of standard deviations.

The process mean may move away from μ, as in figure 15.2; we assume that σ does not change. Our goal is to detect when the mean deviates beyond the band between $\mu + \theta\sigma$ and $\mu - \theta\sigma$.

Assume, as is often the case, that we cannot directly observe the process mean. Instead we track it by taking a sample of bolts in each batch. This sampling is of course an imperfect proxy for the process, which is why our process may fall outside the band for some time before we realize this; see the long thin "outside band" period in figure 15.2.

Our goal is to find a method for tracking the process mean in the profit-maximizing way. To do this, let us first define a cycle as a period when the process mean is within the band, followed by a period when it is outside. Figure 15.2 shows two cycles.

The generic sampling procedure is simple: take n bolts from each batch, calculate the average bolt length, check whether the average strays beyond some specified band *for the sample*. Since we are dealing with a sample now, this band has a standard deviation of $\sigma/\sqrt{n}$ instead of the process's σ, and we use a different band specification of t standard deviations instead of θ standard deviations. Let us say:

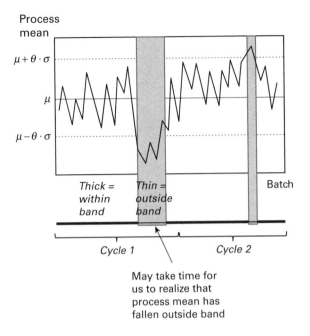

Figure 15.2
Process mean.

N = batch size,

n = sample size,

c = cost of sampling each bolt,

t = width of the control band, in number of sample standard deviations ($\sigma/\sqrt{n}$) around our desired mean μ.

In other words, we check whether the sample mean has strayed below some lower control limit (LCL) $\mu - t\sigma/\sqrt{n}$ or upper control limit (UCL) $\mu + t\sigma/\sqrt{n}$.

Figure 15.3 shows how the sample mean goes out of band. Point A is a false alarm; the process mean is actually still within band. Point B is a true alarm, although it comes quite late, after the process mean has been out of band for a while. C and D are false and true alarms. After true alarms, we fix the process so that its mean returns to μ (more precisely: we think we fix it, since we cannot observe the real process mean), and that brings us to a new cycle.

The question in designing the sampling procedure is: How do we decide n and t? The economic tradeoff is similar to what we had for output control. A bigger n implies a higher cost of sampling, but it buys greater accuracy. A bigger t reduces the probability of false alarms, but it also reduces that of true alarms.

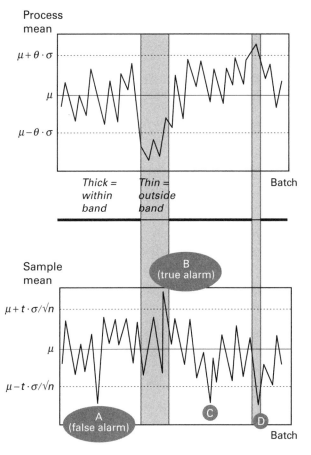

Figure 15.3
Process and sample means.

We want n and t to maximize the expected profit per batch; a batch may be good (process mean within band) or bad (otherwise). To define this profit, we first illustrate with net revenues of each type of situation:

Good batch, process mean within band = $100/bolt,

Bad batch, process mean outside band = −$2/bolt,

False alarm, sample mean outside band even though process mean is within band = −$6/bolt,

True alarm, sample mean outside band, correctly detecting that the process mean is outside band = −$1/bolt,

Sampling = −$1/bolt.

The cost of a bad batch may include cost of materials less the salvage value of selling away the bad batch. The cost of a false alarm is on top of getting a good batch, and might include the cost of fruitlessly searching for why the process deviated when it actually did not. The cost of a true alarm is on top of getting of a bad batch, and may include both the diagnosis and the fixing of the process.

The profit per batch, using $E(.)$ the expectation operator, is:

Profit per batch = $\{N[\$100 \times E(\text{good batches in a cycle}) - \$2 \times E(\text{bad batches in a cycle}) - \$6 \times E(\text{false alarms in a cycle}) - \$1 \times E(\text{true alarms in a cycle})] - n \times \$1\}$ / $E(\text{batches in entire cycle})$.

The periods of good batches are represented by the thick black lines in the middle of figure 15.3; the periods of bad batches are the thin lines; point A is an example of a false alarm and B of a true alarm. We bear in mind that $E(\text{true alarms in a cycle})$ is 1, since there is only one true alarm, the one that ends the cycle. Also, $E(\text{batches in entire cycle})$ is $E(\text{good batches in a cycle}) + E(\text{bad batches in a cycle})$.

To determine $E(\text{good batches in a cycle})$, we need to specify:

p = probability of process staying within the band.

So the number of good-batch periods has a geometric distribution:

$P(\text{good batches in a cycle} = g) = p^g (1 - p)$.

Notice that we do not count the last batch, which is a bad one. From the expectation formula of a geometric variable, we get:[3]

$E(\text{good batches in a cycle}) = p/(1 - p)$.

To find $E(\text{bad batches in a cycle})$, we use a similar technique. But this time, the probability is that of the sample mean staying within band when the process mean is out of band. We use these notations:

Sample mean = $\overline{X}$,

Process mean = $E(\overline{X})$.

The process mean is the expected value of the sample mean, because of the statistical law of iterated expectations. Let us use q to denote the probability of blissful ignorance of bad batches:

$q = P(\text{sample mean within band} \mid \text{process mean outside band})$

$$= P\left(|\bar{X} - \mu| \le \frac{t\sigma}{\sqrt{n}} \mid E(\bar{X}) = \mu + \theta\sigma\right)$$

$$= P\left(-t - \theta\sqrt{n} \le \frac{\bar{X} - \mu - \theta\sigma}{\sigma/\sqrt{n}} \le t - \theta\sqrt{n} \mid E(\bar{X}) = \mu + \theta\sigma\right)$$

$$= \Phi\left(t - \theta\sqrt{n}\right) - \Phi\left(-t - \theta\sqrt{n}\right),$$

where, as usual, Φ is the cumulative density function of the standard normal distribution. So we have a similar geometric distribution:

P(bad batches in a cycle = b) = $q^{b-1}(1 - q)$.

As before, the expectation is:

E(bad batches in a cycle) = $1/(1 - q)$.

Moving on to E(false alarms in a cycle): first, the probability:

$$P(\text{false alarm}) = P\left(|\bar{X} - \mu| > \frac{t\sigma}{\sqrt{n}} \mid E(\bar{X}) = \mu\right)$$

$$= P\left(\left|\frac{\bar{X} - \mu}{\sigma\sqrt{n}}\right| > t \mid E(\bar{X}) = \mu\right)$$

$$= P(|Z| > t) = 2\Phi(-t).$$

Then multiple the probability by E(periods of good batches):

E(false alarms in a cycle) = $2\Phi(-t)p/(1 - p)$.

Now we are done. To recap:

Profit per batch = $\{N[\$100 \times p/(1 - p) - \$2 \times 1/(1 - q) - \$6 \times 2\Phi(-t)p/(1 - p) - \$1 \times 1] - n \times \$1\} / [p/(1 - p) + 1/(1 - q)]$.

For example, if $p = 0.1$ and $\theta = 10$ (this last tolerance is a managerial decision, usually based on historical estimates), we can plot the optimal t for every n, as in figure 15.4. The figure also shows that as n reduces, we need a larger optimal t, as we would expect.

15.3   Innovation Management

Innovation, like quality, is often deemphasized in turnaround situations. But few would deny that for a turnaround to be sustainable, it has to put in place mechanisms to manage innovation. The particularly challenging issue during turnaround is that there is

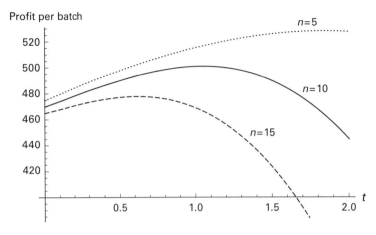

Figure 15.4
Profit per batch for various thresholds t and sample sizes n.

considerably less room for error in innovation management, and therefore a higher premium for getting it right.

We focus on "getting it right" in three areas: selecting projects to pursue, developing products, and commercializing the products.

15.3.1   Selecting Projects to Pursue: The LPTU Model

Christoph Loch, Michael Pich, Christian Terwiesch of Wharton, and Michael Urbschat of INSEAD (collectively, LPTU) describe a case study of how BMW's R&D department selects the best projects that can contribute to plugging the gap in various dimensions (e.g., control, weight, cost) of various types of transmission systems (e.g., four-speed auto, continuously variable).

We can state these parameters:

g_{jk} = gap to be filled, in dimension j of transmission k,

p_{ij} = expected extent to which project i plugs the gap in dimension j, which is the same for all transmissions,

w_{jk} = importance weight of dimension j in transmission k.

The selection of projects is done with a mathematical program. We have the following decision variables:

Y_i = 1 if project i is selected and 0 otherwise

X_{ik} = 1 if project i is targeted at transmission k and 0 otherwise

S_{jk} = remaining shortfall after project contributions, in dimension j of transmission k.

The objective is to minimize $\sum_j \sum_k w_{jk} S_{jk}$ subject to a number of constraints. The first two set up constraints on the decision variables. The first is an accounting identity to construct S_{jk}, where e_{jk} is the excess gap and is constrained to be nonnegative:

$$S_{jk} = g_{jk} - \sum_i [p_{ij} X_{ik}] + e_{jk},$$

$$X_{ik} = \{0,1\},\ Y_i = \{0,1\},\ S_{jk} \geq 0,\ e_{jk} \geq 0.$$

A project can only target a transmission type if it is selected:

$$\sum_k [X_{ik}] \leq \sum_k [1] Y_i.$$

The total resource commitment for all projects must also be below the total available resources:

c_i = resource requirement, in \$ equivalent, to do project I,

C = total resources available (in \$ equivalent),

$$\sum_i c_i Y_i \leq C.$$

Finally, we include some illustrative interproject constraints. For example, if project n cannot be selected together with some M projects in the set Ω, we write:

$$M - M X_{nk} \geq \sum_{i \in \Omega,} X_{ik}.$$

If a set of projects Ψ are mutually exclusive, then we have:

$$\sum_{i \in \Psi,} X_{ik} \leq 1.$$

Loch et al. also note that the model is valued not only for selecting projects but for allowing BMW managers to clarify options, formulate the problem, and conduct sensitivity analyses.

15.3.2   Developing Products: The Terwiesch-Xu model

Christian Terwiesch of Wharton and Yi Xu of the University of Maryland articulated how we can organize to develop products. They lay out some fundamental design options:

• ***Open or internal innovation?***   In open innovation, we—the "seeker"—seek new product ideas developed by outsiders—the "solvers." Internal innovation instead is the

Table 15.3
Types of Problems in the Terwiesch-Xu Model

	Technical Uncertainty (will it work?)	Market Uncertainty (will seeker like it?)	Critical Inputs			
			Expertise	Effort	Number of Trials	Example
Expertise-based	Low	Low	Yes	Yes	No	Modify existing process for new factory
Ideation	Low	High	No	Yes	Yes only if solver is also seeker*	Design next-generation bike
Trial-and-error	High	Low	No	No	Yes	Develop pill to reduce gray hair

* If the solver is not the seeker, given the high market uncertainty (i.e., the seeker may not even like the submitted product idea), there is no incentive for the solver to introduce even more uncertainty by holding trials.

traditional mode, in which the seeker is also the solver. For open innovation, additional design options are available.

• *Self- or intermediary-managed.* For example, QVC and Staples sought new product ideas over the Internet by themselves, while other seekers may use an intermediary such as InnoCentive, a web-based outfit that offers rewards for solving research problems posed by seeker companies.

• *Number of solvers* to be allowed (may be restricted by imposing some submission fee, for instance).

• *Fixed or royalty-based reward*, for the solver who posed the winning submission.

What design do we use? That depends on the type of problem. Table 15.3 shows three generic types. These depend on the type of uncertainty, and on the critical inputs needed by the solver to create a good product. The seeker's goal is to get the best submission.

The Terwiesch-Xu model suggests some powerful insights into the optimal design of product development. Consider first the choice between open or internal innovation, and, if open, the choice between self- or intermediary-managed innovation. Figure 15.5, panel (a), shows the optimal design for expertise-based and ideation problems. While the form is the same for both problem types, the region for internal innovation is smaller for expertise-based problems. This is because there is greater value to finding a better expert among outside solvers.

When the solver's effort has high return and low cost, not surprisingly, the seeker should solve the problem herself, at the top left ("internal"). If the cost of effort is high, then the best option is to use open innovation. But which open design: self- or intermediary-managed? Intermediary-managed open innovation has the advantage of getting more solvers, but having more solvers incurs greater "negative externality"—that is, a solver puts in less effort if there are too many competing solvers. Intermediaries also cost a

(a) Expertise-based and ideation problems

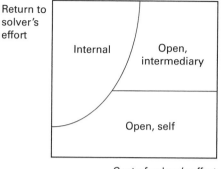

(b) Trial-and-error problems

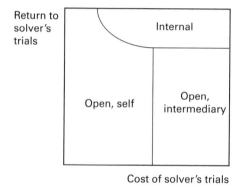

Figure 15.5
Optimal designs.

fee that could be more costly than self-management. But if the return to effort is high, both these problems are overcome, and intermediary-managed innovation is better than self-managed.

With trial-and-error types of problems, even the form of optimal design is different; see figure 15.5, panel (b). As before, internal innovation is optimal if the return to trials is high enough. Otherwise, we use open innovation. But this time, the demarcation of the remaining space is based on cost rather than return. This is again because it is more important to get many trials across all solvers, rather than a solver with many trials. The former is driven more by the cost of trials rather than the return. So for a low enough cost, self-managed open innovation is optimal.

What about the other design options: whether to restrict the number of solvers and whether to use fixed or royalty-based reward?

The model predicts that having more solvers is almost always better, because the negative externality of solvers putting in less effort when there are more competing solvers is usually overwhelmed by other factors. For expertise-based problems, the diversity of having many solvers obtains a greater likelihood of getting good expertise. For ideation problems, having more solvers, even if each solver might be more restrained in putting in maximal effort, still leads to greater likelihood of getting a submission that the seeker desires. And obviously for trial-and-error problems, the more trials, the better. More solvers are not better, however, if the seeker places sufficient weight not only on the best submission but on the average quality of submissions; the latter might be important if the seeker is really creating new products out of all submissions.

With regard to the reward system, royalty-based is better for ideation and trial-and-error problems, since solvers are now incentivized not only to win but to share in the size of the outcome. Royalty-based rewards are still good when there are many solvers, but its superiority over fixed rewards is diminished because, with many solvers, other factors—negative externality and the importance of solver diversity—turn out to outweigh the reward consideration. For expertise-based problems, royalty-based and fixed rewards are about the same, because the key consideration is the endowed expertise among the solver base.

15.3.3   Advanced Topic: Commercializing Products: The Cohen-Eliashberg-Ho Model

Morris Cohen and Jehoshua Eliashberg of Wharton and Teck-hua Ho of Berkeley developed an influential model of how companies should trade off spending more time to make a new product better against commercializing a less-than-perfect one faster to capture revenues earlier. We adapt their model here.

Suppose we have a current product, with quality Q_0, and wish to develop a new, better one having quality Q_1; see figure 15.6.

The new product has a profit-making window that ends at T, so if we denote the time of commercialization as T_C, we have time $(T - T_C)$ to make profit from the new product. The tradeoff is: if we introduce the new product with an early T_C, its quality Q_1 will suffer, hurting our new product's profitability. So what's the optimum T_C?

To find that, we maximize the profit between time 0 and T. This profit has two components: profits from selling the current and new products, and the cost of developing the new product. The former, as we will see, is easy. To deal with the latter, we assume that the cost of quality improvement depends on two things:

L = labor input

α = labor productivity; if this is a fraction, we have the familiar diminishing marginal product of labor.

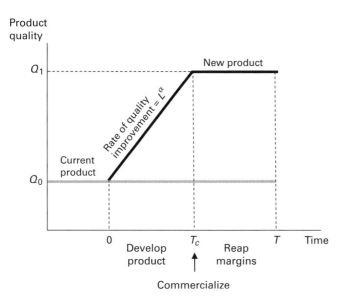

Figure 15.6
Quality improvement of current and new product over time, in the Cohen-Eliashberg-Ho model.

To clarify, we can write $Q_1 = Q_0 + L^\alpha T_C$. The profit is then:

$$T_C M \frac{Q_0}{Q_0 + Q_c} m_0 \quad + \quad (T - T_C) M \frac{Q_1}{Q_1 + Q_c} m_1 \quad - \quad T_C L w$$

current product profit   *new product profit*   *development cost,*

where:

M = market demand rate. For example, $T_D M$ would be the market demand over time period T_D;

Q_C = quality of competitors' product. In the model, the market share when our quality is Q_0 is $Q_0/(Q_0 + Q_C)$;

m_0, m_1 = margins for old and new products;

w = wages for the two stages of quality improvements.

The optimal T_C is given by the following,[4] where we write $Q_0 + Q_c$ as Q_{0c}:

$$T_C^* = \frac{\left\{ \begin{array}{c} \sqrt{L^{2\alpha} M m_1 Q_c Q_{0c} (Q_{0c} + L^\alpha T)[M(m_1 Q_{0c} - m_0 Q_0) + L Q_{0c} w]} \\ -L^{\alpha+1} Q_{0c}^2 w + L^2 M Q_{0c} (m_0 Q_0 - m_1 Q_{0c}) \end{array} \right\}}{L^{2\alpha} [L Q_{0c} w - M(m_0 Q_0 - m_1 Q_{0c})]}$$

This rather intimidating expression is surprisingly helpful. Among other things, it reveals some compelling insights:

- T_C^* **changes only by the square root of T,** because we see that T appears only once, in the square root of the numerator. So if the window of opportunity T shrinks to half, our optimal time to commercialization T_C shrinks to only $\sqrt{1/2} = 71\%$ of its original duration.

- T_C^* **increases with M and m_0, and decreases with w and L.** In other words, if the market is big or the current product is strong, it is optimal to slow down time to market. On the other hand, if it is costly to innovate, we should commercialize quickly. Therefore, a sweeping "faster is better" is not always right. We have to check how changes in these inputs counteract each other to determine the optimal time to market. The relationship between T_C^* and other variables are sometimes increasing, other times decreasing.

- **Minimized break-even time is smaller than T_C^*.** Some businesses like HP have suggested that the T_C that minimizes break-even time (that is, the T_C for which the profit is first zero) is the optimal one. It turns out that such a minimized break-even time is smaller than our profit-maximizing T_C^*.

As we have just seen, the model can be useful in testing many hypotheses about how we should trade off the time to commercialization T_C against quality Q_1.

15.4   Revenue Management

We take as given our investment in capacity. Here we focus on how we can maximize revenues by: (1) allocating our capacity to different product tiers (think of economy versus first-class airline seats, or advanced-purchase versus regular opera tickets), and (2) accepting reservations beyond our capacity (think of overbooking in hotels or restaurants).

Since we focus on operational issues, we will not discuss many other aspects of revenue management that focus on price as a decision variable, such as peak load pricing (when we have too much capacity) and markdowns (when we have too much inventory). Put another way, we take prices as given, as in a competitive market.

15.4.1   Value-Maximizing Allocation of Capacity to Product Tiers

Suppose we have 100 hotel rooms to sell, at either the regular price of \$400 per night or an advanced-sale price of \$300 per night. It is important that these two customer segments can be separated. This is easy here, because the advanced price is available only until, say, two weeks before the stay. How many rooms should we allocate for the regular price?

To maximize NPV, at every period (say, every day), we have to balance the costs of overstocking and understocking these regular-priced rooms. This immediately recalls the newsvendor analysis in section 12.4. As before, let us set:

C_o = overstocking cost = \$400/night,

C_u = understocking cost = 400 − 300 = \$100/night,

service probability = $C_u/(C_u + C_o)$ = 100/(100 + 400) = 0.2.

Next, we find the mean and standard deviation of the regular-priced rooms. Let us say these are:

mean = 65,

standard deviation = 10.

Assuming that this is a normal distribution, we have:

Z = normsinv(0.2) from Excel = −0.842,

optimal number of regular-priced rooms = 65 − 0.842 × 10 = 57.

15.4.2 Value-Maximizing Amount of Overbooking

Continuing our previous hotel example, we now want to account for no-shows: some clients reserve rooms but do not show up. One solution is to allow some overbooking. But how many overbook reservations should we offer? Again, to maximize NPV, at every period we have to balance the costs of overbooking and underbooking.

We assume we can risk-pool regular and advanced-sale rooms—e.g., a no-show of an advanced-sale room might be compensated by a show of a regular room. Recall that we have the following:

regular rooms = 57, priced at \$400/night,

advanced-sale rooms = 43, priced at \$300/night.

One component of overbooking cost is the cost of reimbursing the guest who arrives but cannot get a room. Assume these overbooking costs:

regular rooms = \$200/night,

advanced-sale rooms = \$150/night.

So we have the following:

$$C_o = \text{overbooking cost} = \frac{57}{100}200 + \frac{43}{100}150 = \$178.5/\text{night},$$

$$C_u = \text{underbooking cost} = \frac{57}{100}400 + \frac{43}{100}300 = \$357/\text{night},$$

service probability = $C_u/(C_u + C_o)$ = 178.5/(357 + 178.5) = 0.33.

As before, we find the mean and standard deviation, but this time we want the distribution of both regular and advanced-sale no-shows. Say we have these:

mean = 10,

standard deviation = 3.

Suppose this distribution is normal. We have:

Z = normsinv(0.33) from Excel = −0.431,

optimal number of overbooked rooms = $10 − 0.431 \times 3 = 9$.

There are of course more complexities than the examples above can convey. For example, what if clients register in groups? What if there is some leakage from one product tier to another? By combining the above technique with those described elsewhere (e.g., real options), we can more accurately management revenues.

15.4.3   Advanced Topic: The Pricing of Warranties

Recall from section 10.3.5 how we arrive at warranty reserves, based on how long the warranty period is. But how long should the warranty be? This depends on the customer's pricing of warranty. Specifically (and reusing notation from section 10.3.5), we denote:

- MTTF = mean time between failures in months,
- w = length of the warranty period in months,
- p = the unit price to the customer with warranty,
- p^- = the unit price to the customer without warranty.

The customer's willingness to pay $p − p^-$ more for a warranty of length w (i.e., the price of warranty) allows us to determine w.

We assume that a customer uses the product continuously. That is, if the unit fails, the customer gets a new unit, either through the warranty program or via a new purchase.

Notice that we now use the customer's perspective, which is different from the producer's perspective in section 10.3.5. There, a producer's concern ends when the warranty expires. But here the customer's perspective can be different. Take, for example, the customer buying units under a free replacement warranty, in which she gets a free replacement unit if her unit fails during the warranty period. On warranty expiration, she continues using the unit until it fails, at which time she buys another unit and the cycle continues. Therefore, the customer's concern may last beyond the warranty period.

Let us return to calculating w, which depends on the price of warranty—i.e., what the customer is willing to pay for a unit with and without warranty. Recall that there are two main types of warranties: a free replacement policy, in which the failed unit is replaced free of charge, and a pro-rata policy, in which the customer receives a rebate equal to p prorated with the remaining warranty time (recall figure 10.7).

Start with free replacement warranties: we equate the customer's per-month cost for a unit without and with warranty; from the equation, we find w.

If the customer buys a unit without warranty, she pays $\$p^-$ to use a unit over MTTF months until the unit breaks, so she in effect pays $\$p^-$/MTTF per month. If the customer buys a unit with warranty, she pays $\$p$ but enjoys use over a cycle. The first part of the cycle is covered by warranty, which lasts w months. The second is a unit (it could be the original or a replaced unit) lasting beyond the warranty period. Assuming that the failure rate is random, the time to failure is memoryless, and is MTTF months. So the time cost is $\$p/(w + \text{MTTF})$ per month.

For the right w, the customer should be indifferent to the two costs:

$$\text{no warranty} = \frac{p^-}{\text{MTTF}} = \frac{p}{w + \text{MTTF}} = \text{free replacement warranty.}$$

From this equation, the warranty period w is given by:

$$w = \text{MTTF}\left(\frac{p}{p^-} - 1\right).$$

Put another way, if we were selling free replacement warranties, we should set our warranty time price at $(p - p^-)/w$.

Now let us consider pro-rata warranties. If the customer buys a unit without warranty, her cost is $\$p^-$/MTTF per month, as before. If the customer buys a unit with warranty, the cost depends on whether the unit breaks during or after w. Let us denote:

t = time the unit breaks (0 is the time of purchase).

If the unit breaks during warranty—that is, for t between 0 and w—the customer pays p but gets a rebate of $p(1 - t/w)$ (see section 10.3.5), so she pays pt/w net. If the unit breaks after warranty—for t from w to infinity—the cost is p.

To get the expected cost, we multiply these costs by the probability of failure at time t (reproducing that in section 10.3.5):

$P(\text{unit fails at time } t) = e^{-t/\text{MTTF}}/\text{MTTF.}$

Therefore, the expected cost is:

$$\int_0^w \left(\frac{e^{-\frac{t}{\text{MTTF}}}}{\text{MTTF}}\right)\frac{pt}{w}\,dt + \int_w^\infty \left(\frac{e^{-\frac{t}{\text{MTTF}}}}{\text{MTTF}}\right)p\,dt = \frac{p}{w}\left[\text{MTTF} - e^{-\frac{w}{\text{MTTF}}}(\text{MTTF} + w)\right] + p\left(e^{-\frac{w}{\text{MTTF}}}\right).$$

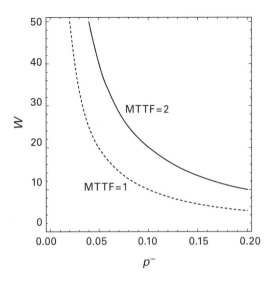

Figure 15.7
Warranty period for various unit prices and MTTF values.

The customer's effective cost per unit time is expected cost (above) divided by MTTF, the expected time to failure:

$$\frac{\left\{\frac{p}{w}\left[\text{MTTF} - e^{-\frac{w}{\text{MTTF}}}(\text{MTTF}+w)\right] + p\left(e^{-\frac{w}{\text{MTTF}}}\right)\right\}}{\text{MTTF}} = \frac{p}{w}\left(1 - e^{-\frac{w}{\text{MTTF}}}\right).$$

As before, we equate the two time costs to get w:

$$\text{no warranty} = \frac{p^-}{\text{MTTF}} = \frac{p}{w}\left(1 - e^{-\frac{w}{\text{MTTF}}}\right) = \text{pro rata warranty}.$$

This time, we cannot get a closed-form formula for w, but we can plot w for various values of p^- and MTTF as in figure 15.7, in which we normalize p to \$1. As expected, w decreases as p^- gets closer to p so that the customer's willingness to pay for the warranty is reduced. But w increases with MTTF, as expected.

15.5   Performance Management

We first outline the broader issue of governance, then focus on three tools of performance management: operational incentives, process auditing, and measures that balance financial and operational considerations.

The issue of governance arises because of the separation between a principal and an agent who works for the principal. External governance concerns issues between holders of equity/debt and the firm's management. Internal governance concerns issues between higher management (say a CEO) and lower (say a divisional manager).

Governance issues arise mostly because of issues of agency (misalignment of interests between an agent and a principal) and information asymmetry (the principal does not know exactly what the agent is doing).

There are several possible results:

- *Empire-building.*   Agents hoard resources and overinvest in plants with questionable returns or in fruitless acquisitions and diversifications. They do this to maximize their job security (called "entrenchment" in the research literature) or reputation ("career concerns"), among many other reasons.

- *Short-termism.*   We described this in section 4.4. For example, agents holding shares in the business might overinvest in the business for short-term boosts in earnings or sales, even if these come at the expense of longer-term results.

- *Shirking.*   Here, the idea is that agents prefer to do less rather than more. This can lead to underinvestment when agents do not execute profitable opportunities, or overinvestment when agents do not cut losses.

- *Herding.*   Suppose some agents are better than others, in terms of information they have and actions they take. An unfortunate consequence of information asymmetry is that the principal—not knowing which agent is good and which is not—would rationally judge that agents who act like others are more likely to be good. So even good agents tend to "follow the herd," hurting the efficient allocation of investments.

There are some generic approaches to address governance. Some apply to external governance, some to internal, and some to both:

- *Constrain free cash flow.*   It has been empirically established that firms constrained in financing invest less. To constrain agency, the CEO may restrict the actions of his supervisees, board directors may ask that the firm disgorge excess cash, or the firm may take on debt, because this needs regular repayments and the debt overhang limits the additional financing that the firm can obtain. What is less certain is whether the constraint is reducing overinvestment (which would be good) or is really introducing underinvestment (bad). But if we know that overinvestment is likely, then this is certainly a possible approach.

- *Covenants, claim rankings, and distress.*   Many financiers—especially debt providers—introduce covenants so that the firm needs to gain explicit approval from the debt holders for materially significant actions such as large investments. Further, financiers have explicit rankings of claims on the firm, to further discourage overly risky investments that can push the firm into distress, with negative consequences for the agent.

• **Norms.**   We should not forget that cultural issues can provide strong constraints on behavior. Strong company loyalty, high morale, low staff turnover, slower expansion, and feedback systems all address agency issues.

• **Incentives.**   The crux in designing incentives is to balance a number of conflicting goals:

> Encouraging an agent to work hard and take appropriate risks, but curbing the agent from taking too much inappropriate risks. For example, if a manager is given a bonus for sales but not penalized for overstock, the manager might take inappropriate risks by stocking up as much as possible.

> Providing for the agent's risk aversion: employees work rather than become entrepreneurs themselves because they are more risk averse; they prefer a stable to a volatile income stream, even if the expected value of the volatile stream is higher.

> Getting the agent to reveal true information (e.g., sales forecast, the agent's true potential) despite the possibility that this information may be used against the agent (e.g., there may be a penalty for not meeting the forecast, or the forecast may be upped for the next period).

We show an example of how to create incentives in the next section.

• **Auditing.**   As mentioned earlier, a source of agency problems is information asymmetry. Such problems may be reduced to the extent that we have a disciplined approach to gathering more information. Below, we delve into auditing processes.

• **Measures.**   One of the main complaints about incentive systems is that they are too narrowly defined. In the final subsection, we focus on the "balanced scorecard" as an antidote to this problem.

15.5.1   The Gonik Incentive Scheme

As mentioned, incentive design has to address a few issues. Jacob Gonik of IBM Brazil proposed an approach that has more than doubled revenues since the transition from a traditional salary-plus-bonus scheme. The Gonik scheme has been subject to rigorous scrutiny in the research literature.

The issue is that a sales staff's performance is determined by several components indistinguishable to the principal: effort, territory potential, and noise, such as uncertainty in the economy.

The Gonik scheme begins with the firm deciding how much to compensate, assuming maximum effort by the salesperson, for various sales levels, due to differing sales potential in the salesperson's territory. Then the firm asks the salesperson to announce her forecast at the beginning of the sales period. Importantly, her compensation is such that it is highest if she meets her forecast; see figure 15.8. This means that there is no incentive to provide

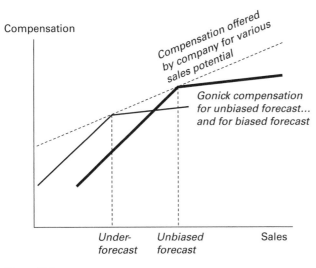

Figure 15.8
The Gonik incentive scheme. Adapted from Chen (2005).

a biased forecast. In the figure, we see that the highest compensation for the sales staff is obtained only when she provides an unbiased forecast and exerts maximum effort.

Although it is primarily designed for sales staff, the Gonik scheme may be modified for other types of staff.

15.5.2 Time Equations and the Process Audit

We next consider processes. A useful way to measure process efficiency is activity-based costing, or ABC. Traditionally, ABC asks workers to split their time spent on various activities (e.g., a worker might spend 22% of each day to process credit card applications) and cost these out (e.g., if a worker costs $55,000 per year, then that worker's cost in processing the applications is $55,000 × 22% = $12,100 each person-year). With such information, we streamline activities that seem out of line in costs—when these are compared, say, between workers in the same unit, or between like activities, or even between firms—or where cost trends are worsening.

One concern with traditional ABC is that workers tend to underestimate their underutilization, and they find it extraordinarily difficult to estimate the time they spend on transactions of varying complexities. In time-driven ABC, workers' estimates are different: (1) instead of estimating the percentage of time, they estimate the amount of time; (2) instead of estimating for a day, they estimate the time spent on a single unit (e.g., one credit card application); and (3) instead of estimating for a variety of complex transactions, they estimate the time spent on the simplest, most common transaction. The insight in the last point is that workers find it easier to estimate what additional time they need for additional complexity. An example of such a *time equation* is:

time to process one credit card application = 6 minutes,

[+ 10 minutes if applicant's credit score is below 550],

[+ 5 minutes if applicant does not also have a deposit account].

Time equations also provide an even clearer basis for efficiency improvement programs, and for additional pricing for more complex work.

Still, time equations give only a cost perspective to processes. Michael Hammer (2007) suggested a number of further dimensions for auditing a process; see table 15.4.

15.5.3   The Balanced Scorecard

Just as the process audit provides a more complete way to audit a process, the balanced scorecard provides a more complete view of the business on a recurrent basis.

Table 15.4
Dimensions of a Process Audit

Dimension	Subdimension	Average	Best Practice
Design	Purpose	Patches from legacy, no explicit purpose	Fits supply chain processes; end-to-end
	Context	Identified inputs, outputs, suppliers, customers	Mutually defined expectations with customers, suppliers
	Documentation	Documented functions	Electronic, collaborative analyses
Performers	Knowledge	Can identify performance metrics	Familiar with interfirm performance too
	Skills	Local problem solving	Change management too
	Behavior	Allegiance to functions	Seeks end-to-end improvements
Owner	Identity	Individual or group informally charged with improvements	Member of the firm's senior decision-making body
	Activities	Communicates to all performers, sponsors small-scale changes	Develops rolling strategic plan, collaborates with supply chain counterparts
	Authority	Encourages functional managers to make changes	Controls process's budget and personnel assignments
Infrastructure	Information systems	Fragmented legacy IT support	Modular IT architecture supporting supply chain
	Human resource systems	Rewards functional excellence	Hires, develops, rewards end-to-end and supply chain improvements
Metrics	Definition	Some basic cost and quality metrics	Metrics derived from supply chain goals
	Uses	Track functional performance, identify causes	Regularly refreshed; also for strategic planning

Adapted from Hammer (2007).

Table 15.5
Balanced Scorecard of Electronic Circuits Incorporated

Goals	Measures	Goals	Measures
Financial perspective		**Internal business perspective**	
Survive	Cash flow	Technology capability	Manufacturing geometry versus competition
Succeed	Quarterly sales growth and operating income by division	Manufacturing excellence	Cycle time, unit cost, yield
Prosper	Increased market share and ROE	Design productivity	Silicon efficiency, engineering efficiency
Customer perspective		**Innovation, learning perspective**	
New products	% of sales from new products, % of sales from proprietary products	Technology leadership	Time to develop next generation
Responsive supply	On-time delivery defined by customer	Manufacturing learning	Process time to maturity
Preferred suppliers	Share of key accounts' purchases; ranking by key accounts	Product focus	% of products that equal 80% of sales
Customer partnerships	Number of cooperative engineering efforts	Time to market	New product introduction versus competition

Source: Kaplan and Norton (1992).

Table 15.5 shows an example for Electronic Circuits Incorporated, a semiconductor manufacturer. There are several important considerations in choosing measures for the scorecard. The first is that the measures, as much as possible, should be leading indicators of performance. The chapters in part 1 of this book all provide some guidance on what these indicators might be. The appendix provides additional guidance on industry-specific indicators.

Second, as far as possible the measures should be mutually exclusive and collectively exhaustive. By drawing up a tree, for example, we can achieve this purpose (recall section 7.2.1).

Third, it may seem that a plethora of measures let managers avoid thinking hard about tradeoffs, which is the core of strategy. However, many practical users of the balanced scorecard address this issue by assigning different thresholds to tradeoffs. Measures with higher thresholds are areas of priority; those with lower thresholds require attention only if they fall below those thresholds.

15.6 Investor Management

No matter how much a business thinks its turnaround is on track, it is difficult to convey that credibly to investors (by which we include their proxies, such as analysts). The issue (recall section 4.2) is twofold: (1) information asymmetry, in that outsiders (investors without board seats, analysts) inherently cannot be as informed about a business as insiders (managers, investors with board seats); and (2) agency, in that insiders often have incentives to misrepresent the true situation of the business to outsiders.

Therefore, if we are to have a sustainable turnaround, it seems that we should at least consider the issue of how to properly manage outside investors. From the previous discussion, we can tackle the twin issues of information asymmetry and agency.

It seems obvious that firms should disclose more information and on a more timely basis. But greater disclosure has its own issues:

• *Cost of compliance* (e.g., hiring auditors) and production (e.g., hiring more bookkeepers),

• *Cost of exposing* proprietary information to the competition, suppliers, customers, or regulators,

• *Equally low credibility* of additional information disclosed; indeed, there is often the problem of outsiders second-guessing why a business is offering to disclose more,

• *Other sources* of information—such as the public media—are available anyway,

• *Risk of unauthorized disclosure,* including disclosure in a format that may be construed as providing insider information.

Similarly, the approach of reducing agency has its own issues. We give examples of these, reviewing some sources of agency described in section 15.5:

• *Empire-building.*   One approach is to impose self-discipline. For example, CUC International, on finding it difficult to persuade outside investors of the long-term attractiveness of its proposed marketing investments, decided to lever up its balance sheet, including recapitalizing its equity and buying back shares. But this exposed the business to other costs, such as the greater probability of distress.

• *Short-termism.*   Managerial compensation could be vested over a longer term; but this would blunt the sharpness of incentives, and introduce more noise into the incentive design.

• *Shirking.*   Managerial compensation could have a higher performance-based component; but the correspondingly reduced fixed-salary component would force too much risk onto risk-averse managers.

• *Herding.*   One approach, which also addresses the other agency issues, is to take the business private; but this reduces the wealth diversification of the manager-entrepreneur, again putting too much risk onto her.

In short, it is not easy at all to increase the credibility of messages to outside investors.

15.6.1   Tailoring Management by Investor Segment

One approach to managing the challenges just described is to tailor investor management by segment. Palter, Rehm, and Shih (2008) provide an example of such segmentation,

Table 15.6
Average Characteristics of Investor Segments

Investor Segment	Intrinsic	Mechanical	Trading-Oriented
Examples	Warren Buffett, venture capital, private equity*	Computer-run and closet index funds	Day traders
Percent of US equity (segments not exhaustive)	20	32	35
Concentration (investment as % of portfolio)	2–10	<1	<1
Primary basis of investment decisions	Fundamental analysis	Financial ratios	News
Impact on market	Via opinion	Via trading intensity	Via trading intensity
Investment per buy-side analyst	4–10	100–150	>20
Investment holding period	3–8 years	Months	Days, hours
Trading volume per segment ($trillion/year)	3	11	6
Trading volume per investor ($billion/year)	6	88	6
Trading volume per investment per investor ($million/day)	79–109	1	1

Source: Palter, Rehm, and Shih (2008).
* Palter, Rehm, and Shih's analysis focuses on public securities, but venture capital and private equity investors mostly fall in this category.

summarized in table 15.6, which shows the characteristics of intrinsic, mechanical, and trading-oriented investors.

Importantly, intrinsic investors are more willing to listen and discuss a business's prospects, making it more worthwhile to engage them. Their advantage is in gaining a fuller understanding of the operations and economics of their investees, so a subject like operations forensics fits with their interests.

At the opposite extreme, mechanical investors rarely take management's qualitative discussions into direct consideration, and instead base their investments mainly on financial ratios. Even for closet index funds—institutional investors whose portfolios resemble index funds because these portfolios are enormous—that have analysts to supplement computerized trading, the analysts follow a large number of investments, making it difficult for them to analyze businesses in detail.

Finally, trading-oriented investors care about news about the business, but it is not their trading strategy to get too deep into the news.

The segmentation provides a considered guideline for managing investors. For intrinsic investors, there is value in engaging them frequently, frankly, and deeply. The extent of engagement might be similar to that for venture capitalists; see table 15.7. While clearly it is legally only possible to communicate the same information to all investors at the same time, it is useful to get from—not deliver to—intrinsic investors information that can be helpful to the business.

Table 15.7
Intensity of Contact between Venture Capital Firm's Five Lead Partners and Seven Investee Companies

Characteristics of Contact	Mean	Standard Deviation
Number of visits per year	3.85	1.68
Length of each visit (hours)	2.43	0.79
Number of telephone calls per year	9.43	3.21
Length of each call (minutes)	12.14	4.88

Source: Sweeting and Wong (1997).

This approach concentrates senior management time on listening to and crafting messages for intrinsic investors. It also allows investor relations to focus on: (1) ensuring that messages intended for one segment do not get misinterpreted by another, and (2) focusing their energies on messaging for mechanical and especially trading-oriented investors. Finally, it also implies that senior management engage investors at locations where intrinsic investors are more likely to gather, such as conferences at product association meetings, industry conferences, and money centers.

Finally, it bears recalling that the set of investors can be endogenously selected to some extent. For example, if intrinsic investors are the target, then it would be inconsistent to spend senior management time meeting with index funds. Some analysts may find it inconvenient that only a company's investor relations staff—and not its senior executives—can meet some of the analysts' highest-trading clients. However, there is some evidence that companies with an investor selection approach do not lose analyst following, because most analysts work for a diverse enough set of investors that the analysts can find the right investors for the right companies.

15.6.2   Some Operationally Related Investor Relations Initiatives

At the beginning of this section, we listed some initiatives to overcome information asymmetry and agency problems, although we also described some of the challenges in implementing these initiatives. Here, we make that list more complete by focusing on operationally related initiatives:

• *Appoint operationally savvy board directors.*   Such directors have the obvious value of bringing expertise, both in directing the company and in communicating with investors.

• *Complement in-house investor relations* with outside investor relations with expertise in managing intrinsic investors. Research also shows that strong investor relations focus on increasing visibility and management access, rather than increasing disclosure.

• *Provide selective disclosure of operational metrics.*   For example, if a business is consistently ahead of its industry in inventory management, then it makes sense to disclose the aging profile of its inventory.

Finally, we should mention a radical approach: at the extreme, some companies have gone private when it is too challenging to have investors understand the operations of the business.

15.7   Takeaways

Turning around is only the first step. In this chapter, we focus on recurrent processes that need to be in place to sustain a successful turnaround. These include:

• *Quality management.*   We develop formulas for the profit-maximizing level of controlling output quality and controlling process quality.

• *Innovation management.*   We describe a linear programming approach to selecting innovations to pursue, a model for organizing the development of the innovations (e.g., in-house, outsourced to a collection of outsiders), and a model of commercializing the developed innovation (i.e., whether to push an innovation out faster, or to develop it more before commercialization).

• *Revenue management.*   We provide formulations for allocating capacity to different product tiers (first class versus economy class) and for overbooking capacities, so as to maximize revenues in the face of uncertain demand.

• *Performance   management.* How   do   we   measure   and   track   operational improvements?

• *Investor management.*   How do we tell an operational narrative to an audience that might be skeptical, uninterested, or not ready?

We also describe operations- and organization-oriented turnarounds. There is some evidence that neither by itself is sufficient for sustaining turnaround. Instead, we need both, which is best done sequentially, operational followed by organizational.

15.8   Survey of Prior Research in One Paragraph

There is a paucity of rigorous research on turnarounds. Michael Beer and Nitin Nohria's paper is one of the soundest ones. The quality movement was started by famous names: W. Edwards Deming, Joseph M. Juran, Kaoru Ishikawa, Taiichi Ohno, Walter A. Shewhart, Shigeo Shingo, Eiji Toyoda, Eitan Zemel, and others. The texts by Steve Nahmias and by Wally Hopp and Mark Spearman contain excellent discussions of modern quality management. Garrett van Ryzin and his students have done much to establish the state of the art in revenue management. Mark Ferguson and his associates describe a fascinating case of using revenue management in Harrah's Cherokee Casino & Hotel. Rajiv Banker, Dennis Campbell, Chris Ittner, Bob Kaplan, David Larcker, and Marshall Meyer are some of the leaders in research on performance management. The discussion of the Gonik scheme is due to Fangruo Chen. Brian Bushee and Greg Miller are authorities on investor relations.

15.9 Further Reading

Banker, R. D., I. R. Bardhan, H. Chang, and S. Lin. 2006. "Plant Information Systems, Manufacturing Capabilities and Plant Performance." *Management Information Systems Quarterly* 30 (2): 7.

Beer, M., and N. Nohria. 2000. "Cracking the Code of Change." *Harvard Business Review* 78 (3): 133–141.

Bushee, B. J., and G. S. Miller. 2007. "Investor Relations, Firm Visibility, and Investor Following." *Journal of Accounting and Economics* 34: 149–180.

Campbell, D., S. M. Datar, S. L. Kulp, and V. G. Narayanan. 2006. "The Strategic Information Content of Non-Financial Performance Measures." Working paper, Harvard Business School, Boston.

Chen, F. 2005. "Salesforce Incentives, Market Information, and Production/Inventory Planning." *Management Science* 51 (1): 60–75.

Cohen, M. A., J. Eliashberg, and T. H. Ho. 1996. "New Product Development: The Performance and Time-to-Market Tradeoff." *Management Science* 42 (2): 173–186.

Hammer, M. 2007. "The Process Audit." *Harvard Business Review* 85 (4): 111–123.

Hopp, W. J., and M. L. Spearman. 2001. *Factory Physics*. Boston: McGraw-Hill/Irwin.

Ittner, C. D., and D. F. Larcker. 1998. "Are Nonfinancial Measures Leading Indicators of Financial Performance? An Analysis of Customer Satisfaction." *Journal of Accounting Research* 36 (suppl.): 1–35.

Ittner, C. D., and D. F. Larcker. 1997. "The Performance Effects of Process Management Techniques." *Management Science* 43 (4): 522–534.

Ittner, C. D., D. F. Larcker, and M. W. Meyer. 2003. "Subjectivity and the Weighting of Performance Measures: Evidence from a Balanced Scorecard." *Accounting Review* 78 (3): 725–758.

Kaplan, R. S., and S. R. Anderson. 2004. "Time-Driven Activity-Based Costing." *Harvard Business Review* 82 (11): 131–138.

Kaplan, R. S., and D. P. Norton. 1995. "Putting the Balanced Scorecard to Work." In D. G. Shaw et al., eds., *The Performance Measurement, Management, and Appraisal Sourcebook*, 66. Amherst, MA: Human Resource Development Press.

Kaplan, R. S., and D. P. Norton. 1992. "The Balanced Scorecard: Measures that Drive Performance." *Harvard Business Review* 70 (1): 71–79.

Loch, C. H., M. T. Pich, C. Terwiesch, and M. Urbschat. 2001. "Selecting R&D Projects at BMW: A Case Study of Adopting Mathematical Programming Models." *IEEE Transactions on Engineering Management* 48 (1): 70–80.

Metters, R., C. Queenan, M. Ferguson, L. Harrison, J. Higbie, S. Ward, B. Barfield, T. Farley, H. A. Kuyumcu, and A. Duggasani. 2008. "The 'Killer Application' of Revenue Management: Harrah's Cherokee Casino & Hotel." *Interfaces* 38 (3): 161–175.

Nahmias, S. 2005. *Production and Operations Analysis*. 5th ed. Boston: McGraw-Hill/Irwin.

Palter, R. N., W. Rehm, and J. Shih. 2008. "Communicating with the Right Investors." *McKinsey Quarterly* 2: 64.

Pisano, G. P. 1994. "Knowledge, Integration, and the Locus of Learning: An Empirical Analysis of Process Development." *Strategic Management Journal* 15 (S1): 85–100.

Sweeting, R. C., and C. F. Wong. 1997. "A UK 'Hands-Off' Venture Capital Firm and the Handling of Post-Investment Investor-Investee Relationships." *Journal of Management Studies* 34 (1): 125–152.

Talluri, K. T., and G. Van Ryzin. 2005. *The Theory and Practice of Revenue Management*. New York: Springer.

Terwiesch, C., and K. Ulrich. 2009. *Innovation Tournaments: Creating, Selecting, and Developing Exceptional Opportunities*. Boston: Harvard Business School Press.

Terwiesch, C., and Y. Xu. 2008. "Innovation Contests, Open Innovation, and Multiagent Problem Solving." *Management Science* 54 (9): 1529–1543.

Von Hippel, E., and E. A. Von Hippel. 1988. *The Sources of Innovation*. New York: Oxford University Press.

Zemell, E. 1992. "Yes, Virginia, There Really Is Total Quality Management." Anheuser-Bush Distinguished Lecture Series, SEI Center for Advanced Studies in Management, Wharton School, Philadelphia.

Appendix A   Industry ROA Trees

In section 3.1, we described return on assets (ROA) trees in several industries to illustrate how operational indicators at the leaves of these trees could affect various measures of performance, such as earnings and ultimately ROA. Here we provide a more complete description of high-level ROA trees for various other industries.

A.1   ROA Tree for Retail Banking

Figure A.1 shows the ROA tree for a typical retail bank. It shows that retail banks have several major products, of which deposits and loans generate mostly interest revenues. Banks also get fee income from transfers, investments, services, and penalty charges. We can categorize expenses into bank, customer, and transaction levels. Bank-level expenses are the most aggregate and transaction-level the least; so the former approximates fixed costs and the latter variable costs.

To keep this discussion manageable, we limit it to ROA drivers that are specific to retail banking.

A.1.1   Pricing Deposits and Loans with Interbank Cost and Price of Funds

We should price deposits independently of loans, using the interbank rate as the price of funds for deposits and the cost of funds for loans. If we were to simply price them together, taking the loan rate minus the deposit rate as the joint profit of deposits and loans, we would confound the net revenues of the two products. We call these "net revenues" because they are net of the price or cost of funds.

Operationally, the key here is to keep the maturities of deposits and loans matched with their respective price and cost of funds. For example, ten-year loans should be matched to ten-year funds with the respective cost. Unless a bank is betting on interest rates by taking positions on mismatched maturities, it is important to constantly buy and sell funds to keep maturities matched.

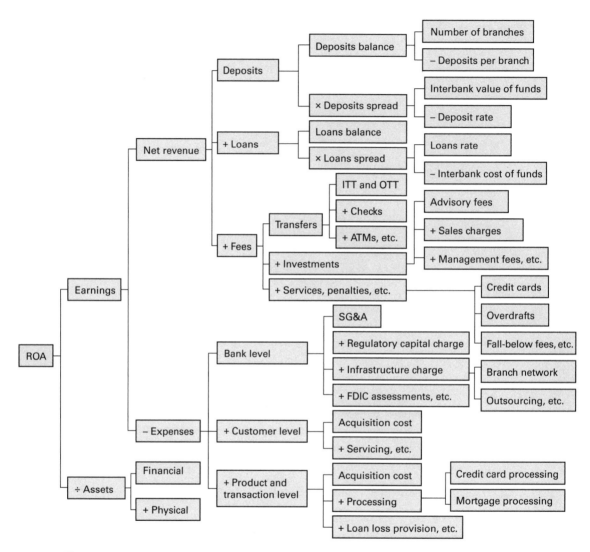

Figure A.1
ROA tree for a retail bank.

A.1.2 FDIC Assessments and Regulatory Capital

There are several types of expense that figure prominently in banks. One is the Federal Deposit Insurance Corporation (FDIC) assessment for deposit insurance. In 2009, this was 0.05% of some defined level of capital. This might seem small but, as we see below, the ROA of retail banks is usually within 1%. As another indication, a 2009 proposal by the FDIC to increase this to 0.2% "was resisted by regional bankers who said the fee could wipe out half of their profit."[1]

Another expense specific to banks is the charge for regulatory capital. Regulatory capital is the counterpart to deposit insurance in forming a cushion against loan risks. The Basel I scheme requires:

$$\text{Tier 1 capital ratio} = \frac{\text{common stock, disclosed reserves}}{\text{risk-adjusted assets}} \geq 6\%$$

$$\text{Tier 2 capital ratio} = \frac{\text{Tier 1, undisclosed reserves}}{\text{risk-adjusted assets}} \geq 10\%.$$

Risk-adjusted assets are obtained by assigning different weights to different asset classes, ranging from zero weight (0%) for cash equivalents to a high weight (100%) for clean loans—i.e., loans not secured with collateral. Table A.1 shows the Tier 1 ratio for some banks.

A.1.3 Efficiency Ratio and Branch Network Size

Two particularly prominent components retail bank infrastructure are branch networks and outsourced facilities. We discuss details of branch networks in chapter 14.

Here we just note that a common measure of bank productivity called the efficiency ratio—defined as noninterest expense divided by the sum of net interest income and non-interest income—tends to improve with branch network size. Table A.1 illustrates this relationship, with US Bancorp, which has 2,791 branches, with the best (lowest) efficiency ratio of 47%. There are of course exceptions, such as Sierra Bancorp, whose good ratio despite having a small branch network perhaps contributes to its high ROA.

Table A.1 presents some measures in the ROA tree of several US regional banks. Banks with more than 1% ROA are generally considered top performers (shown in the top half of the table).

The table illustrates a familiar theme of this book: that there is no single silver bullet, and that a business needs to do many things right in order to be a top performer. For example, while the top four banks appear to be generally more efficient in generating deposits than the bottom four, just deposit-generating efficiency is insufficient: Comerica has one of the industry's best efficiency ratios in this regard but still appears in the bottom four.

Table A.1
Examples of ROA Drivers for Some Banks

Higher ROA firms

	Westamerica Bancorp	US Bancorp	FirstMerit	Sierra Bancorp
ROA (%)	1.39	1.17	1.11	1.05
Efficiency ratio (%)	52	47	59	49
Number of branches	86	2,791	163	23
Revenues ($mil)	171	11,447	485	53
Credit card fee ($mil)	11	2,190	47	2.1
Tier 1 capital ratio (%)	11	11	10	12
Deposits/branch ($mil)	36	57	47	46

Lower ROA firms

	Comerica	Bank of Commerce Holdings	MB Financial	Columbia Banking System
ROA (%)	0.33	0.32	0.19	0.19
Efficiency ratio (%)	66	64	61	60
Number of branches	439	5	72	53
Revenues ($mil)	2,022	18	194	109
Credit card fee ($mil)	58	0.4	18	8.0
Tier 1 capital ratio (%)	11	12	12	13
Deposits/branch ($mil)	96	111	90	45

Source: Capital IQ, for US regional banks that have available data for the columns, for calendar year 2008.

A.2   ROA Tree for a Restaurant

Figure A.2 shows the ROA tree for a restaurant. Table A.2 shows data for some sample restaurants. We first describe some ROA drivers unique to restaurants, then offer some general observations about the table.

A.2.1   Revenues: Dupes with Coupons and Covers with Differing Tops

There are two ways to see what drives restaurant revenues. One is the product view, which is to look at sales volume. This is driven by dupes—the orders sent to the kitchen—and the average price of each dupe. Dupes are also collectively called the sales mix: how many orders of what menu items. The average price is driven by how customers order. For example, coupons—also called early birds—are those who might order low-ticket items, and having many of these would reduce the average price of dupes.

The other is the customer view: the number of covers—restaurant jargon for customers— per time period. This is driven by three factors. The first is the number of tables. Then there is table turn, which is how quickly the tables are used for each customer "top" (a "top" is a party of customers). In calculating turn, we might include off-hours, if we want

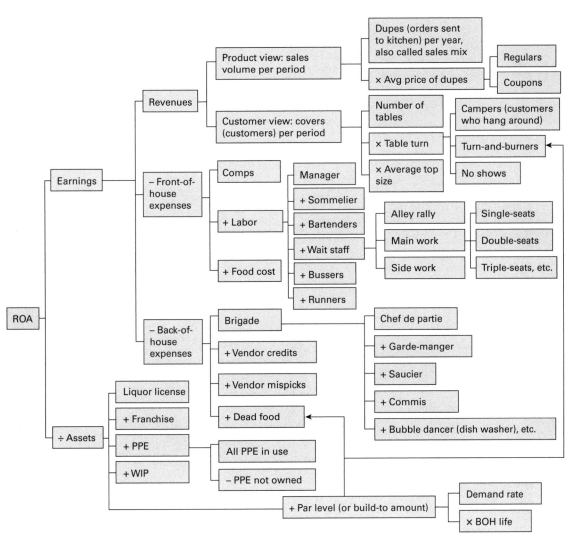

Figure A.2
ROA tree for a restaurant.

Table A.2
Examples of ROA Drivers for Some Restaurants

	EPL	Panera Bread	Yum! Brands	McDonald's	Tim Hortons
ROA (%)	3.79	10.6	13.1	13.6	14.2
Inventory turnover	122.6	75.7	63	125.7	33
Restaurants	413	1,325	36,292	31,967	3,437
Same-restaurant sales growth (%)	0.2	5.5	3	6.9	4.4
Owned restaurants	165	562	7,568	6,502	34
Franchise restaurants	248	763	28,079	21,328	3,403
Average-week sales/restaurant ($000)	—	39	—	—	—
Operating margin (%)	−9	8.7	—	27.4	21.7

Source: Capital IQ, for US restaurant chains that have available data for the columns, for calendar year 2008.

to consider utilization on a 24-hour basis. The third factor is top size—that is, how many customers are there in each top.

Table turn depends on how quickly we can set up a table for the next top. But mostly it depends on how long each top takes to clear the table. Here there is a mix. Campers are those who hang around long. Turn-and-burners are customers who finish quickly. And no-shows do not even show up, and could significantly reduce our table turn.

A.2.2   FOH Expenses: Comps, Food Costs, and Labor

Expenses in a restaurant may be divided into those at the front of the house (FOH) where customers are seated and those at the back of the house (BOH). FOH expenses often constitute the largest expense item for restaurants, so we need to explore them in more depth.

FOH expenses consist mainly of labor, although comps and food costs can be critical. Comp is an abbreviation for compensation, such as a second try at an oyster dish that is bad or a complimentary dessert. Food costs are the costs of the contents that go into served food.

Labor consists primarily of the wait staff. These spend most of their time on main work, which is waiting on customers. The utilization in this respect may be increased when wait staff are double-seated—that is, when one person waits on two tables—or even triple-seated. Wait staff also spend their time in the alley rally, the meeting usually held at the start of restaurant hours. Then there is side work, such as replenishing condiments at tables or even cleaning bathrooms.

There are usually other FOH staff. For example, the manager assumes overall responsibility for the restaurant, and the sommelier is the wine wait staff. Then there are bartenders, bussers, and runners whose responsibility is primarily to carry food to tables.

A.2.3   BOH Expenses: The Brigade, Dead Food, and Vendor Credits and Mispicks

At the back of the house (BOH), the most prominent expense is the brigade. This is the crew which primarily includes the chefs de partie, the chiefs at each cooking station, the garde-manger who takes care of cold preparations and desserts, the saucier who is responsible for sauces, the commis who help out, and others who do not cook, such as the "bubble dancer" who washes dishes.

Another tangible expense is wasted food, often called dead food. Vendor credits—sometimes called trade credits—are credits given by suppliers, but at a cost to the restaurant in the form of forgone discount on the invoices.

Another major BOH expense is vendor mispicks. These are inaccurate deliveries of supplies, perhaps because of wrong items (stock-keeping units or SKUs) or wrong quantities. The cost incurred in addressing these—such as labor time—can be high.

A.2.4   Assets: Liquor Licenses, PPE, WIP, and Par Level

Licenses are an important type of asset possessed by restaurants. Since beverages usually form a good portion of a restaurant's profits, the liquor license is especially important.

Then there is the value of the franchise. Notice again that our definition of assets includes not just those on financial statements, but also soft assets such as franchise value.

Next, we have property, plant, and equipment (PPE). An important consideration here is how much of the PPE really does not belong to the business, but to third parties such as franchisees. By using third-party PPE, a restaurant can boost its own ROA.

Of the food in production, work in progress (WIP) represents food under preparation, while par level—also called build-to amount—represents prepared food that is held for sale. The par level can be determined with Little's Law, a standard in operations management texts (see also section 7.2.3):

$$\text{inventory} = \text{flow rate} \times \text{flow time}.$$

Here inventory is the par level, flow rate is the demand rate, and flow time is the back-of-house life of the prepared food, which is how long the food stays in the BOH until it is sold.

Notice how the par level affects table turn. We show a link only to the turn-and-burners, because for these customers the par level is likely to be the bottleneck; for campers who stick around, serving food quicker is unlikely to raise ROA. The par level also affects the amount of dead food, since having too much prepared food means that more of it is likely to be wasted.

We see how these drivers work in table A.2, which shows the restaurant chain with the highest ROA on the right. As in other fields, businesses rarely prosper because of a single performance driver. Tim Hortons actually has the worst inventory turn among the five examples, but it more than compensates by having a low proportion of properties owned and a decent operating margin.

A.3   ROA Tree for Gaming

Figure A.3 shows the financial and operational drivers for ROA in gaming. Table A.3 shows the figures for some drivers in four gaming companies, ranked from left to right in terms of ROA. Here we focus on aspects specific to the gaming industry, leaving discussion of the rooms and food-and-beverage business lines to other sections that discuss hotel and restaurant ROA trees.

A.3.1   Win, Drop, Hold Ratio, and the House Advantage

In the gaming industry, gross profit is called win. Drop is the bet placed by customers. To be precise, drop needs to account for the floating amount of chips on the casino floor, such

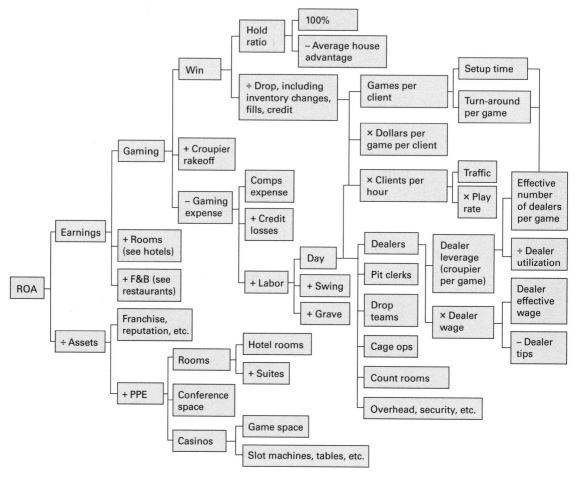

Figure A.3
ROA tree for a gaming house.

Table A.3
Examples of ROA Drivers for Some Gaming Companies

	Las Vegas Sands	MGM Mirage	Wynn Resorts	Ameristar Casinos
Return on assets (%)	0.9	2.7	3.3	5.0
Number of suites	10,282	1,117	2,034	423
Meeting and conference space (mil sq ft)	3.5	2.9	0.3	0.02
Owned casinos	5	17	3	8
Casinos	5	21	3	8
Gaming space (mil sq ft)	1.07	2.12	0.39	0.52
Slot machines	6,280	35,735	4,020	13,855
Tables	1,450	1,928	600	302
Gaming hold ratio (%)	31	46	34	53
Room margin (%)	80	72	76	80
Gaming win ($mil)	3,192	2,976	2,262	1,297
Gaming expenses	2,214	1,619	1,491	605
Food and beverage revenues ($mil)	369	1,582	359	157
Food and beverage expenses	187	931	207	75
Food and beverage promotional costs	71	289	80	63
Inventory turnover	114	34	20	93
Rooms revenues ($mil)	767	1,907	327	56
Rooms expenses	155	534	78	11
Rooms promotional costs	44	91	36	12

Source: COMPUSTAT, for calendar year 2008.

as hopper fills in slot machines and credit provided to clients. The hold ratio is win divided by drop. The hold ratio is another way to look at the house advantage, which is the expected amount of takings by the gaming house for every dollar of drop. Table A.3 shows that AmeriStar Casinos has the highest ROA among the four gaming houses analyzed, and also has the best hold ratio of 53%.

While the hold ratio may be fixed at the industry level, the drop could be operationally determined by individual gaming houses. The drop is a multiple of three factors: games per client, dollars per game per client, and clients per hour. Games per client is determined by the amount of time it takes to execute a game. This includes setup time and the time it takes to turn around the game. As a casino observer notes, "I recently played at a table where the dealer did three things that I would bet makes his employer more money. He shuffled quickly, he dealt quickly and he only cut one deck out of a six-deck shoe, as opposed to the norm in that casino of cutting out 1 1/2 to 2 decks. I'd be willing to bet he makes more money for that casino than his colleagues."[2]

The other operational lever is clients per hour, which is determined by the traffic through the casino and the play rate, which is the number of people in the traffic who choose to play—i.e., who become clients. This is equivalent to the conversion rate concept in other industries (e.g., see section A.9).

A.3.2 Croupier Rakeoffs

In some games such as *paigou*, clients play against each other rather than against the gaming house. The house's take is a percentage—or rakeoff—of the stakes played.

While we do not show the details of the drivers of rakeoff in figure A.3, it is not surprising that these are similar to those for win. That is, one part is the commission rate (analogous to the hold ratio) and the other is the drop.

A.3.3 Comps Expense and Credit Losses

Comps expense is the promotional expense incurred to bring in clients. This may include giving premier customers extra chips or discounted rooms.

Credit losses may be incurred just as with any financial institution: credit is granted to clients who may not pay up.

Operationally, the optimal amount of comps expense may be analyzed using revenue management techniques, because these expenses could be viewed as a tradeoff between lower pricing and greater volume, given uncertain demand. Some of issues are discussed in section 15.4.1.

A.3.4 Labor Expenses: Dealer Leverage and Utilization

As shown in figure A.3, there are three major types of labor: those who work the day shift, those in the graveyard shift (or simply called the "grave shift"), and those who are part-timers and work flexible "swing shifts."

The operational crew in each gaming shift includes the dealers, pit clerks, drop teams, cage operations (cashiers in the cages), and count room staff (who count chips and receipts). Then there is the overhead, security, and other staff. As an example, the key driver for the number of dealers is the dealer leverage or its equivalent for various games, and the dealer wage. The former is determined by actual dealers hired, even if the utilization of these dealers might be low if poorly scheduled (and it is the effective leverage that determines drivers like setup and turnaround time, as shown in figure A.3).

The other driver of dealer cost is dealer wage. Here we can subtract from the wage that dealers take home the amount of tips the dealer gets.

A.4 ROA Tree for Home Building

Figure A.4 shows the ROA tree for a typical home builder. Table A.4 shows data for five home builders, ranked left to right by ROA. It might be worth mentioning that sales and developments in 2008 were meager, perhaps explaining the low (mostly negative) ROAs in these figures.

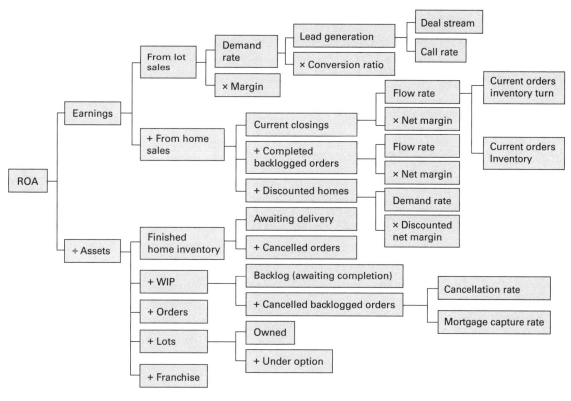

Figure A.4
ROA tree for a home builder.

A.4.1 Backlogs, Cancellation Rate, and Mortgage Capture Rate

One of the hardest metrics to interpret is the backlog. On the one hand, a large backlog of orders is decidedly good news. It suggests that the home builder has a pipeline of future profits. But a backlog also suggests more insidious problems. It could arise from a home builder inept in forecasting demand and managing capacity. It exposes the home builder to cancellation of the orders. Such cancellations can be especially high if the mortgage capture rate—the percentage of customers using mortgage financing—is high.

In a sense, this conundrum resembles that for inventory: large holdings suggest that a firm expects large impending sales, but they could also reflect an inept firm. We describe the mechanics of this in chapter 4.

A.4.2 Lot Banks and Options

Many home builders purchase lots on which to develop homes. Some others focus only on development, without taking on the inventory risk of holding on to lots. For those who

Table A.4
Examples of ROA Drivers for Some Home Builders

	Standard Pacific	Beazer Homes	MDC Holdings	Toll Brothers	NVR
ROA (%)	−0.55	−0.36	−0.15	−0.05	0.05
Finished home inventory turn	1.63	1.45	2.16	0.74	5.13
Backlog (average price $000)	301	241	325	648	317
Backlog (units)	642	1,358	533	2,046	3,164
Closings (average price $000)	330	249	303	655	338
Deliveries/closings (units)	4,607	7,692	4,488	4,743	10,741
Finished homes/work in progress	632	1,052	416	2,586	393
Land under development ($mil)	628	0	222	1,300	0
Inventory not owned ($mil)	43	107	0	223	144
Total inventory ($mil)	1,303	1,652	637	4,127	545
Undeveloped inventory owned ($mil)	0	493	0	19	8
Lots owned	19,306	39,627	7,577	32,081	
Lots under option	2,519	10,504	2,358	7,703	45,000
Orders (average price $000)			288	549	311
Orders (units)	3,946	6,065	3,074	2,927	8,760
Cancellation rate (%)	26		45		
Mortgage capture rate (%)		78		66	

Source: COMPUSTAT, for calendar year 2008.

purchase lots, clearly a high inventory turn helps the ROA. This might have been what happened at NVR in table A.4, where a turn of 5.13 was associated with a high 0.05% ROA.

Interestingly, some of the higher-performing home builders such as NVR and Toll Brothers also have large numbers of lots under option.

A.5   ROA Tree for Hotel Groups

Figure A.5 shows the ROA tree for a typical hotel group. ROA performance hinges on a few critical drivers. Table A.5 shows these for five hotel groups.

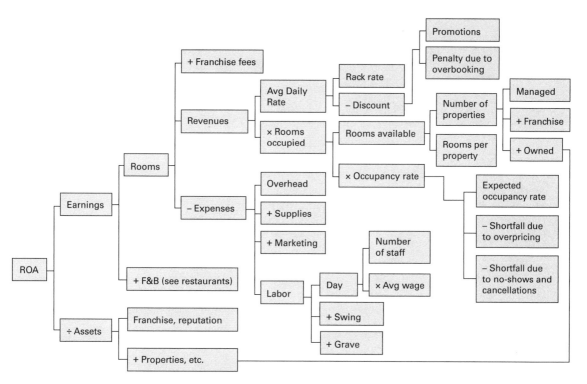

Figure A.5
ROA tree for a hotel.

Table A.5
Examples of ROA Drivers for Some Hotel Groups

	Red Lion	Marriott	Wyndham	Starwood	Choice Hotels
ROA (%)	0.00	0.04	−0.11	0.03	0.305
Inventory turn	115	6	5	4	
Average daily rate ($)	90.1	146.0	69.5	185.2	74.1
Number of properties	47	3,111	7,043	942	5,827
Revenue/available room	55	101	36	125	41
Number of rooms (000)	8.9	548	593	285	473
Occupancy rate	61.1	69.5	51.4	67.6	55.3
Owned properties		41			
Franchise properties		2,079			
Managed properties		1,058			

Source: COMPUSTAT, for calendar year 2008.

A.5.1   Occupancy Rate

The occupancy rate is the proportion of rooms that are sold out of the available rooms. More generally, we can consider other revenue properties—such as conference facilities, restaurant seats, retail space—along with rooms.

   The occupancy rate is partially driven by market demand, which we can call the expected occupancy rate, but there are operational issues that can reduce the effective occupancy rate. One is shortfall due to overpricing beyond what the market will bear. In an effort to forecast demand, we could have overestimated the strength of that demand. Conversely, there could also be shortfalls due to no-shows and cancellations. If we have not overbooked enough, these shortfalls will cut into our occupancy rate.

A.5.2   Rack Rates and Discounts

While the rack rate may be high, hotels tend to have a multitude of discounts. One is promotions offered to travel agents, groups, early reservations, and other opportunities. "Discounts" could also come in the form of penalties for overly aggressive overbooking. For example, we may have to give bigger rooms to guests at a lower price.

   Of course there are other operational issues, such as turnaround time for rooms. But these generally have a smaller impact on ROA; for example, a faster room turnaround might allow guests to check in earlier, but that alone is unlikely to improve ROA unless it is part of a broader strategic initiative to enhance guests' experiences.

A.6   ROA Tree for Healthcare

Figure A.6 shows an ROA tree for a typical healthcare provider. This time, we provide alternative ways of viewing different drivers. For example, revenues can be decomposed from a financing view—the sources of payment to the healthcare provider—or a patient view—whether the treatment is inpatient or outpatient.

A.6.1   Outcomes: Service, Clinical, and Process

We also mention "outcomes history" as an asset in that it builds a reputation for the provider. Of course, negative outcomes can be a liability. Table A.6 shows a range of measures for these outcomes. Importantly, these outcomes not only form a provider's assets or liabilities but can also affect revenues, as a higher reputation may lead to a greater number of visits.

A.6.2   Length of Stay: The Demand and Supply Views

Figure A.6 shows two ways of looking at the average length of stay. In the demand view, we consider patients, dividing the number of patient-days by the number of patients.

   In the supply view, we consider beds. Recall Little's Law: flow time = inventory / flow rate. Here, inventory is the beds in service and flow rate is the bed usage rate (how quickly

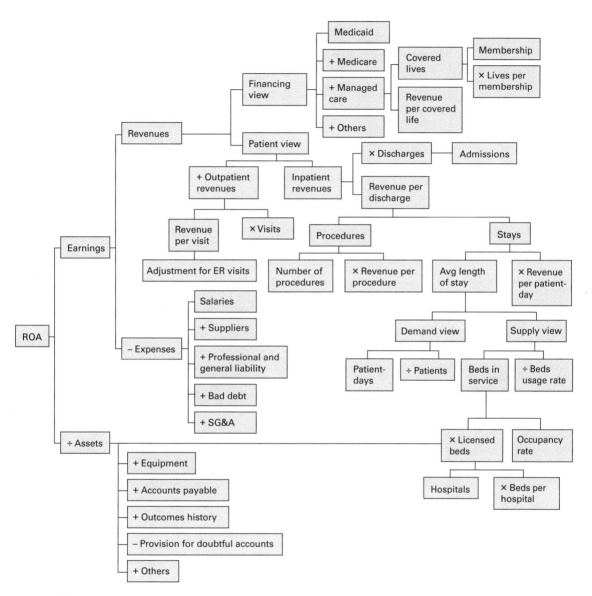

Figure A.6
ROA tree for a healthcare provider.

Table A.6
Healthcare Outcome Measures

Service outcomes
% referrals
Satisfaction with stay
Clinical outcomes
Mortality rate; CABG (coronary artery bypass graft) rate
Readmission rate
Central venous catheter infection rate
ORYX® measures for acute care
Aspirin administration within 24 hours post-MI (myocardial infarction)
Positive blood cultures in NICU (neonatal intensive care unit)
Birth trauma among high-risk women
Cesarean-section rates; C-section infection rates
Surgical site nosocomial infection rate
Stage of cancer at diagnosis
Process outcomes
Percent of transfusions having reactions
Accurate performance of transfusion protocols
Adverse drug reactions
Medicine error severity ratio
Autopsy rate
Correlation between pathology and autopsy reports
Employee exposures to blood and bodily fluids
Hours of emergency room diversion
Code response time
Restraint use rate
Specimen rejection rate
Abnormal mammogram turnaround time

Source: www.dashboardspy.com, accessed December 28, 2009. Note: ORYX® is not an acronym, and refers to a set of performance measures proposed by a joint commission.

the beds turn around). The former can be further decomposed into the number of beds in capacity ("licensed beds") and the percentage of them actually occupied.

Table A.7 shows ROA drivers for four healthcare providers. As before, we see that it is a combination of drivers, not a single one, that determines ROA. For example, MedCath Corp. has the highest ROA in the group. It achieves this by being generally good on a number of critical metrics, such as occupancy rate, bad debt, and salaries.

A.7   ROA Tree for the Semiconductor Industry

Figure A.7 is an illustrative ROA tree for a semiconductor manufacturer. Table A.8 shows some actual figures, ranked as usual by ROA.

A.7.1   Book-to-Bill Ratio and Backlogged Orders

The book-to-bill ratio is the ratio of the value of orders on the order book to the value of orders billed. A ratio of more than one means that new orders more than replace old ones

Table A.7
Examples of ROA Drivers for Some Healthcare Providers

	Tenet	SunLink	HCA	MedCath
ROA (%)	0.003	0.014	0.028	0.032
Medicaid (% of revenue)	8	14	8	4
Medicare (% of revenue)	25	42	29	39
Managed care (% of revenue)	55	0	53	
Other (% of revenue)	11	44	10	57
Revenue growth (%)			7	2
Outpatient service (% of revenue)				
Admissions (000)	527	9	1,542	29
Admissions growth (%)	1.2		0.9	
Average daily census (patient days)			20,795	
Bad debt (% of revenue)	7.2	13.9	12.0	7.1
Beds in service		588		464
Licensed beds	13,411	402	38,504	509
Patient days (mil)	2.6	0.0	7.6	0.1
Number of procedures (000)	361	4	1,291	24
Hospitals	48	10	271	7
Occupancy rate (%)	53	21	54	63
ER visits (mil)			5.25	
Outpatient visits (mil)	3.8		5.2	
Length of stay (days)	5	4	5	4
Salaries (% of revenue)	44	47	40	33
Supplies (% of revenue)	18	9	16	28
Inventory turn	45.6	22.4	32.6	33.5

Source: COMPUSTAT, for calendar year 2008.

and the business is growing, while a ratio of less than one means otherwise. Not surprisingly, the book-to-bill ratio is eagerly watched by analysts. In figure A.7 we show that the value of backlogged orders can be calculated by multiplying the book-to-bill ratio by the value of orders.

The value of backlogged orders can be derived using another "value view." As the figure shows, it is simply the number of backlogged orders multiplied by the average price of these orders.

Of course, the book-to-bill ratio is not the only indicator of performance. As table A.8 shows, ASM Pacific Technology has the highest ROA among the five companies shown, though its book-to-bill ratio is mediocre. The company has, however, an impressive inventory turnover ratio of 3.49, which partially contributes to its high ROA.

A.8 ROA Tree for Oil Exploration and Development

The oil business provides a different perspective on ROA trees. We focus on metrics that are specific to the oil industry.

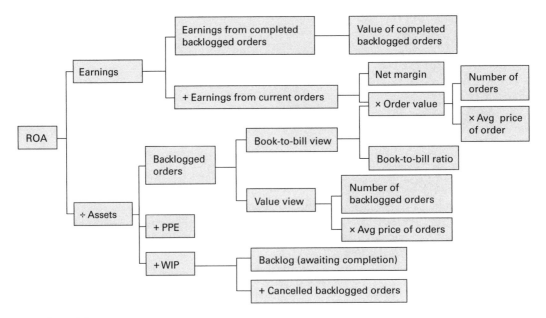

Figure A.7
ROA tree for a semiconductor manufacturer.

Table A.8
Examples of ROA Drivers for Some Semiconductor Manufacturers

	BE Semiconductor	Veeco	SUSS MicroTec	ASM International	ASM Pacific Technology
ROA (%)	−0.881	2.06	2.4	5.3	17.1
Inventory turnover	2.11	2.74	1.68	2.37	3.49
Book-to-bill ratio	0.85	0.96	0.93	0.85	0.86
Order value ($mil)	176.5	424.4	194.2	891.1	74.6
Change in order value (%)	−21.4	−6	−7.1	−31	−21.7
Bookings ($mil)	175	424			887
Backlog value ($mil)	35.5	147.2	97.4	126.7	6.84
Warranty reserves end ($mil)	3.73	6.89	2.67	13.9	

Source: Capital IQ, for calendar year 2008.

A.8.1   Netback, FDA, and the Recycle Ratio

Earnings are usually calculated as a multiple of "netback" (profit per barrel) and oil production volume. Netback is determined by oil prices less expenses.

There is also an oft-used term called the recycle ratio, which is netback divided by the "find, development, and acquisition" (FDA) cost.

A.8.2   Reserves and Decline Rate

On the asset side, the principal components are reserves and infrastructure. Reserves are usually divided by their likelihood of yielding oil, from possible to probable to proven. Part of the proven reserves are put into production and part not.

In the oil industry, production is driven by the size of reserves being developed and the yield—i.e., the percentage of reserves that is extracted by year. A crucial operating metric is the *decline rate*, which captures how much reserves shrink over time.

Infrastructure is commonly divided into various equipment from the oil field to the customer. Some elements, such as the number of wells, are both a direct infrastructure asset as well as a driver of the size of possible reserves. Of course, as a driver of reserves, wells must be successful (that is, yield adequate amounts of oil). The success rate of wells is another critical operational metric.

Table A.9 shows figures for some oil companies. Those in the top half of the table have higher ROAs than those in the bottom half. Three of the low-ROA firms—Cabot Oil & Gas, Cross Canyon Energy, and Chesapeake Energy—have the highest costs for their production volume. We see that costs—whether for finding, developing, or acquiring reserves—are generally lower when scaled by production. The other low-ROA firm—Pioneer Natural Resources Company—has the lowest ratio of sales to production (62%), which might have overwhelmed its production scale.

A.9   ROA Tree for Retailing

Figure A.9 shows an ROA tree for a typical retailer. Its earnings are driven by the difference between gross margin and expenses. Gross margin includes revenues from different channels, less the cost of goods sold (COGS). As with many other businesses, retailing also has many intangible assets such as customer goodwill and reputation, a notable example of which is the retailer's brand franchise. Some other important drivers not shown in the ROA tree—including inventory turn, product mix, and labor scheduling and utilization—are discussed in the course of this book.

Table A.10 shows data for some retailers, with higher-ROA retailers in the top half of the table and lower-ROA in the bottom. Even with this limited data we can see some patterns. For example, the higher-ROA retailers tend to couple higher sales per square foot

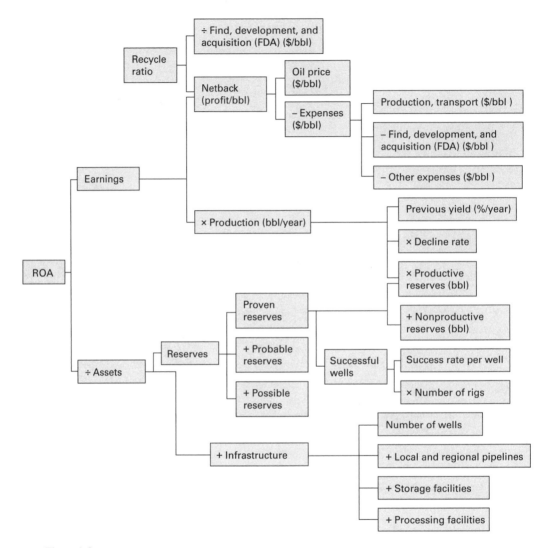

Figure A.8
ROA tree for an oil company.

Table A.9
Examples of ROA Drivers for Some Oil Companies

Higher-ROA firms

	Occidental Petroleum	Crimson Exploration	Belden & Blake	Questar
ROA (%)	19	11	11	10
Production (mil bbl)	171	0.5	0.3	3
Find costs ($mil)	341	2.5	2.5	60
Development costs ($mil)	4,100	87	27	1,060
Acquisition costs, proven ($mil)	1,831	61	1.5	603
Acquisition costs, unproven ($mil)	1,710	57	0.8	125
Proven reserves (mil bbl)	2,211	2.6	3.8	32
Developed reserves (mil bbl)	1,675	1.6	3.6	24
Price/bbl (hedged) ($)	88	84	94	73
Net productive wells	22,252	28	715	485
Sales volume (mil bbl)	170	0.5	0.3	3.3

Lower-ROA firms

	Cabot Oil & Gas	Cross Canyon Energy	Pioneer Natural Resources	Chesapeake Energy
ROA (%)	6.8	5.5	5.2	2.6
Production (mil bbl)	0.8	0.1	18	11
Find costs ($mil)	89	0.0	427	612
Development costs ($mil)	594	0.7	897	5,185
Acquisition costs, proven ($mil)	606	43	88	355
Acquisition costs, unproven ($mil)	153	9	50	8,129
Proven reserves (mil bbl)	9.3	0.5	463	121
Developed reserves (mil bbl)	6.7	0.3	226	85
Price/bbl (hedged) ($)	89	100	76	71
Net productive wells	158	2.0	4,569	3,840
Sales volume (mil bbl)	0.8	0.1	11.2	11

Source: Capital IQ, for US oil companies that have available data for the columns, for calendar year 2008.

with higher margins, whereas the lower-ROA retailers may have one but not the other. Duane Reade's otherwise excellent operating metrics shown in the table are hampered by its high expenses (not shown).

A.9.1 Same-Store Sales Growth

For many analysts, an important consideration is whether store revenues come from "same-store sales growth" or from new stores. The former is generally considered a higher-quality contributor.

While same-store sales growth is a *general* driver of ROA, single metrics are unlikely to determine an *individual* retailer's ROA. For example, table A.10 shows that some

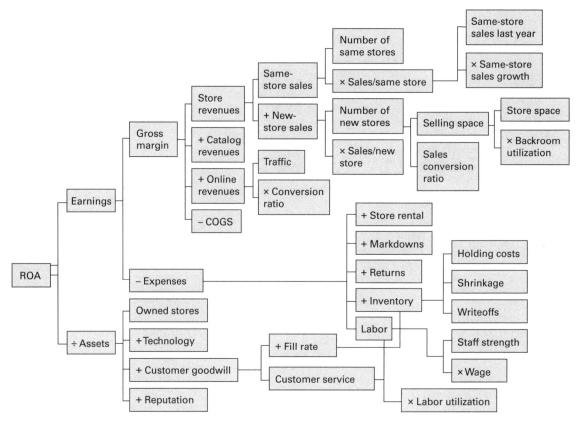

Figure A.9
ROA tree for retailing.

retailers with higher ROAs have low same-store sales growth; Big Lots achieved an 11% ROA despite having just 0.5% same-store growth, while Dollar General has a 4.4% ROA with 9% same-store growth.

A.9.2   Sales Conversion

On the store front, an important operational metric is the ratio of converting sales space to sales. On the online front, an equivalent metric is converting clicks to purchases.

    An important idea is that the *path* a customer takes in a store ("shopping path") or on a website ("click stream") can determine the likelihood of her purchasing a product. Wharton researchers in one case study have dispelled some myths about such paths. For example, it turns out that grocery shoppers do not comb through all aisles in an up-and-down fashion as commonly thought, but weave through only selected ones. Even shoppers

Table A.10
Examples of ROA Drivers for Some Retailers

Higher-ROA firms

	Dollar Tree	Big Lots	PetSmart	Advance Auto Parts
ROA (%)	12	11	10	9.0
Store space (mil sf)	30	29	25	25
Sales per sf ($)	158	160	202	211
Stores	3,591	1,339	1,112	3,368
Inventory turnover Ratio	4.64	3.76	6.07	1.70
Same-store sales growth (%)	4.1	0.5	3.8	1.5
Gross margin (%)	34	40	30	48
Revenues ($mil)	5,059	4,630	5,290	5,461

Lower-ROA firms

	Hot Topic	Dollar General	Hancock Fabrics	Duane Reade
ROA (%)	5.7	4.4	1.3	0.1
Store space (mil sf)	1.6	58.8	3.2	1.7
Sales per sf ($)	444	180	74	1,010
Stores	840	8,362	263	251
Inventory turnover Ratio	5.40	5.47	1.44	5.76
Same-store sales growth (%)	1.0	9.0	2.5	4.2
Gross margin (%)	36	29	43	31
Revenues ($mil)	761	11,456	275	1,837

Source: Capital IQ, for US retailers that have available data for the columns, for calendar year 2008.

who travel through most aisles do short "excursions" into most of them rather than going up one and down another, suggesting that products in the center of aisles have a lot less face time with customers than commonly thought.

A follow-on idea is the *conversion funnel*. The concept is twofold: proactively manage the paths that customers travel and create facings—such as physical shelves or web pages—that encourage sales. For example, WebTrends™ finds that T-Mobile's web customers tend to drop off on the accessories page, and that removing this page increases online orders by 27%.

A.9.3 Space Utilization

The proportion of sales to backroom space in a store is another operational driver of ROA. For example, Wal-Mart's "Inventory Deload" initiative aims to reduce inventory throughout its distribution path, from cross-docking in warehouses (incoming trucks will directly transfer their loads to outgoing trucks at warehouse docks) to shrinking backroom space to constrain inventory accumulation and maximize sales space.

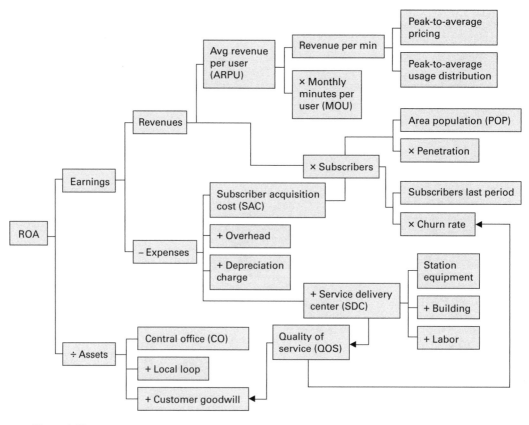

Figure A.10
ROA tree for telecom.

A.10   ROA Tree for Telecom

In figure A.10, we see a typical ROA tree for a telecom company. We leave the tree at a generic enough level to cover both wired and wireless firms. Some characteristics of these are shown in table A.11.

The telecom industry is distinctive for its large asset investments. We see this in the ROA tree, in the form of the central office and local loop. The other parts of the tree bear some resemblance to those of retailers. Below, we focus on the distinguishing features of telecom.

A.10.1   ARPU, MOU, POP, and Churn

Telecom revenues are driven by a multiple of the average revenue per user (ARPU) and the number of subscribers. ARPU is driven by the monthly minutes per user (MOU) and

Table A.11
Examples of ROA Drivers for Some Telecom Providers

Telephone and cable

	General Communication	Virgin Media
ROA (%)	2.57	0.62
Inventory turnover	42.2	22.3
Revenue ($mil)	575.4	5,851
Gross margin %	64.7	54.5
Penetration (%)	64.4	28.7
Homes passed (mil)	0.23	12.6
Broadband penetration (% of THP)	45.2	29.2
Subscribers, broadband (mil)	0.10	3.68
Subscribers, basic cable (mil)	0.15	3.62
Subscribers, telephony (mil)	0.24	4.1

Wireless

	T-Mobile USA	MetroPCS	iPCS
ROA (%)	4.7	5.0	4.5
Inventory turnover	8.88	11.8	63.7
Revenue ($mil)	21,885	2,751.5	525.5
Gross margin %	61	43.2	34.9
Penetration	11.37	3.58	5.53
ARPU ($)	51.0	41.4	48.7
SAC ($)	290	127	383
Churn (%)	2.9	4.7	2.3
Subscribers (mil)	32.8	5.37	0.691

revenues, which are in turn driven by peak-to-average pricing (we discuss these in detail in section 15.4.1).

The number of subscribers can be seen in two ways. One is to consider the penetration of the area population (POP). Another is to consider the time pattern: what percent of this period's subscriber base is different from last period's, referred to as the churn rate. The former is a valuable external perspective when we consider market share. The latter is a valuable internal perspective when we consider what we have to do to retain customers (see section 8.3).

A.10.2   SAC, SDC, and Depreciation Charges

Among the expenses, the most prominent are subscriber acquisition costs (SAC), the service delivery center (SDC), and depreciation charges. SAC is especially important in businesses where churn is high, and wireless is one of them. In table A.11, MetroPCS is fortunate to keep its SAC down to compensate for its high churn rate. iPCS, on the other hand, has a high SAC despite a low churn, and a lower ROA of 4.5%.

The SDC governs quality levels—called quality of service or QOS in the industry—which in turn determines customer goodwill, an asset to the firm. As the ROA tree shows, QOS also determines churn rate. This makes for a complicated web of interactions, which is a point we want to make.

A.11   ROA Tree for Life Insurance

In many respects, insurance resembles banking. Instead of deposits and interest income, we have "insurance in force" and premiums; but claims only happen when customers incur losses. Instead of loans, insurers place out investments, which like loans, have returns, losses, and the need to provide for potential losses. And like banks, insurers have customer acquisition and underwriting costs (for banks, underwriting is usually associated with credit products such as loans).

Table A.12 shows available data for some life insurers. The scarcity of data does not allow us to pinpoint any meaningful operational factors for success, but there is some basis for hypotheses. For example, Torchmark has a very high ROA despite having a small insurance-in-force, but it also seems to have controlled its claims very well. MetLife is

Table A.12
Examples of ROA Drivers for Some Life Insurers

Higher-ROA firms

	Torchmark	AFLAC	Unum Group	StanCorp Financial Group
ROA (%)	3.16	1.67	1.21	1.19
Insurance in force ($bil)	146	119	590	305
Premium revenue ($bil)	2.8	14.9	7.8	2.1
Acquisition, underwriting costs ($bil)	0.5	2.2	0.8	0.2
Insurance liabilities ($bil)	8.8	65	36	5.3
Gross claims ($bil)	0.2	55	49	7.2

Lower-ROA firms

	MetLife	Delphi Financial Group	Presidential Life	Conseco
ROA (%)	0.74	0.67	0.41	0.18
Insurance in force ($bil)	3,667	152	1.5	53
Premium revenue ($bil)	31	1.4	0	3.3
Acquisition, underwriting costs ($bil)	3.8	0.2	0	0.4
Insurance liabilities ($bil)	133	2.6	0.1	9.9
Gross claims ($bil)	8	2.2	0	1.3

Source: Capital IQ, for US life insurers that have available data for the columns, for calendar year 2008.

obviously enormous and may have benefited tremendously from its scale: its acquisition and underwriting costs are proportionately smaller, and so are its reserves.

A.12 ROA Tree for Securities Brokerage

Even within the same broad financial services industry we can observe different operational drivers, some of which are different mostly in name (as in banking versus insurance) but others in substance (as in banking versus brokerage).

Figure A.11 shows an ROA tree for a securities broker. Brokers may have many lines of business, but we focus on the most common: brokerage. Brokerage fees are driven by

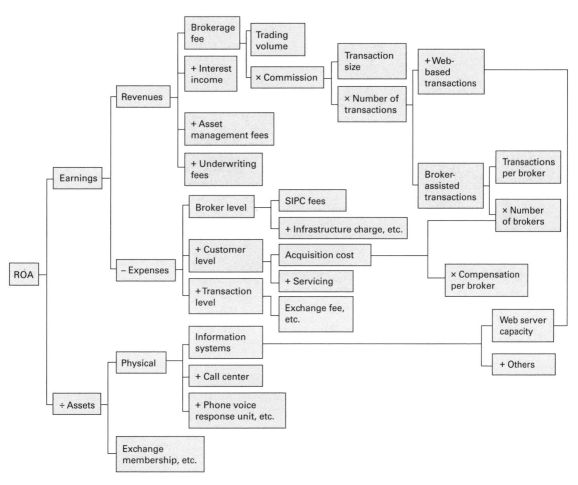

Figure A.11
ROA tree for a securities broker.

commission percentage and trading volume, the latter in turn driven by transaction size and the number of transactions. The number of transactions can be divided into transactions executed through the web and through brokers. Those through brokers are in turn determined by the average transactions brought in by each broker and the number of brokers.

The other lines of business may include interest income from proprietary trading and fees from managing client assets and from underwriting activities.

Like a bank, a broker may have expenses at different levels. Some are unique to brokers, such as the fees payable to the Securities Investor Protection Corporation (SIPC), the equivalent of FDIC for banks. Another unique feature is exchange fees, some of which are per transaction. These are payable to the exchange (say the New York Stock Exchange) for consummating the transaction.

Brokers vary widely in asset bases. A trading-oriented securities broker is likely to support web-based transactions, in which case it likely requires a range of technology assets, from web servers and call centers to phone voice response units. Another asset unique to securities brokers is the membership in exchanges.

Table A.13 shows the data for a few brokers. Their ROAs span a wide range. Among other things, we note Morgan Stanley's quite different business mix: it has a very large underwriting business. Raymond James is also different, earning most of its revenues from financial advice rather than traditional securities brokerage.

This points to another value of the ROA tree: to discern differences in business mix and how they lead to differences in ROAs.

Morgan Stanley and Raymond James have the highest compensation per employee (at $262,000 and $236,000 per employee), which could be one of many contributory reasons to their lower ROAs.

Table A.13
Examples of ROA Drivers for Some Securities Brokers

	Jones Financial Companies	Stifel Financial Corp.	Raymond James Financial	Morgan Stanley Group
ROA (%)	4.87	3.63	1.36	0.21
Transaction volume ($mil)	528	293	6	1,260
Commissions ($mil)	1,349	330	1,634	4,463
Underwriting fees ($mil)	81	91	95	4,092
Compensation, benefits ($mil)	2,133	546	1,673	12,306
Number of employees	17,488	3,371	7,100	46,964

Source: Capital IQ, for US securities brokers that have available data for the columns, for calendar year 2008.

A.13   ROA Tree for Pharmaceuticals

Here we consider fully integrated pharmaceutical companies, or FIPCOs, rather than the newer generation of biotech firms that focus solely on research. There is a wide heterogeneity among pharmaceutical firms; for better focus, we describe macromolecule firms.

Product-wise, these firms produce some or all of three main groups of drugs: replacement hormones, recombinant proteins, and monoclonal antibodies (MAb). These all have different economics—as do drugs with different therapeutic indications, such as those for general medicine, metabolic disorders, oncology, inflammation, vascular medicine, or immunology.

Technology-wise, they can also be very different. The technologies may be categorized by their application at two stages:

• Target identification and validation. Technologies include genomics, proteomics, systems biology, and RNAi.

• Lead identification and optimization. Examples include rDBA, MAb, rational drug design, combinatorial chemistry, high-throughput screening (HTS), bioinformatics, and combinatorial chemistry.

Figure A.12 shows a high-level ROA tree for a pharmaceuticals company. We should caution here that, more than in most industries previously described, ROA may not be the most relevant single performance measure. The pharmaceuticals industry has a long lag between research and development (R&D) and marketing revenues. The ROA view may work at steady state, but that condition is rare. Therefore, it should be complemented by other measures, including direct operational measures.

As usual, we focus on ROA drivers unique to the industry. Not surprisingly, the key is in managing the risks of getting drugs from R&D to marketing. This process consists of several phases:

• Target identification. The goal is to pinpoint the molecule which the therapeutic compound should bind with for efficacy.

• Lead compound identification. Here, we find the compound to pursue. We may base this on a number of criteria, such as efficacy, safety, competitiveness, and cost of manufacturing.

• Preclinical trials. These are either in vitro or in animal subjects, rather than in vivo in human subjects.

• Phase 1. The goal is to see whether there are side effects. This is often done with healthy volunteers.

• Phase 2. The goal is to assess efficacy, at various dosages. This is often done on actual patients.

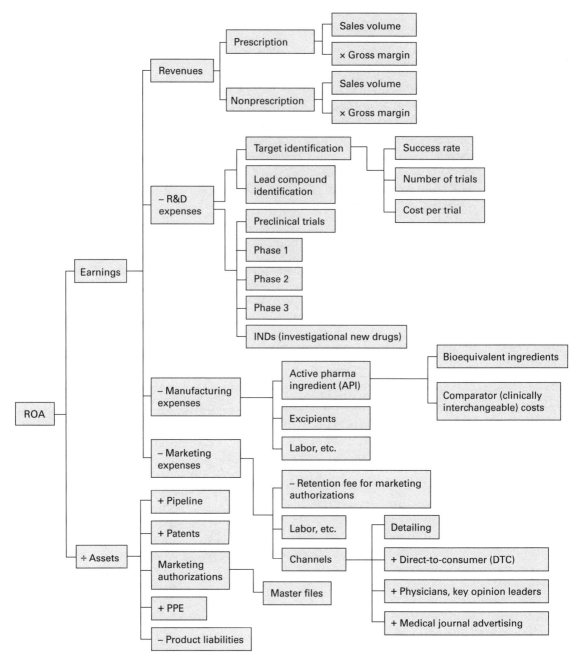

Figure A.12
ROA tree for a pharmaceuticals company.

Table A.14
Examples of ROA Drivers for Some Pharmaceutical Companies

	Vical	Elan	Roche	Shire	AstraZeneca	Sucampo
ROA (%)	−31	−4.04	11.5	11.6	12.8	14.9
Inventory turnover	—	14.8	2.28	2.48	3.24	—
Products in discovery research	2	3	—	—	—	—
Products in pre-registration	1	4	6	4	8	1
Products in preclinical trials	1	3	100	3	46	4
Products in Phase I	4	9	42	1	34	1
Products in Phase II	3	7	27	4	31	2
Products in Phase III	2	5	39	5	14	1
Patent applications	87	—	—	—	—	52
Patents	68	1,700	—	58	—	98
Products launched in 2008	—	1	29	2	—	—
Products approved in 2008	—	1	13	1	2	2

Source: Capital IQ, for US pharmaceutical companies that have available data for the columns, for calendar year 2008.

- Phase 3. Here, the objective is to see whether the compound works on a representative large sample of thousands.

- Investigational new drug (IND). At this stage, the business submits the compound for regulatory approval. On approval, the compound gets a "marketing authorization" to be sold.

Table A.14 describes real data for six pharmaceutical companies.

A.13.1 Risks in the Path from R&D to IND Status

The ROA is primarily driven by how much time and cost it takes to get drugs to pass through each stage in figure A.12. That in turn depends on the success rate of the trials, the number of trials, and the cost of each trial.

The success rates depend on the phase of development:

- Pre-Phase 1: Out of 3,000 to 10,000 molecules studied, 5 to 10 may prove effective for a given problem.
- Phase 1. The success rate is just 10% at this stage.
- Phase 2. The success rate is about 50%.
- Phase 3. The success rate is about 70% now.

The number of trials depends on the number of compounds and how many revisions each compound gets after an initial failure.

The cost per trial varies. For example, Phase 1 trials might cost about $15,700 per volunteer; Phase 2, $19,300 per patient; and Phase 3, over $26,000 per patient.[3]

A.13.2   Manufacturing Expenses: APIs and Excipients

While the pharmaceutical business has manufacturing expenses resembling those of other industries, it has two expenses unique to pharmaceuticals.

The first is the active pharmaceutical ingredient (API), which, as its name suggests, is the chemically or biologically active component of a drug. This is subject to high regulatory standards, with standardized practices such as "good manufacturing practices" (GMP), including in-process checks by regulatory auditors. Therefore, while the API might be sourced more cheaply through an alternate supplier, like other manufacturing inputs, here the options are generally much narrower.

Excipients are the inert ingredients in a drug that make it suitable for administration. Examples include binders, distegrants, glidants, preservatives, sugars, gums, gels, or even printing ink. Again, these are subject not only to internal but to regulatory standards.

A.14   Further Reading

Eadington, W. R. 1999. "The Economics of Casino Gambling." *Journal of Economic Perspectives* 13 (3): 173–192.

Girotra, K., C. Terwiesch, and K. T. Ulrich. 2007. "Valuing R&D Projects in a Portfolio: Evidence from the Pharmaceutical Industry." *Management Science* 53 (9): 1452–1466.

Loveman, G. 2003. "Diamonds in the Data Mine." *Harvard Business Review* 81 (5): 109–113.

Pisano, G. P. 2006. *Science Business: The Promise, the Reality, and the Future of Biotech*. Boston: Harvard Business School Press.

Zeller, T. L., B. B. Stanko, and W. O. Cleverley. 1996. "A Revised Classification Pattern of Hospital Financial Ratios." *Journal of Accounting and Public Policy* 15 (2): 161–181.

Appendix B   Resources

This list is not meant to be exhaustive, but could be a useful start. Except for the books, the items here are mostly available free of charge. Some Internet links may not work after the publication of this book. Please send feedback and suggestions for updating this list to opsforensics@gmail.com. While we cannot guarantee that all suggestions will be incorporated into the list, we will always be grateful for them.

B.1   Sample Due Diligence Checklists

1. *www.1000ventures.com*   This has a glossary and has a useful due diligence checklist at: http://www.1000ventures.com/venture_financing/due_diligence_checklist_byvpa.html

2. *www.meritusventures.com*   This has a good due diligence checklist at www.meritusventures.com/template_assets/pdf/diligence.pdf. "In addition to equity investments, Meritus Ventures can provide operational assistance (OA) to its actual and potential portfolio companies at no cost to those companies" (accessed January 7, 2010).

3. *office.microsoft.com*   Yes, Microsoft has a template for due diligence checklists. http://office.microsoft.com/en-us/templates/TC011734851033.aspx?pid=CT1025305 81033

4. *www.corp21.com*   Another due diligence checklist at www.corp21.com/download/ DueDiligence.pdf

5. *www.annarborusa.org*   Ann Arbor offers a sample too: http://www.annarborusa.org/ funding-incentives/pre-seed-fund/due-diligence-checklist/

6. *www.heartlandangels.com*   This is a short list for angel investors: http://www.heartlandangels.com/investors/due_diligence_checklist.html

7. *www.mgma.com*   This list is targeted to medical practices: http://www.mgma.com/ WorkArea/DownloadAsset.aspx?id=12710

8. *www.charity-commission.gov.uk*   This regulator of charities in the UK has a useful list for non-profits: www.charitycommission.gov.uk/library/chkduedil.pdf

9. *www.rmkb.com*   Ropers, Majeski, Kohn & Bentley is a law firm, with a useful list here: http://www.rmkb.com/tasks/sites/rmkb/assets/image/15.Due%20Diligence%20Checklist.pdf

B.2   Books

There are no books that speak directly to the issues here, but some good texts in operations management, accounting, and private equity are excellent references.

B.2.1   Operations Management

10. Cachon, G., and C. Terwiesch. 2006. *Matching Supply with Demand: An Introduction to Operations Management.* New York: McGraw-Hill. I believe this is the best operations management text for MBAs.

11. Hopp, W. J., and M. L. Spearman. 2001. *Factory Physics.* Boston: McGraw-Hill/Irwin. This text has had immense success with executives and is probably the best text in that genre.

12. Van Mieghem, J. A. 2008. *Operations Strategy: Principles and Practice.* Belmont, MA: Dynamic Ideas. This is the best book I know of on the subject.

B.2.2   Private Equity, Finance, Accounting

13. Metrick, A. 2007. *Venture Capital and the Finance of Innovation.* New York: Wiley. I consider this the best on the market.

14. Copeland, T. E., T. Koller, and J. Murrin, J. 2000. *Valuation: Measuring and Managing the Value of Companies.* New York: Wiley. This focuses on financial valuation, but has excellent chapters on return on invested capital (ROIC) trees.

15. MIT Open Courseware, course 15.501, Introduction to Financial and Managerial Accounting, http://ocw.mit.edu/OcwWeb/Sloan-School-of-Management/15-501Spring-2004/LectureNotes/index.htm. MIT is admirably generous in offering its material free. These lecture notes are by Sugata Roychowdhury, a leading scholar on the manipulation of real phenomena such as sales instead of accounting figures.

16. Another MIT Open Courseware course: 15.535, Business Analysis Using Financial Statements, http://ocw.mit.edu/courses/sloan-school-of-management/15-535-business-analysis-using-financial-statements-spring-2003/ This splendid set of lecture notes is by Peter Wysocki.

B.2.3   Econometrics and Analytics

17. Wooldridge, J. M. 2008. *Introductory Econometrics: A Modern Approach.* Mason, OH: South-Western Publishing. This is positively the best first course on econometrics.

18. MIT Open Courseware, course 15.053, Optimization Methods in Management Science, http://ocw.mit.edu/courses/sloan-school-of-management/15-053-optimization-methods -in-management-science-spring-2007/ These are valuable, accessible lecture notes on how to formulate and optimize decisions.

B.3   Journals, Magazines, Academic Research

19. *Management Science*   This is the premier journal in operations management. Its editor in chief is Gerard Cachon of Wharton.

20. *Manufacturing and Service Operations Management*   This is another top journal in operations management (OM), and differs from *Management Science* by being more focused on OM.

21. *Journal of Accounting and Economics*   This is one of the top journals in accounting and also has quite accessible statements of the latest research.

22. *Journal of Forensic Accounting*   This accessible journal is useful for "accounting that is suitable for legal review, offering the highest level of assurance, and including the now generally accepted connotation of having been arrived at in a scientific fashion."

23. *Private Equity Analyst*   With this magazine, "go 'behind the scenes' at leading institutions and private investment firms and find out exactly what is driving this dynamic market."

24. Sol C. Snider Entrepreneurial Research Center at Wharton. This is "the first center dedicated to the study of entrepreneurship" and produces a wealth of state-of-the-art research.

25. Center for Private Equity and Entrepreneurship at the Tuck School of Business at Dartmouth. This is a highly respected center, at mba.tuck.dartmouth.edu/pecenter

B.4   Consultants and Information Sources

19. *www.minecost.com*   A rich source of information for building industry cost curves in competitive cost analyses in the commodities industry.

20. *www.auditintegrity.net*   "Audit Integrity was founded in 2002 to develop risk management tools based on a statistical analysis of corporate integrity."

21. *www.ratefinancials.com*   "An independent firm that rates and ranks the financial reporting of public companies."

22. *www.dnb.com*   "D&B (NYSE:DNB) is the world's leading source of commercial information and insight on businesses." They are particularly known for their information on the credit situation of businesses, obtained from suppliers and customers.

23. *www.onesource.com*   This information source provides easily readable financials and news about public and many private businesses.

24. *www.compustat.com*   This data provider has some industry-specific data, some of which is used in this book.

25. *www.Capital IQ.com*   This data provider has been acquired by Compustat and is particularly useful for its industry-specific collection. It is the source for some of the operational data in the book.

26. *www.forensicaccounting.com*   Alan Zysman's forensic accounting website is highly informative.

27. *operations-extranet.mckinsey.com*   This McKinsey extranet has a free login facility and contains a trove of operations material from a management consultant's perspective.

28. *www.bain.com*   Look under the Publications/Articles tab to find thoughtful articles on related topics, such as corporate renewal, private equity, and operational improvements.

B.5   Directories, Trade Associations, Standards

29. *www.turnaround.org*   The Turnaround Management Association "is the only international non-profit association dedicated to corporate renewal and turnaround management. Established in 1988, TMA has more than 9,000 members in 46 chapters."

30. *www.glgroup.com*   The Gerson Lehrman Group is a community of experts who provide in-depth industry knowledge.

31. *www.mavenresearch.com*   This group functions more like a broker, between those who need in-depth operational knowledge and those who have such information.

32. *www.guidepointglobal.com*   This group also has a network of experts around the world who can answer in-depth questions from private equity firms and financial analysts.

33. *Generally Accepted Auditing Standards*   The American Institute of Certified Public Accountants publishes these at http://www.aicpa.org/Research/Standards/AuditAttest/ DownloadableDocuments/AU-00350.pdf

34. *Generally Accepted Accounting Standards*   These are at http://www.fasab.gov/ accepted.html

35. *www.nvca.org*   The National Venture Capital Association contains useful industry statistics.

36. *Tuck Valuation Standard*   This provides an emerging standard for valuation standards for private equity and venture capital. At mba.tuck.dartmouth.edu/pecenter/research

B.6 Software

37. Data envelopment analysis   Paul Jensen has a very useful, very clear set of operations research tools, including that for DEA. http://www.me.utexas.edu/~jensen/ORMM/omie/index.html

B.7 Others

38. Sequoia Capital's slide presentation on "R.I.P. Good Times"   This is one of three highly circulated documents (see the other two below) that investors send to their portfolio companies on the need to manage burn rate in a recession, and how to do this. http://techcrunch.com/2008/10/10/sequoia-capitals-56-slide-powerpoint-presentation-of-doom/

39. Angel investor Ron Conway's email on managing burn rate   Another famous email on the subject. http://techcrunch.com/2008/10/08/angel-investor-ron-conway-adresses-his-portfolio-companies-over-financial-meltdown/

40. Benchmark Capital's Bill Gurley's email on managing burn rate   One more famous email on the subject. http://techcrunch.com/2008/10/09/benchmark-capital-advises-startups-to-conserve-capital/

Appendix C Glossary

While we assume that the reader has some familiarity with operations management concepts, the following glossary might serve as a useful reminder. Please refer to the index for the pages where these terms are used in the text.

Term	Definition	Examples or Intuition
Activity	Work step that adds value to making a unit. Also called station, step, or task.	Nursing station that treats patients
Activity capacity	How fast an activity *can* treat units. Activity capacity = 1/activity time × number of resources.	4 patients/hour may be how fast a nursing station can treat patients
Activity time	How long it takes one resource to treat a unit. This excludes any waiting time.	Time it takes to treat a patient (might be 30 minutes/patient)
Batch size, B	Number of units made together after every setup. For an activity with setup time S, the optimal B is that which gets the activity to reach flow rate $R = B/(S + B \times$ activity time).	Make 20 model T cars after setting up the line for the model
Bottleneck	Activity with highest utilization, which is also the activity with the highest implied utilization. By this definition, an activity is a bottleneck even if it has spare capacity that is unused, as in a demand-constrained process.	When demand rate is the same across all activities (e.g., in a process with a simple line of activities), bottleneck is that activity with slowest capacity. If all activities have just one resource, bottleneck is that activity with longest activity time.
Buffer	Holding area in which units wait to be treated.	Any waiting area in hospital, as long as the patient is not being treated
Coefficient of variation	Measure of variability. We scale this by the mean, so this is standard deviation ÷ mean.	2 (notice this is a ratio)
Cost of direct labor	Labor wages paid during time it takes to produce a unit. Includes payment for idle time, since we have to pay wages for that time too. Formula is total wages/hr ÷ flow rate in units/hr. Unless otherwise stated, this is cost of direct labor *per unit*.	$200 per patient
cv_a	Coefficient of variation for interarrival time a. Measures variability of a: do units come at regular intervals, or in lumps?	

Term	Definition	Examples or Intuition
cv_p	Coefficient of variation for processing time p.	
Cycle time, CT	Time it takes for a unit to be produced by a process; equal to 1/flow rate.	20 minutes per patient. This is from the view of a hospital's CEO, standing outside the hospital's exit and counting how long it takes for patients to emerge.
Demand rate	How fast we *want* the process to make units. In this book, we take this as given.	200 patients per day (hospital needs to process)
Erlang loss fraction, $P_m(p/a)$	Fraction of throughput lost because arriving units drop out when servers are busy. This is obtained by looking up an Erlang loss table, using p/a, the ratio of processing to interarrival times, and m, the number of servers.	40% of patients diverted to another hospital when a hospital is busy
Flow rate, R	How fast a process *actually* produces units, equal to 1/cycle time. This is smaller of process capacity and demand rate. Also called throughput.	200 patients a day (actually being processed)
Flow time, T	Elapsed time for a unit to move from first activity to last, including waits in between.	23 hours, from patient's (not hospital's) perspective
Idle time	Time paid to resources but not spent on producing units. Unless otherwise stated, this is idle time *per unit*. Elapsed time to make one unit is cycle time; during this time, number of person-minutes paid to resources is number of resources × cycle time. During this time, the unit gets treated over activity time (by one resource . . . remember, no multitasking).	4 person-hours per patient (could be 2 persons idle over 2 hours, 1 person idle over 4 hours, etc., depending on how process is configured)
Implied utilization	Portion of an activity's capacity used to meet demand rate; if capacity is below demand rate, portion that needs to be added to meet demand rate.	When demand rate exceeds activity capacity, this is more than 100%
Interarrival time, a	Time between units arriving at a server. This is a variable with a distribution that has a mean and a coefficient of variation. If there is no throughput loss, the average a is also the average cycle time CT.	Mean $a = 3$ minutes per unit (notice we usually refer to the mean a, not a specific value of a for a specific unit)
Inventory, I	Number of units within a boundary (activity, buffer, process, company, etc.). Unless otherwise stated, we think of this as average inventory.	Average number of patients in a hospital. Could be measured in dollar terms (e.g., $46 million at end of 2004); or as days of inventory (e.g., 26 days of inventory), as in inventory/COGS, where COGS is in days.
Inventory cost per period (%), also called inventory percent charge per period	Analogous to an interest charge, so it has a time period. Remember this is a charge on units held as inventory, not units sold.	6% a year (note: dimension here is just percent per year, not per dollar)
Inventory cost per unit sold ($)	Converts inventory cost per unit sold from % term to $ term, but multiplies by the value of a unit sold at cost (i.e., COGS).	If COGS of a unit sold is $100 and inventory cost per unit sold is 2% of each unit sold, then inventory cost is $2 per unit sold

Term	Definition	Examples or Intuition
Inventory cost per unit sold (%)	Inventory percent charge for each unit sold; equals inventory cost per period ÷ inventory turn. Numerator is for units held; denominator converts units held to units sold.	2% of each unit sold
Inventory turn	How many units sold per period by holding a unit of inventory during the period. For a company, this is COGS/inventory (for denominator, we often simply use end-of-period inventory).	3 times per year (make sure you are aware of the time period used)
Labor content	Number of person-hours spent treating a unit to produce it (could be at an activity or process level); equal to activity time (or for a process, the sum of all activity times), where activity time is expended by one resource at any one time (recall "no multitasking"). Unless otherwise stated, this is labor content *per unit*.	16 person-hours per patient. Since it is always one person acting on the patient at any one time, this is patient literally receiving 16 hours of activity time (not, for example, 2 persons treating patient for 8 hours).
Labor utilization	Portion of an activity's available person-hours (per hour) being used to make units (per hour); equal to flow rate × activity time ÷ number of resources. For a process, we use activity times and number of resources across all activities in the formula. Equivalent to labor content ÷ (labor content + idle time).	Up to 100%
Little's Law	Within a boundary (process, activity, company, etc.), inventory = flow rate × flow time. These are for averages.	As a mnemonic, use I = Remember × That!
Newsvendor formula	Formula to determine optimal inventory stocking level to balance over- and understocking costs.	If over- and understocking costs are C_o and C_u, optimal stocking level corresponding to a service probability of $C_u/(C_u + C_o)$
Process	Sequence of activities and buffers.	Series of activities that a patient goes through in a hospital
Process capacity	How fast a process *can* make units, determined by capacity of the bottleneck activity.	300 patients a day (hospital is capable of processing)
Processing time, p	Same as activity time; term used in queuing and throughput loss analysis.	
Queue	Same as term used in queuing and throughput loss analysis.	Waiting area in hospital
Queue wait time, T_q	How long average unit waits before being treated by a server: $\dfrac{p}{m}\dfrac{u^{\sqrt{2(m+1)-1}}}{1-u}\dfrac{cv_a^2+cv_p^2}{2}$, where p is processing time, m is number of servers, u is server utilization, cv_a and cv_p are coefficients of variation for interarrival and processing times.	
Resource	Workers or machines at an activity, each of which either works on one unit or is idle (no multiple resources on one unit or multiple units by one resource simultaneously).	Nurse; we assume the nurse has accompanying tools to treat a patient (we do not count tools as resources)
Server (number of servers denoted m)	Same as resource; term used in queuing and throughput loss analysis.	Check-in counter

Term	Definition	Examples or Intuition
Server utilization	How much of servers' capacity m/p is used, on average. In queueing analysis with no throughput loss, this is $1/a \div m/p = p/(ma)$.	In queueing analysis, we assume that utilization is 100% or less. Otherwise, queue can get infinitely big.
Service probability	Cumulative probability that inventory stocking level can meet demand.	Probability that a newsvendor stocks enough newspapers to meet demand
Setup time, S	Downtime during which process produces no unit.	Preventive maintenance time; downtime at a production line to switch from making one car model to another
Steady state	A running process that is not starting from an empty process, nor ending its run.	A process that runs 24/7/365
Throughput loss	What happens when units that cannot be immediately served drop out, instead of queueing to be served.	Ambulance diversion, in which patient is sent elsewhere when hospital (server) is busy
Unit	Item to which an activity adds value.	Patient
Utilization	The portion of an activity's capacity used to make units; equal to flow rate ÷ activity capacity.	Up to 100%

Notes

Chapter 1

1. Peter Kafka, "Expert Network Gerson Lehrman Sells Stake: $875 Million Valuation," www.businessinsider.com, December 18, 2007. Accessed November 16, 2010.

2. Patrick Jenkins and Paul J. Davies, "HSBC close to dropping plan to buy Nedbank," *Financial Times*, October 15, 2010.

3. Using "data envelopment analysis" (see section 9.4.1).

4. Using queueing theory (see section 7.2.3).

5. See section 2.1.5.

6. See section 4.5.

7. P. Hodkinson, "Delicate Operations: Partners Differ on How to Manage Their Firms' Investments," *Financial News*, July 27, 2009.

8. http://portfoliooperations.blogspot.com/2007/10/henry-kravis-explains-how-kkr-adds.htmlu, accessed January 2, 2010.

9. KKR Private Equity Investor LP fourth quarter 2008 financial results conference call.

10. Hodkinson, "Delicate Operations."

11. J. Marino, "Q&A Dean Nelson: KKR's Special Ops; Henry Kravis and George Roberts May Be the Architects, but Dean Roberts Is the Guy on the Ground Ensuring Investments Are Built to Spec," *Mergers & Acquisitions: The Dealmakers Journal,* June 1, 2009.

12. http://portfoliooperations.blogspot.com/2007/10/henry-kravis-explains-how-kkr-adds.htmlu, accessed January 2, 2010.

13. Ibid.

14. H. Sender, "Street Sleuth: HCA Deal Spotlights Low-Profile Bain Capital—in Contrast to Big-Name Rivals, Private-Equity Firm's Staff Often Bring Operations Expertise," *Wall Street Journal*, August 1, 2006.

15. Ibid.

16. We direct readers' attention to organizations such as the Turnaround Management Association (www.turnaround.org) for more information (see Appendix B.5).

Chapter 2

1. This colorful example is from A. H. Millichamp's *Auditing* (Thomson Learning, 2002).

2. For example, see section 3.1.2.

3. If we have annual COGS, we can easily convert that to daily COGS by dividing annual COGS by the number of days in a year.

4. While "days of inventory" is obviously measured in days, "inventory turn" is often measured in times per years.

5. See also section 4.4.

6. http://portfoliooperations.blogspot.com/2007/10/henry-kravis-explains-how-kkr-adds.htmlu, accessed January 2, 2010.

Chapter 3

1. As we are primarily interested in operations, we ignore a third term common in finance texts, assets/equity, which captures financial leverage. The combination of all three terms forms the DuPont formula: ROE = (net profit/COGS) × (COGS/assets) × (assets/equity).

2. This is Little's Law (see the discussion in section A.2.4 in the appendix), and it holds under some liberal assumptions.

3. "What Makes Southwest Airlines Fly," an interview with Herb Kelleher at Knowledge@Wharton, June 4, 2003.

4. Ibid.

5. John Paczkowski, "2011 iPad Sales: 25 Million? 18 Million? Well, a Big Number, Anyway," *AllThingsD*, July 8, 2010.

6. "How Apple's iPad Sales Break Down by Quarter," *Washington Post*, August 24, 2012.

7. Of course, there is also the forensics of getting deeper into $demand_t$, but since we focus on operations rather than marketing, we do not discuss that here. Here we use the simple assumption that $demand_t$ is positively correlated with $demand_{t+1}$ as shown in the figure.

8. To see this, denote unit cost by c and cumulative units by u. If c drops exponentially with u, the curve can be specified as $c = u^{-a}$, where a is some constant. Taking logs on both sides, we get $\log(c) = -a \log(u)$, which is a straight-line relationship between $\log(c)$ and $\log(u)$.

9. You might recall that the surface area of a sphere is $4\pi r^2$ where r is the radius; and its volume is $4/3\ \pi r^3$.

Chapter 4

1. Julie Schlosser, "King of the Retail Jungle," *Fortune*, April 4, 2005.

2. Jennifer Ablan, "Smart Shopper," *Barron's*, December 13, 2004.

3. We use "manipulation" and eschew less loaded words such as "management" to bring clarity to the discussion: specifically, retailers could decide to do different things than what equity holders intend. To the extent that equity holders are *not* the parties to whom retail managers should answer, then "manipulation" should be taken as a neutral word.

4. This is the result from standard inventory management formulations, such as the "newsvendor formula."

Chapter 5

1. The "Seven Dwarfs" were later reduced to "the BUNCH": Burroughs, UNIVAC, NCR, CDC, and Honeywell.

Chapter 6

1. See Altman (1968).

2. In Altman's original paper, e is cast as a ratio, but a through d are percentages. So his coefficients for a through d are one-hundredth the size of the ones cited here.

3. Net interest payments would be included, since these impact whether a company can continue to run (is a "going concern" in accounting parlance). In any case, net interest payments count under "Cash flow from *operating* activities" under the US GAAP standard, even if not under the IAS 7 standard.

Chapter 7

1. To see this, set $-1p + 2(1 - p) = 0$. Keeping only p on the left side, we get $-p - 2p = -2$, or $p = 2/3$.

2. The queueing time is approximately

$$\frac{p}{m} \frac{u^{\sqrt{2(m+1)}-1}}{1-u} \frac{cv_a^2 + cv_p^2}{2},$$

where p is the average processing time of a server, m the number of servers, u the server utilization ($= p/(ma)$, where a is the average interarrival time), and cv_a^2 and cv_p^2 are the squared coefficients of variation (variance divided by mean) of a and p, respectively.

Chapter 9

1. http://www.leanpackaging.com/, accessed June 20, 2011.

2. Quoted in Bob Emiliani, "Meaningless Victory," www.leanCEO.com, accessed June 4, 2012.

3. This is not true if the linear program is "degenerate." When degeneracy happens, we get different weights depending on which hospital's leanness ratio we maximize. Fortunately, this only means that we get different right answers to the same question, rather than wrong answers.

Chapter 10

1. To simplify exposition, we use phrases like "covariance of the business and the market" rather than the longer but more precise "covariance of the business's cash flows with the market portfolio's cash flows."

2. There is one area of finance where risks amplify, and it is similar to the situation here. That is the study of contagion in a financial system.

Chapter 11

1. This is a continuously compounded variance, not the variance from discrete outcomes. In this case, the upside is $1,500/1,200 = 1.25$. Then σ is given by $\log(1.25) = 0.223$.

2. The subsequent cash flows are obtained using a standard deviation, assumed here to be \$0.5 million. If these cash flows follow a random walk, we can model the ups and downs as follows: in every year, the upward move is $e^{0.5} = 1.65$ times the previous cash flow, and the downward move is $1/e^{0.5} = 0.61$ of the same.

3. This is an abstract version of a situation encountered by Loews Corporation, which bought a chain of theaters from MGM and converted some of these to hotels.

Chapter 12

1. batcat, January 30, 2009, in AppleInsider.com.

Chapter 13

1. From www.chicago-consulting.com; accessed October 16, 2010.

2. In general, P_m is the fraction of customers lost when we have m servers and is called the Erlang loss. We write:

$$r = D/C, P_m = \frac{r^m}{m!} / \left(1 + \frac{r^1}{1!} + \frac{r^2}{2!} + \cdots + \frac{r^m}{m!} \right).$$

3. Profit is maximized when we differentiate the profit function by C and set that differential to zero.

4. See note 2 of chapter 7 for details of this same formula for waiting time.

5. $\frac{cv_D^2 + cv_C^2}{2}$ is 1 when each squared coefficient of variation is 1, which holds when demand and capacity times (i.e., customer interarrival time and processing time) are random.

6. We can also model falling sales—such as using fractional powers of t—but will avoid this complexity here.

Chapter 14

1. For example, we might use geometric programming. See Boyd et al. (2007).

Chapter 15

1. Beer and Nohria (2000) called our "operational" turnaround "economic," but this type of turnaround has at least as much to do with operations—processes, organizational structure, planning, execution—as it does with incentives.

2. Floyd Norris, "Will Justice Department Go After Dunlap?," *New York Times*, September 6, 2002.

3. This expectation is obtained as

$$\sum_{k=0}^{\infty} p^k (1-p)k = (1-p)\sum_{k=0}^{\infty} p^k k.$$

We can extract the k in the summation by using a differential, so the expectation is

$$(1-p)p\frac{d}{dp}\left(-\sum_{k=0}^{\infty} p^k \right) = -(1-p)p\frac{d}{dp}\left(\frac{1}{1-p} \right)$$

using the standard sum of an infinite series. Since

$$\frac{d}{dp}\left(\frac{1}{1-p} \right) = -\frac{1}{(1-p)^2},$$

the expectation is $p/(1-p)$.

4. As usual, to find the optimal, we differentiate the profit expression by T_C, set that differential to zero, and then recast it with T_C on the left-hand side.

Appendix A

1. "F.D.I.C. Charges Banks New Fee to Replenish Fund," *New York Times*, May 22, 2009.

2. http://www.bj21.com/bj_reference/pages/questionforcasinomanagement.shtml, accessed December 28, 2009.

3. http://www.pharmpro.com, accessed December 31, 2009.

Index

Page numbers followed by b, f, and t indicate boxes, figures, and tables, respectively. Glossary page numbers are italicized.